INTERNATIONAL DEVELOPMENT IN FOCUS

Leveraging Export Diversification in Fragile Countries

The Emerging Value Chains of Mali, Chad, Niger, and Guinea

JOSÉ R. LÓPEZ-CÁLIX

Contents

Acknowledgments   ix
About the Author   xi
Key Messages   xiii
Abbreviations   xvii

Overview   **1**
Notes   16
References   16

CHAPTER 1   **Development Context for Export Diversification in Mali, Chad, Niger, and Guinea**   **17**
Challenges in the quest of export diversification   17
Annex 1A   29
Notes   31
References   31

CHAPTER 2   **Why Export Diversification Matters to MCNG Countries**   **33**
Why past diversification efforts failed   34
Rationale for export diversification   36
Notes   39
References   40

CHAPTER 3   **Conceptual Approach: The Export Diversification Ladder and Structural Transformation**   **41**
What theory says about export diversification and growth   41
The export diversification ladder   43
Diversification and structural change dynamics   44
Notes   49
References   49

CHAPTER 4   **Micro Foundations (1): Identifying Opportunities for Export Diversification**   **51**
Previous efforts at identifying new exports   52
Applying revealed comparative advantage analysis   52
Applying product space analysis: A complementary approach   55
Applying the fitness approach: Another complementary approach   56
Opportunities for export diversification   57
Annex 4A: Technical definitions   59
Notes   60
References   61

CHAPTER 5   **Micro Foundations (2): Upgrading Agricultural Value Chains   63**
Introduction   64
The position of Mali, Chad, Niger, and Guinea in the typology of global value chains   65
How are global value chains in the key agriculture sector organized?   69
How do the value chains differ in each country?   71
What are the relevant actors at national and regional levels?   73
Scope for diversification: Specific upgrading strategies and policy options   76
Notes   80
References   80

CHAPTER 6   **Macro Foundations (1): Revisiting Trade Policy and Logistics   83**
Background   84
Pitfalls in the trade policy framework of MCNG countries   86
Trade logistics and facilitation   90
Policy options   94
Notes   99
References   99

CHAPTER 7   **Macro Foundations (2): Business Environment and Firms' Productivity   101**
Major obstacles to the investment climate observed in the MCNG countries   102
Measuring the quality of business regulations   108
Cross-country comparisons of firms' productivity   110
Main policy options   115
Notes   120
References   120

CHAPTER 8   **Revamping Export Diversification Policies in MCNG Countries: A GVC 2.0 Cluster-Based Approach   121**
Need for a new GVC 2.0 development approach to projects in MCNG countries   122
New GVC 2.0 development approach: Introducing cluster-based policies   123
What works and what does not with market incentives   126
Implementing the GVC 2.0 development approach to success and the priority agenda   128
Maximizing Finance for Development and the key role IFC can play in attracting foreign direct investment to GVC 2.0 development   132
Notes   139
References   140

Bibliography   *141*

Boxes

O.1   Learning from failure: The case of COPEOL in Guinea   2
O.2   Learning from a promising start-up: The case of SOGUIPAH in Guinea   3
5.1   Benchmarking-based methodology for classifying global value chains   64
5.2   Learning from best practices worldwide for process and product upgrading   75
6.1   High informality in regional trade in West Africa   84
6.2   The role of border bazaars   89
6.3   Estimating the fiscal impact of trade reform: The case of Niger   91

Figures

O.1 Since 2016, Mali, Chad, Niger, and Guinea have been classified in the "Alert" category in the Fragile States Index 5
O.2 Per capita GDP income levels in Niger, Mali, and Chad have broadly stagnated over 35 years 7
O.3 Export diversification ladder 8
O.4 Decomposition of labor productivity growth in Niger, 1990–2015, and other world regions, 1990–2005 9
1.1 Human Capital Index in Sub-Saharan Africa (low-income countries only) 21
1.2 Degree of export diversification, 2015 21
1.3 Exports, by product, 2015 22
1.4 Exports destinations, 2015 23
1.5 Growth in oil vs. non-oil exports in Chad 23
1.6 Nonresource export growth in Guinea, Niger, and Mali 24
1.7 World export shares of selected regions, 2002–06 25
1.8 Regional exports of selected regions 25
1.9 Share of foreign value added in exports, 2008–12 26
1.10 Sub-Saharan Africa: Depth of integration into global value chains, average 1991–95 vs. 2008–12 26
1.11 Inward FDI flows over time for MCNG countries, 2007–16 27
1.12 FDI typology: Share of Mali's greenfield FDI by type, 2012–16 28
1.13 FDI typology: Share of Mali's greenfield FDI by type and sector, 2012–16 28
1.14 FDI typology: Share of Guinea's greenfield FDI by type, 2012–16 28
1.15 FDI typology: Share of Guinea's greenfield FDI by type and sector, 2012–16 28
2.1 Since 2016, Mali, Chad, Niger, and Guinea have been classified in the "Alert" category in the Fragile States Index 34
2.2 Niger, Mali, and Chad per capita GDP income levels have broadly stagnated over 35 years 35
2.3 Oil price slumps have dramatically deteriorated Chad's fiscal position 37
2.4 Rainfall and GDP growth: Niger's growth has featured wide booms and busts, due largely to the fact that the economy relies on rainfall and the price of uranium 37
3.1 Export diversification ladder 43
3.2 Manufacturing value added in Chad vs. Sub-Saharan Africa 45
3.3 Mali's industrialization is stagnating 46
3.4 Guinea: Correlation between sectoral productivity and changes in employment share, 2006–15 47
3.5 Niger and Chad's correlation sector productivity and changes in employment, 1990–2015 and 2005–15 48
3.6 Chad: Decomposition of labor productivity growth, 2005–15 48
3.7 Decomposition of labor productivity growth between Niger, 1990–2015, and world regions, 1990–2005 48
4.1 Product space for Chad, Guinea, Mali, and Niger, 2014–15 56
4.2 Mali, Chad, and Niger's economic fitness, 2012–17 58
5.1 Governance in agricultural commodities value chains in Chad, Mali, Niger, and Guinea 70
5.2 Typical product diversification path from live bovine meat for countries with Niger's capabilities 77
5.3 Typical product diversification path from sesame seed and shelled cashew for countries with Mali's capabilities 78
5.4 Typical product diversification path from sesame seed and gum arabic for countries with Chad's capabilities 78
6.1 Chad's trading partners: Predicted vs. actual exports 85
6.2 Niger's trading partners 85
6.3 Average tariffs by stage of production, 2016 88
6.4 Mali, Niger, and Chad's logistics performance 92
7.1 Top 5 major (or very severe) constraints in Chad, Guinea, Mali, and Niger 102
7.2 Political instability: Rated as a top-ranked obstacle to business operations 103
7.3 Corruption: Rated as a major or very severe constraint 104

7.4   Informality: Rated as a major or very severe constraint   105
7.5   Firms competing against unregistered or informal firms   105
7.6   Electricity: Power outages rated as a major or very severe constraint   106
7.7   Access to finance: Rated as a major or very severe constraint   107
7.8   Comparative Doing Business rankings and distance to frontier   108
7.9   Labor productivity in Mali, Niger, Guinea, and comparator countries   111
7.10   Labor productivity in Mali, Niger, and Guinea compared to countries at
       similar levels of development   112
7.11   Manufacturing labor costs in Guinea, Mali, and Niger   112
7.12   Larger firms are the most productive in Mali, Niger, and Guinea   113
7.13   Exporters are more productive than nonexporters in Mali, Niger, and Guinea   114
7.14   Niger features a lower share of export-to-total firms than Mali and Guinea   114
7.15   Foreign-owned firms are more productive in Mali, Niger, and Guinea than
       domestic firms   115
7.16   Few manufacturing firms in Niger and Guinea are foreign-owned   115
8.1   Mali: Supporting large-scale pilot projects in the mango sector: How the
       Joint Implementation Plan is supporting the mango value chain   135
8.2   Chad: Illustrative structure of a risk-sharing facility based on a collateral
       management agency   137
8.3   Example of integrated value chain developer: Sustainable Agriculture, Food
       Security, and Linkages (Solidaridad) in the aquaculture, dairy, and horticulture
       sector of Bangladesh   138

Maps

1.1   Market potential of West African agglomerates   18
1.2   Mali: Main logistics corridors for cashew and sesame in the south of the
       country away from the conflict-prone north   20
1A.1   Niger: Meat and onion value chain (October 2018)   29
1A.2   Chad: Arabic gum and sesame seeds value chain (October 2018)   30

Tables

O.1   Cluster-based typology of export diversification policies   11
O.2   Revamped main export diversification policies in Mali, Chad, Niger, and
       Guinea ("game changers")   12
1.1   Export diversification share in total exports of MCNG countries, 2015   22
2.1   Average values of trade-to-GDP ratio   38
2.2   Potential impact on the per capita GDP growth of
       Chad, Mali, and Niger   38
4.1   Average revealed comparative advantage by sector in
       Chad, Guinea, Mali, and Niger, 2015   53
4.2   Summary of selected products with higher potential for export
       diversification   54
5.1   Population, incomes, and value-added shares, 2000 vs. 2015:
       Mali, Niger, Chad, Guinea, and comparator countries   66
5.2   Global value chain share as buyer and seller, 2000 vs. 2011:
       Mali, Niger, Chad, Guinea, and comparator countries   67
5.3   Upstreamness of imports and exports and gap, 2000 vs. 2014:
       Mali, Niger, Chad, Guinea, and comparator countries   68
5.4   Characteristics of selected global value chains   70
5.5   Importance of selected value chains in Chad, Mali, and Niger   71
5.6   Characteristics of selected value chains and constraints   72
5.7   Value chain segments, lead actors, and chain governance   74
5.8   Upgrading components of the cluster approach and policy options   79
6.1   Average tariff rates in Niger   86
6.2   Comparative simple and weighted tariffs in regional groupings, 2016   87
6.3   Trading across borders: Indicators   93
6.4   Road harassment in selected West African countries   94
6.5   Matrix of policy interventions in trade policy for export diversification   95

7.1   Selected corruption indicators: Comparators and Sub-Saharan Africa   104
7.2   Interactions with tax administrations   105
7.3   Electricity: Indicators   106
7.4   Selected access to finance indicators and regional benchmarking   107
7.5   Starting a business: Indicators   109
7.6   Construction permits: Indicators   109
7.7   Paying taxes: Indicators   110
7.8   Obtaining credit: Indicators   110
7.9   Access to electricity: Indicators   110
7.10   Main policy recommendations of Doing Business 2019   116
8.1   SWOT study of Chad's sesame seed and gum arabic value chains   125
8.2   Cluster-based typology of export diversification policies   125
8.3   Comparing international good practices in investment incentives:
        Application to Niger   127
8.4   Main nontax market incentives to global value chains in the manufacturing
        sector in Morocco, Turkey, and Tunisia   129
8.5   Theory of change of revamped main export diversification policies in
        Mali, Chad, Niger, and Guinea ("game changers")   130
8.6   The cascade decision-making approach for agricultural value chains   133
8.7   Guinea: Customized MFD reform agenda for IFC and World Bank, 2019   136

Acknowledgments

This flagship regional report is the result of a joint team effort by the Macroeconomic, Trade, and Investment Global Practice and the Finance, Competitiveness, and Innovation Global Practice. It also benefited from the support of the Poverty Global Practice, the Governance Global Practice, and the International Finance Corporation, which contributed with reference papers, presentations, case studies, and other relevant technical notes and inputs, as well as participated in a number of discussions with key counterparts. The team is most grateful for the generous collaboration of the Malian, Chadian, Nigerien, and Guinean authorities, in particular the representatives of their ministries of agriculture, commerce, economy and finance, mines and industry, and planning, their national institutes of statistics, export promotion national agencies, and chambers of industry and commerce, all of whom provided valuable mission support and written inputs and took part in candid discussion throughout the preparation of the study.

This summary report was prepared by a team comprising multiple Global Practices, led by José R. López-Cálix (Lead Economist and former Program Leader). Main contributors (core team) were Ephraim Kebede (Consultant) for chapter 4, Ghada Ahmed (Consultant) for chapter 5, Nihal Pitigala (Consultant) for chapter 6, and Mehdi Benyagoub (Private Sector Specialist) for chapter 7. Valuable inputs and thoughtful technical advice were provided by Jean-Christophe Maur (Senior Economist and Co-Task Team Leader). Specific inputs from the extended team, most of them developed in more detail in the previous individual country studies, were provided by Mariama Cire Sylla (Private Sector Specialist); Mamoudou Nagnalen Barry (Young Professional) for the overview; Maria Reinholdt Andersen (Consultant), Nelly Bachelot (Consultant), and Irum Touqeer (Public Sector Specialist) for chapter 1; Fiseha Haile Gebregziabher (Economist), Dinar Prihardini (Economist), Hans Lofgren (Consultant), and Asif Islam (Economist) for chapter 2; Salma Daki (Consultant), Olivier Béguy (Senior Economist), and Abdoul Ganiou Mijiyawa (Senior Economist) for chapter 3; Masud Cader (Senior Portfolio Officer) for chapter 4; Daria Taglioni (Principal Country Economist) and Bonaventure Fandohan (Consultant) for chapter 5; Silvia Muzi (Program Coordinator), George Clarke (Consultant), and Lauren Clark (Consultant) for chapter 7; Mahaman Sani (Private Sector Specialist), Xavier Forneris (Senior Private Sector Specialist), Mukhtar Gulamhussein (Investment Officer), and Alexandre Laure (Senior Private Sector Specialist) for chapter 8.

Other contributors to the individual country studies included Luc Razafimandimby (Senior Economist), Markus Kitzmuller (Senior Economist), Susana Sánchez (Senior Economist), Olivier Béguy (Senior Economist), Marcel Nshimiyimana (Economist), Olanrewaju Kassim (Economist), Boulel Touré (Economist), Nancy Benjamin (Consultant), Thomas Bossuroy (Economist), Aly Sanoh (Senior Economist/Statistician), Fatoumata Fadika (Financial Sector Specialist), Ziva Razafintsalama (Senior Agricultural Economist), Johannes Hoogeveen (Lead Economist), Yaye Ngouye Ndao Ep Diagné (Operations Officer), Gael Raballand (Lead Public Sector Specialist), Gildas Bopahbe Deudibe (Consultant), Kirstin Roster (Strategy Analyst), Gemechu Ayana Aga (Economist), and Yosuke Kotsuji (Senior Investment Officer). Their respective individual contributions are detailed in each of the country reports and background notes.

Lars Christian Moller (Practice Manager) provided close monitoring, technical advice, and enthusiastic encouragement, whereas Consolate Rusagara (Practice Manager), Rashmi Shankar (Practice Manager), Michel Rogy (Program Leader), Christophe Lemière (Program Leader), Madio Fall (Acting Program Leader), Mehita Sylla (Country Manager), Sabrina Birner (Consultant), and Paul NoumbaUm (former Country Director) all advised the team at various stages of the process or provided inputs into various chapters and drafts. Soukeyna Kane (Country Director), François Nankobogo (Country Manager), Joëlle Dehasse (Country Manager), Rachidi Radji (Country Manager), Boubacar Walbani (Senior Operation Officer), and Michael Hamaide (Senior Country Officer) provided country guidance and valuable support to the team. Detailed and constructive advice was provided by the peer reviewers of the present report: Paul Brenton (Lead Economist), Vincent Palmade (Lead Economist), Joanne Catherine Gaskell (Senior Agricultural Economist), Hoda Youssef (Senior Economist), and José Daniel Reyes (Senior Economist). This complemented exceptional guidance previously provided by the peer reviewers of the individual country studies. For Chad and Mali: Jakob Engel (Young Professional), Gonzalo Varela (Senior Economist), Jean Michel Marchat (Lead Economist), and César Calderón (Lead Economist). For Niger: Daria Taglioni (Principal Country Economist), Fulbert Tchana (Senior Economist), Vandana Chandra (Consultant, former Senior Economist), and Albert Zeufack (Chief Economist). Maude Jean-Baptiste Valembrun (Program Assistant) did outstanding work on formatting and editing the main document. Micky Ananth (Operation Analyst) was instrumental in monitoring the budget of the whole set of studies. Hawa Maiga (Senior Executive Assistant), Mariama Diabate-Jabbie (Executive Assistant), Fatimata Sy (Senior Program Assistant), Hamsatou Diallo Barke (Executive Assistant), Theresa Bampoe (Program Assistant), and Edmond Badge, Habibatou Gologo, and Mamadou Bah (Communication Officers) also provided valuable logistical support and precious media guidance.

About the Author

José R. López-Cálix, a native of El Salvador, is a seasoned Lead Economist and former Program Leader in the Macroeconomics, Trade, and Investment Global Practice of the World Bank. López-Cálix obtained his PhD, MSc, and bachelor's degrees, with majors in international finance, trade, and econometrics, from the Catholic University of Louvain, Belgium, and the University of Pittsburg in the United States. Before working for the World Bank, his professional career included working in a number of international organizations, including the U.S. Agency for International Development, the U.S. Congress, the Canadian International Development Agency, and the Inter-American Development Bank. He also worked as Chief Research Director in the Central American Monetary Council and as visiting professor in several U.S. universities and the Central American Institute of Business Administration (INCAE) in Costa Rica. He has more than 25 years of experience working in the Latin America and the Caribbean, Middle East and North Africa, South Asia, and Sub-Saharan Africa regions of the World Bank, including multiple fragile and conflict-prone economies. He is the author of multiple books, academic articles, and reports and the recipient of multiple awards as an innovator for designing, testing, and successfully implementing analytical tools that have become mainstream within the World Bank and worldwide. These tools include an early-warning system of currency/fiscal crises, public expenditure tracking surveys, social service delivery surveys, export firm surveys, budgetary protection for priority social programs, a multivariable index of subnational (local) development, and most recently, a global value chain 2.0 (GVC 2.0) spatially integrated approach for attracting foreign direct investment and private sector participation to agribusiness development and export diversification in fragile settings.

Key Messages

This report describes the key policies of four fragile countries—Mali, Chad, Niger, and Guinea (henceforth the MCNG countries)—aiming to successfully leverage export diversification in order to foster economic growth. Following several unsuccessful attempts at diversifying their economies since the 1990s, in recent years, these countries have decided to reengage with actively diversifying their exports.

International experience shows conclusive evidence of the poor economic performance of fragile and resource-abundant African countries when compared to nonfragile, nonresource peers. Thus, while large-scale production of natural (mostly mining) resources offers substantial opportunities, it also comes with major shortcomings that prevent sustained high growth. These shortcomings hit particularly hard in countries finding themselves in conflict-prone situations motivated by either greed (where the benefits derived from resource-based growth justify the opportunity cost of fighting) or grievances (with resources appropriated by narrow elites).

Shortcomings include the tendency to grow beyond the economy's potential in cycles of booming prices, high gross domestic product (GDP) growth and fiscal volatility that translates into a fragile fiscal stance and limited fiscal space for public investment, a resource curse that favors production of noncompetitive, nontradable goods, and a growth pattern biased toward rent-seeking and low job-creation activities. Furthermore, all MCNG countries are landlocked (except Guinea) and feature small domestic markets.

To change direction, all MCNG countries have reached national consensus around respective Visions 2030–35, aiming, among others, to diversify their exports as a possible way out of this curse. This report fully supports such visions. Below, we do not summarize its main conclusions but rather emphasize 10 messages which can shape the design of national policies toward export diversification. The report focuses on the promotion of carefully selected agribusiness global value chains (GVCs) under a renewed cluster-based approach that can foster high and sustainable economic growth in fragile countries such as those covered by this report.

First message. Literature shows a strong correlation between export concentration and short-lived growth acceleration and between export diversification and high, sustained, inclusive growth. Over the last decades, natural resource exports have accounted for a major share of total MCNG exports. Estimates made for this report for Niger and Mali conclude that under their present resource-based export model, these economies will achieve (at best) modest, highly volatile average growth rates over the next decade. In contrast, nonmining, export-oriented diversification policies will allow them to reach high and sustained growth rates.

Second message. The so-called "resource curse" remains an obstacle to structural change, including labor reallocation from low to high productive activities, the mirror image of export diversification. While mining activities are poor job creators, above 75 percent of MCNG populations continue to rely on agriculture for their livelihoods, working as subsistence farmers or in low-productive informal activities. However, estimates made for this report show that modest (but positive) structural change in Chad, Niger, and Guinea has been led by other sectors, which has created employment in trade, construction, and public and financial services.

Third message. Exclusive strategies led by modern services or broad industrialization are unlikely to accelerate structural change in MCNG countries. Shifting resources from low-productive sectors such as agriculture or informal trade to high-productive modern services sectors requires skilled labor, which is scarce in these economies; while shifting resources from low-productive agriculture to broad manufacturing industries also seems unpromising because of these countries' failed record of import substitution policies with regard to the subregion and the poor financial performance of state-owned enterprises involved in productive activities.

Fourth message. In contrast, an outward-oriented agribusiness strategy can deliver diversification and create abundant, better-paying jobs for both low- and high-skilled workers. Such an agribusiness strategy would be based on a mix of: (i) improved access to agricultural inputs and new production technologies to increase productivity; (ii) new value chain crops and related industries gradually producing more sophisticated agribusiness exports; (iii) an improved, modern backbone of financial, transportation, and communications services; and (iv) an enhanced business climate effectively attracting targeted foreign direct investment (FDI).

Fifth message. To achieve this aim, the MCNG countries should consider embarking on a four-step export diversification strategy. From simple to more complex endeavors, taking these complementary steps would require upgrading the country's capacity for: (i) exporting more of the same; (ii) opening new markets (regional and global) abroad; (iii) piloting emerging, more sophisticated export winners, especially agri-based products; and (iv) moving into a fully-fledged GVC-based agribusiness diversification strategy.

Sixth message. Reducing export product and market concentration (the first two steps) can be implemented in the short term. All MCNG countries, albeit to varying degrees, are among the most product-concentrated and least market-diversified economies in Sub-Saharan Africa. In the particular case of Chad, both diversification indexes are deteriorating. A revamped export promotion policy should initially help increase the production of emerging nonmining exports. In parallel, new markets should be explored by gathering commercial intelligence and databases, approaching new FDI business partners, and facilitating upgraded interactions between buyers and sellers. While neighboring markets remain a priority for agri-export marketing, estimates show that MCNG countries are underexporting to the United States, India, France, Thailand, and Singapore. North African countries such as Morocco and Tunisia could also offer opportunities.

Seventh message. When it comes to piloting new and higher-value-added (complex) products (step 3), selectivity is more important than a policy of dispersed and costly expansion of untargeted export promotion. Alternatively, adopting an open-ended approach would make little difference because MCNG countries have few options as only about a dozen agri-based products per country appear to have a revealed comparative advantage (RCA), including gum arabic, sesame seed, maize, raw cotton, woven fabrics, and artificial fiber wadding. Potential winners in the list of agrifoods to be upgraded are cereals, jams, jellies, tropical fruit juices, sugar, and vegetable oils. The potential of livestock is also relevant despite the fact that it does not appear to have a RCA, most likely due to data shortcomings.

Eighth message. In the process of carefully selecting competitive GVCs, each MCNG country has identified a list of potential export products. Under agreement with the relevant authorities, this report singles out gum arabic and sesame seed for Chad, bovine meat and onions for Niger, and sesame and cashew for Mali. Although all of these products have a RCA as well as high potential, they are not the only ones on the list. However, in general, all emerging value chains are in their infancy and feature low participation in global (or even regional) markets. Hence, a starting point will require working at upgrading selected GVCs. In doing so, the move toward more sophisticated products in value chains will require skills and capabilities these countries will need to develop. Micro constraints to such development include lack of institutional policy support, inconsistent quality, low productivity and production volumes, limited agroprocessing capacity, and absence of leading foreign firms investing in value chain upgrading. In response, MCNG countries need to learn from successful exporting neighboring countries by focusing on attracting strategic investors to develop agrifood processing. Exploring the list of foreign firms involved in agribusiness in Africa would be a starting point.

Ninth message. This report introduces a new, full-fledged global value chain 2.0 (GVC 2.0) cluster-based approach to leveraging export diversification. The four pillars of this cluster-based policy (the fourth step) are: (i) process, product, and market upgrading of strategic (and well-selected) GVCs; (ii) targeted investments (the spatial dimension) in trade infrastructure and logistics corridors; (iii) revamped trade and logistics policies; and (iv) an e-business-friendly investment climate. While the first two pillars were developed above, the last two focus on simplifying trade procedures, reducing land registration costs, better managing public contracts, and allowing e-payments. The implementation of backbone services such as single windows and full application of ASYCUDA (Automated System for Customs Data) World in customs as well as online registration and digital payments for trade-related operations should streamline export procedures and reduce opportunities for corruption. As a complement to such measures, addressing the logistics gaps that plague trade transit is particularly critical for landlocked MCNG countries. The next step is to take into account the spatial dimension of the location of potential GVC production areas, which should not only avoid conflict-prone regions and corridors but also focus on the availability of complementary inputs in infrastructure and backbone services required for their operation. This report therefore proposes focusing mainly on the rehabilitation and maintenance of key corridors linking economic centers to the main ports of Dakar and Abidjan (Mali), Douala (Chad), and Cotonou and Lomé (Niger). Bilateral transit facilities and the elimination of myriad checkpoints along these corridors should improve the efficiency of freight transportation. In the case of Guinea, upgrading Conakry's port facilities and management is a must. Finally, to succeed, MCNG countries need to work at removing macro constraints in trade policy. Policy priorities should aim at lowering the number of tariffs and eliminating myriad corruption-prone nontariff barriers, complying with international trade certifications and traceability standards, and attracting leading regional and international firms with experience in marketing emerging GVCs.

Tenth message. The World Bank Group can play an important role in the implementation of the GVC 2.0 cluster-based strategy. Most World Bank projects on GVC development in MCNG countries have had limited success due to an almost unidimensional approach that promoted separate and often disconnected components of the agricultural export chain. MCNG countries often fail to make dedicated efforts to upgrade producers' organizations, adopt international health and technical product standards, and attract foreign firms. In exchange, the new GVC 2.0 approach features an integrated effort by the International Finance Corporation (IFC), the World Bank and, eventually, the Multilateral Investment Guarantee Agency (MIGA), all of which are World Bank Group members. In particular. IFC's role could be instrumental in attracting FDI. Following a so-called Cascade approach, which advocates the rationale for private and public sector interventions in fostering agribusinesses, the development of pilot Joint Implementation Plans (JIPs) is an example of joint World Bank Group collaboration, already piloted in Mali, where these institutions are involved in promoting mango exports. Other examples of promising joint collaboration are the setting up of risk-sharing facilities, agribusiness clusters, scope insight models, and value chain developer interventions.

Abbreviations

ANIPEX	Nigerian Export Promotion Agency (*Agence Nigérienne de Promotion des Exportations*)
APIM	Malian Investment Promotion Agency (*Agence pour la Promotion des Investissements au Mali*)
ASEAN	Association of Southeast Asian Nations
ASYCUDA	Automated System for Customs Data
CEDIAM	Malian Center for Research and Industrial and Agricultural Development (*Centre d'Étude et de Développement Industriel et Agricole du Mali*)
CEMAC	Economic and Monetary Community for Central Africa (*Communauté Économique et Financière d'Afrique Centrale*)
CET	common external tariff
CFA	Communauté Financière Africaine
CFAF	CFA franc
CFTA	Continental Free Trade Area
CGE	computable general equilibrium
CIT	corporate income tax
COFCO	China Oil and Foodstuffs Corporation
COPEOL	Oilseed Products Exploitation Corporation (*Compagnie pour l'Exploitation des Produits de l'Huile de Palme*)
CREDD	Strategic Framework for Economic Recovery and Sustainable Development (*Cadre Stratégique pour la Relance Économique et le Développement Durable*)
DTF	distance to frontier
DTIS	Diagnostic Trade Integration Study
EAC	East Asian countries
ECOWAS	Economic Community of West African States
EOD	Economic Orientation Document
EPA	Economic Partnership Agreement
EU	European Union
EUR	euro
FDI	foreign direct investment
FTA	free trade agreement
GDP	gross domestic product

GVC	global value chain
IC	investment climate
ICT	information and communications technology
IDA	International Development Association (of the World Bank Group)
IFC	International Finance Corporation (of the World Bank Group)
IMF	International Monetary Fund
IOPEPC	Indian Oilseed and Produce Export Promotion Council
ITC	International Trade Centre
JIP	Joint Implementation Plan
MAD	Moroccan dirham
MCNG	Mali, Chad, Niger, and Guinea
MFD	Maximizing Finance for Development
MIGA	Multilateral Investment Guarantee Agency (of the World Bank Group)
NGO	nongovernmental organization
NIF	tax identification number (*Numéro d'Identification Fiscale*)
NTB	nontariff barrier
OECD	Organisation for Economic Co-operation and Development
PCDA	Agricultural Competitiveness and Diversification Program (*Programme Compétitivité et Diversification Agricoles*)
PPP	public-private partnership
RCA	revealed comparative advantage
REC	Regional Economic Community
RECO	regional economic corridor
RSF	risk-sharing facility
RVC	regional value chain
SMEs	small and medium enterprises
SOGUIPAH	Guinean Oil Palm Corporation (*Société Guinéenne de Palmier à Huile*)
SONIPEV	Nigerien Meat Production and Exportation Corporation (*Société Nigérienne de Production et d'Exportation de Viande*)
SWOT	strengths, weaknesses, opportunities, threats
TFA	Trade Facilitation Agreement
TVI	import verification tax (*Taxe de Vérification des Importations*)
UNCTAD	United Nations Conference on Trade and Development
VAT	value-added tax
VC	value chain
WAEMU	West African Economic and Monetary Union
WTO	World Trade Organization

All dollar amounts are U.S. dollars unless otherwise indicated.

Overview

This regional report describes the key policies Mali, Chad, Niger, and Guinea—the so-called MCNG countries—should follow if they are to successfully leverage export diversification to foster economic growth in fragile and conflict-affected contexts. Following several unsuccessful attempts at diversifying exports since the 1990s, these countries have deepened their dependence on natural resource commodities, mostly minerals: bauxite in Guinea, uranium in Niger, gold in Mali, and oil in Chad. However, the experience of other countries in Africa and other parts of the world shows that while large-scale production of natural resources offers substantial opportunities, it also comes with major shortcomings. These include the tendency to feature unsustained growth accelerations during cycles of booming international prices, high gross domestic product (GDP) growth volatility translating into a fragile fiscal stance, a resource curse (the "Dutch disease") that favors production of non-tradable goods, and a growth pattern biased toward rent-seeking activities, all of which prevent the expansion of competitive products and inclusive job-creating activities. Not surprisingly, all recent National Development Plans—Mali's Vision 2025, Chad's Vision 2030, Niger's Vision 2035, and Guinea's Vision 2040—acknowledge that these countries have little choice but to create competitive and diversified economies. Exports diversification is a way out of this curse on the path to economic diversification and structural change. Below, we do not summarize all the main conclusions of the individual Country Reports but rather emphasize their key findings along with the new cluster-based global value chain (GVC) 2.0 development approach, which has the potential to shape national consensus on the design of competitive export-oriented policies designed to foster sustainable economic growth. However, the task is far from simple. Two introductory case studies will exemplify the complex nature of the major challenges that lie ahead.

Learning from Failure and Success: Two contrasting examples

The stories of Oilseed Products Exploitation Corporation (COPEOL) and Guinean Oil Palm Corporation (SOGUIPAH) exemplify the complex issues faced by exporting firms in fragile MCNG countries even when fully supported by their government (boxes O.1 and O.2). Initially depicted as game changers, the factors behind their respective failure and success immediately reveal some of the major challenges faced by exporting firms in the MCNG subregion. These difficulties can be of a very different nature and degree of severity.

BOX O.1

Learning from failure: The case of COPEOL in Guinea

Many decades ago, the recently independent Republic of Guinea inaugurated the Sincery peanut oil plant, which became the main economic driver in the city of Dabola. The region, which includes the Kouroussa-Dabola-Dinguiraye corridor as well as the neighboring cities of Mamou, Kankan, Siguiri, and Mandiana, produced enough peanuts to meet domestic demand. Located at the heart of the country, the region is blessed with a savanna climate and millions of hectares of arable land allowing the farming of peanuts. The plant benefited the thousands of peanut producers that supplied it, and its output was sold throughout the country, initially using the Kankan-Conakry railroad to reach local and international markets. Sincery was privatized in 1985, when the country moved from a centralized to a free market economy and privatized its state-owned enterprises (SOEs). However, the unpreparedness of the privatization process led to the plant being closed down a few years later.

In 2013, newly elected civilian President Alpha Conde decided to reopen the plant by bringing in the French companies Castel and Sofiproteol, which became its sole owners and registered the company as COPEOL. The city of Dabola expected that the plant would get its economy back on track by producing more peanut oil, while the government expected to reduce imports of lower-quality oils. In principle, the social contract was apt. Unfortunately, as time went by, the reopening of Sincery became a success story on paper only as its operation soon proved challenging. For instance, while featuring a renewed capacity for processing 50,000 tons of peanuts annually, the plant barely reached 10,000 tons, with similar results for exports. Today, after almost six years of activity, hope is fading, and the plant is at risk of closing its doors again.

The peanut oil value chain. COPEOL produces raw peanut oil for export and groundnut cakes for the domestic and subregional markets. The production cycle of COPEOL starts with a dialogue with peanut producers over both the fixed price of a kilogram of peanuts and the support to be provided by COPEOL to these producers. After agreeing a purchasing price following harvesting, COPEOL also provides both in-kind and financial support to farmers, who, in exchange, promise to grow peanuts and to sell them to COPEOL at the agreed price.

Based on the agreed price and the production forecasts received from farmers, COPEOL makes its own output forecast. Once harvesting ends, farmers bring their crop to the plant, with COPEOL recovering its precrop financing before paying for the rest of the crop at the agreed price. Then comes the processing stage, where COPEOL converts the nuts into semifinalized peanut oil and groundnut cakes. Hence, the key challenges for COPEOL are, at the production stage, the reliability of the agreement concluded with the farmers as supply shortages have an adverse impact on the plant's profitability, and at the processing stage, access to a reliable source of energy, inland transportation from Dabola to Conakry (and other cities in Guinea for groundnut cakes), and shipping of the peanut oil sold on the European market, where the final stage of the manufacturing takes place, or the groundnut cakes sold on subregional markets.

What went wrong? Several factors have contributed to COPEOL's risk of failure. First and foremost, few farmers abide by the content of the purchasing agreement during the harvesting period and generally not only refuse to reimburse inputs received but also prefer to sell their crops to other customers than the plant. In fact, when the plant reopened, President Alpha Conde said that "We want the plant to produce 100,000 tons instead of 50,000 tons. To achieve this, we need to support farmers in order to reach that level of production. The army will also farm 4,000 hectares in order to supply the plant." To achieve this target, the government provided assistance to peanut producer associations alongside the assistance received from COPEOL. Despite agreements signed with over 3,000 producers, who are members of the Federation of Peanut Producers of Upper Guinea, COPEOL failed to receive the 25,000–30,000 tons of peanut needed to break even. In fact, receipts did not even reach 3,000 tons. At a meeting organized by the government in May 2016, the president of the producers' association, Mr. Hadja Djénaba Bangoura, explained that the reason for this shortfall was the fall in the purchase price, which "was initially set at Guinean franc 3,000 per kilogram when harvest started in October. However, in December, COPEOL management decided to lower the price to Guinean franc 2,250 per kilogram, which totally

continued

Box O.1, *continued*

discouraged farmers." Only in late 2018 was a new CEO appointed to prevent closure.

Other loopholes requiring government intervention have included the following:

- *Low-quality infrastructure.* As peanuts farms are located in remote areas, the lack or low quality of rural roads not only damages shipments but increases transportation costs from village to market. The producers claimed that the agreed price of the peanut was at the farm gate, while COPEOL argued that it had to be paid after delivery to the plant.

- *Unavailability of a skilled labor force.* Highly skilled labor is needed to run the plant's laboratory. However, short of local staff, the plant continues to rely on expatriate staff from COPEOL subsidiaries in the subregion, which raises its operational costs.

- *Legal gaps on fiscal issues.* According to COPEOL's officials, the company enjoys tax exemptions on productive assets and export products. However, the provision of inputs to producers is considered a commercial transaction (with no exemptions) by the tax authorities, thus creating tax credits (potential liabilities) worth over US$ 200,000 in 2017.

- *Low access to electricity.* Though a mini dam provides electricity to Dabola, the period at which the plant operates at full capacity unfortunately coincides with the low water stream (January to April), when the dam barely functions. COPEOL therefore uses generators, which considerably increases its production costs.

- *Low competitiveness of the peanut oil made in Guinea.* High production costs combined with the lack of subsidies make the selling price of Guinean peanut oil higher than that of competitors' in the subregion, particularly Senegal, where the government provides considerable subsidies.

BOX O.2

Learning from a promising start-up: The case of SOGUIPAH in Guinea

Created in May 1987, the SOGUIPAH is among the few SOEs in the agricultural sector that have survived in such a violence-prone country. The company is entirely owned by the Guinean Government and was created to develop industrial rubber and palm oil plantations in the village of Diecke, in the forested southeast of the country. This is a remote area located more than 1,500 km away from the port of Conakry. It directly employs over 3,500 workers to operate its palm oil and rubber production plants and its own plantations (about 5,000 hectares of rubber and 4,000 of oil palm trees) as well as some rice produced for food security in the area. The company also provides direct support to about 800 small growers (covering an area of about 2,000 hectares) trained in the cultivation of rubber and oil palm. As the plant's processing capacity was only about 16,000 tons per year, the company decided to resort to artisanal processing, which is more labor-intensive, so as to reach 45,000 tons, with 10 artisanal centers employing over 3,000 additional staff. More recently and following financial support from the European Investment Bank to build a new plant, its output has now reached 55,000 tons per annum. Despite challenging local and international environments coupled with volatility in the international price of palm oil, SOGUIPAH has survived and continues to positively impact the area surrounding Diecke, with exports of palm oil multiplying fivefold between 2013 and 2016.

The palm oil value chain. SOGUIPAH produces palm oil and soap for the domestic and regional markets as well as rubber for the international markets. Palm oil is a high-demand product in Guinea because it is consumed daily by many Guinean families as a cooking ingredient. In the company's early years, successive Guinean governments preferred SOGUIPAH to sell its oil on the local market and temporarily banned exports. However, as production increased, both formal and informal (that is, illegal)

continued

Box O.2, *continued*

exports to neighboring countries (Mali, Senegal, Liberia, Sierra Leone, and Guinea-Bissau) as well as western countries in Europe and North America expanded. Officially, customs data report highly variable exports: between 2011 and 2016, SOGUIPAH's palm oil and rubber exports increased from about 500 to 5,000 thousand kilograms and from 10,000 to 15,000 thousand kilograms, respectively. This included contracts with world-class companies in Europe and Asia (such as Michelin), which guaranteed price stability.

Some positives. From planting to final processing of both products, their value chain starts and ends in Diecke, except for their distribution to the domestic, regional, and international markets. Cultivated areas are located in the same part of the country as the plant, thus reducing transportation costs from farm to plant. Such close local control of the production stages of the value chain is one of SOGUIPAH's main strengths. In fact, the company not only owns major oil palm and rubber tree plantations, but it also works closely with small private producers that supply the plant in order to add to its own production of raw material. SOGUIPAH owns about 9,000 hectares of cultivated lands that produce exclusively for its plant. The company has a three-level production system in the region, which benefits its small private suppliers: rice on lowlands, oil palm on plains, and rubber trees on hillsides. The company supports its suppliers in terms of funding (including seed and in-kind support) as well as training. Once the raw agricultural product reaches Diecke, different plants deal with the processing of the rubber and palm oil lines. While the rubber line produces only for export to Asia and Europe, the palm oil line produces mainly for food and soap manufacturing for the domestic market.

What else went right? Several factors contributed to SOGUIPAH's initially promising start. Among these were: (i) building a strong social contract with Diecke's population; (ii) support from international agencies; (iii) favorable natural conditions for developing the production of palm oil and rubber; and (iv) high demand from domestic, regional, and international markets.

- *SOGUIPAH turned its corporate social responsibility into an asset for securing its supply base and working environment.* The company not only provided social infrastructure (hospital, schools, rural roads, water sources, etc.), but also supported local farmers in developing family farms that grow rice and other daily consumption products. The company also provided inputs (seed, fertilizer, pesticide, etc.) to families and built up their basic production skills. Thanks to this social pact, SOGUIPAH's suppliers remained committed to supplying the company in a steady social environment, with few strikes or related violence.

- *SOGUIPAH received support from multiple donor sources.* Loans or technical assistance have been provided by the African Development Bank, the African Development Fund, the Arab Bank for Economic Development in Africa, the French Development Agency, the French Industrial Development Fund, and the European Investment Bank.

- *Favorable natural conditions, including a proper climate and abundant rainfall, favored production.* The country has over 2 million hectares of palm oil trees, of which 90 percent are natural (*Dura palm*). The remaining 10 percent (*Tenera palm*) belongs almost exclusively to SOGUIPAH's supply chain.

- *Existence of steady domestic and foreign markets in which to sell its production despite international price instability helped the company become profitable.* The consumption of palm oil and soap by the Guinean population and that of neighboring countries remained high thanks to consumers' preference for the local product due to the belief that it is organic and healthy.

However, in a fragile environment, major obstacles still limit the project's impact. These include the following: (i) inland transportation costs remain high as most of the company's customers live in Conakry (1,500 km away from the plant) or are incurred in reaching ports for shipping the rubber; (ii) export costs in the port of Conakry are among the highest in the region; (iii) in a few cases, the company has fallen short of meeting Michelin's (a major customer) quality standards as well as other export requirements (packaging, quality control through its laboratory, etc.); (iv) SOGUIPAH was hit by the Ebola epidemic, which broke out in the region where it is located and led to a temporary shortage of labor due to outward migration of workers; (v) farmers continue to suffer from land tenure insecurity; and (vi) the company's financial situation recently had to endure severe price slumps

continued

Box O.2, *continued*

for rubber (on average to about one third of its 2011 peak). Recapitalization and upgrading an obsolete industrial base might require opening up to a public-private partnership (PPP). Overall, a recent evaluation of the project concluded that SOGUIPAH had a highly differentiated impact on farmers, with greater benefits among farmers owning small plots of land rather than large landowners, and positive indirect effects from the emergence of spontaneous plantations by nonproject beneficiaries (Delarue and Cochet 2013).

Major structural challenges have contributed to the failure of past diversification efforts in the MCNG countries

Chief among these is the high frequency of political instability and violent conflicts that has hindered private investment, destroyed infrastructure, and disrupted trade. The 2016 Fragile States Index combines political and socioeconomic indicators such as (among others) the presence of fractionalized elites, collective grievances, the presence of refugees and internally displaced populations, uneven development, demographic pressure, and poverty. The index classified all these countries as "high," in fact in the "Alert" category, in the following (descending) order of severity: Chad, Guinea, Niger, and Mali (figure O.1). More in particular, literature shows a strong, positive, endogenous relationship between fragility and high population growth, which, despite major efforts, makes it likely that the demographic dividend will turn into a demographic misfortune, which will dampen economic growth in these countries.

In fragile contexts, the spatial dimension is an additional constraint. All MCNG countries (except Guinea) face major difficulties in accessing areas of the country affected by violent conflicts, including northern Mali and the Lake Chad area. Increased military outlays also shrink the fiscal space for filling infrastructure gaps countrywide (roads, energy, irrigation, etc.). This implies that selectivity is essential to rehabilitating and maintaining safe logistics corridors to meet export needs.

Other serious structural challenges have also prevented a rapid pace to diversify exports from new productive activities. Mali, Niger, and Chad face adverse geography for developing exports as only Guinea is not landlocked. Given multiple infrastructure and logistics gaps, poor internal connectivity and low access to power raise exporting costs and make access to markets, including neighboring markets, difficult. Security threats keep private and foreign investors away from some areas and disrupt labor flows. Low human capital accompanied by rapid population growth and the low quality of education translate into a mostly low-skilled population. Concentration on products with high export value and limited foreign market diversification lead to low insertion into GVCs, in addition to foreign direct investment (FDI) inflows being concentrated in extractive industries, and only recently for some countries, in specific backbone services.

FIGURE O.1

Since 2016, Mali, Chad, Niger, and Guinea have been classified in the "Alert" category in the Fragile States Index

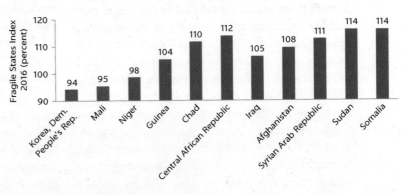

Sources: Fund for Peace 2016.
Note: MCNG = Mali, Chad, Niger, and Guinea.

So far, no MCNG country has received FDI in greenfield agriculture start-ups or in efficiency-seeking projects commonly associated with export diversification.

These common challenges have had some additional negative effects. The high frequency of violent conflicts not only hinders private investment but also shifts government consumption toward military expenditure, which makes it difficult to devote fiscal space to fostering diversification. Similarly, short-lived commodity booms translate not into productive public investment but rather into consumption. Moreover, excessive reliance on natural resources make MCNG economies highly vulnerable to external shocks. Not surprisingly, as soon as governments have made major efforts to affirm democracy, reduce fragility and conflict, and implement sound macro policies, their economic performance has significantly improved, with their attention shifting from short-term macro stability concerns to medium-term economic diversification ambitions.

There are compelling reasons for MCNG countries to urgently diversify their exports as their present growth model, which is based on natural resources, has reached its limits

These initial factors point to the importance of inclusive and diversified growth. The growth model based on natural resources dependence has several shortcomings. Mining activities are capital-intensive, which prevents the majority of the poor, who live in the rural sector, from benefiting from growth acceleration spillovers, including job creation and skills-enhancing effects. Mining extraction is highly dependent on international prices, and boom and busts translate into similar cycles in the nontradable economy, which affects high growth sustainability. These countries also need to create jobs in the agricultural sector, which has the highest population and poverty rates but also untapped job creation potential in agribusiness and possibilities for expanded insertion in global markets. In addition, dependence on natural resources fails to foster the development of the human capital and skills that are the hallmark of every modern economy. Finally, MCNG domestic markets are too small and fragmented to attract specialized FDI in the amounts needed to stimulate the development of an incipient private sector. FDI oriented toward reaching global markets is also badly needed if these countries are to catch up with technological changes and productivity enhancements.

There is conclusive empirical evidence of the poor economic performance of fragile, resource-abundant African countries during the periods 1998–2007 and 2008–2017. This shows that: (i) average economic growth in fragile countries remains lower than in nonfragile countries; (ii) per capita GDP growth in nonresource-abundant countries is higher than that in resource-abundant countries regardless of their condition of fragility, which supports the argument for diversification; (iii) growth in fragile, nonresource-abundant countries remains lower than in nonfragile, nonresource-abundant, which argues in favor of coming out of fragility status; and (iv) growth decelerated in nonfragile, resource-abundant countries while it accelerated in fragile resource-abundant countries, even if in the latter, the likelihood of conflict remains a possibility if resources continue to be appropriated by narrow elites.

Perhaps the most important justification for export diversification is that it would give these countries a chance to reach the expected high, sustained, and inclusive growth aimed at in their respective vision

Over the last 35 years, per capita GDP income levels in Mali, Chad, and Niger have stagnated (and Guinea—not shown in figure O.2—is no exception). An initial macro simulation based on cross-country regressions shows that export diversification is growth-enhancing since beyond reducing fiscal and growth volatility, increased openness would generate significant growth gains for Mali, Niger, and Chad and to a lesser extent Guinea. Based on a popular partial equilibrium model, simple benchmarking indicates that if these countries were to become as open to international trade as, for example, Malaysia or Vietnam, their annual per capita growth rates would increase by 0.9 to 1.8 percentage points (ppts) in Niger, between 1.6 to 2.6 ppts in Mali, and between 0.7 and 1.2 ppts in Chad. When strongly supported by structural reforms, openness brings diversified assets and investment, better quality of institutions, time-bound policies, competition, and less capture. In fact, opening alone would force these countries to counter global business cycles and supply disruptions in far-away locations as these introduce instability in the incorporation of crucial inputs into their production chain.

FIGURE O.2

Per capita GDP income levels in Niger, Mali, and Chad have broadly stagnated over 35 years

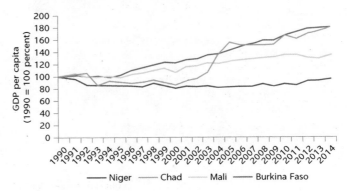

Source: World Bank 2017.
Note: GDP = gross domestic product.

A second macro simulation based on a computable general equilibrium (CGE) model applied individually to Niger and Mali concludes that without export diversification, these countries' economies would be expected to grow at best at an average annual rate of 4.6 and 4.7 percent, respectively, until 2025, modest rates in per capita GDP terms given their 3–4 percent population growth rates. Moreover, such a conclusion is unaffected by positive terms-of-trade shocks. In fact, simulating a positive external environment, that is, a positive terms-of-trade shock consisting of an increase in the price of the products currently exported (or a decrease in the price of imported products), shows that any such growth upsurge would be only temporary and not fundamentally alter the modest average growth rates results obtained under the baseline.[1] These findings confirm that these countries' current natural commodity-based model has limitations.

Conversely, higher average growth rates would result from pro-export diversification policies boosting agricultural productivity or trade facilitation. Through its impact on productivity, investing in irrigation has the potential to increase Niger's average GDP growth from 4.6 to 5.3 percent per annum. The boost to real consumption would be even larger, with average consumption growth increasing by 1 ppt from 4.6 to 5.7 percent per annum. This is explained by the fact that the improvement in agriculture productivity would benefit the incomes of low-skilled rural workers, thus contributing to poverty reduction, as well as those of landowners. Similarly, higher average growth rates, though less pronounced than in the previous case, would arise from improved trade facilitation policies. Results for Mali show similar effects on growth, even if magnitudes vary.

Climbing the ladder of export diversification would reinvigorate structural change

Growth acceleration in the context of export diversification can only succeed if accompanied by structural change. Economic transformation is defined as a continuous rise in per capita output coupled with major shifts in critical economic and demographic variables.[2] One of those shifts is structural change as the rising ratio of average labor productivity from low- to high-productivity activities comes

Export diversification ladder

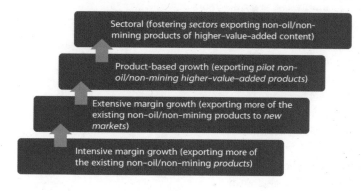

accompanied by labor flows from lower- to higher-productivity subsectors and changes in the composition of exports from low- to high-value-added products.

MCNG countries have many nonmutually exclusive options for export diversification. Based on the lessons from international experience, the organizational representation below (figure O.3) presents a simple typology of export diversification, which helps define what policy choices and mix these countries face. Each government should consider each of these as part of a customized policy mix leading to the design of its own strategy.

The proposed typology considers four steps, in ascending order of complexity, in climbing the export diversification ladder (figure O.3).

- *In the first step*, a country simply aims to export more of what it already produces as nonresource products (growth in its "intensive margin").

- *In the second step*, the country exports more of what it produces as nonresource exports to new markets (growth in its "extensive margin").

- *In exchange, the third step* features a country moving to emerging, often pilot higher-value-added nonresource products. This is the case when countries target the promotion of a few nontraditional exports (or "strategic bets"), commonly agribusinesses in West Africa. This move not only leads to less export concentration on a narrow basket of commodities but unleashes a learning-by-doing productivity enhancement process in the medium term.

- *Finally, in the fourth step*, emerging exports of new, higher-value-added nonresource goods (and eventually services) lead to the recomposition of subsectoral GDP in favor of a higher share of nonresource-based and higher-value-added products, eventually achieving the sectoral diversification of the economy.

It is important to note that the last two steps are normally accompanied by structural change, with, for example, the labor force moving from low- to high-productivity goods or subsectors in the economy.

Interestingly and contrary to a regional trend, in recent decades, all MCNG countries featured positive—albeit slow—structural change, which also accounted for a significant share of labor productivity growth. When compared to regional averages for four groups of countries—Latin America and the Caribbean, High Income, Sub-Saharan Africa, and Asia, MCNG's labor productivity decomposition into a within-sector component due to technological change, capital accumulation, and reduced misallocation, and positive structural change differs from the negative average for other Sub-Saharan Africa countries. Thus, Niger's structural change accounted for about 30 percent of labor productivity growth over the period 1990–2015 (figure O.4), Chad's for about 35 percent over the period 2005–2015, and Guinea's for about 40 percent during 2006–2015. However, it is essential to acknowledge that labor reallocation from agriculture in these countries mainly went to low-productivity subsectors in urban areas such as retail trades and services, thus expanding the informal sector.

In Steps 1 and 2, MCNG countries should make an effort to export higher volumes, perhaps with an eye on regional neighbors (for example, a free trade agreement with Nigeria) while opening new markets in South and East Asia as well as in North Africa.

Since exporting more of the same products and reaching new markets are two logical first steps, a prerequisite should be to identify potential goods or services as well as market opportunities. However, nontraditional opportunities are scarce in MCNG countries because they have the least product-diversified and most market-concentrated export ratios in Sub-Saharan Africa. In a few cases, such ratios have even deteriorated over time. Using a parametric measure of product competitiveness, namely revealed comparative advantage (RCA), allowed us to identify emerging products. This measure was complemented by product space analysis, which determines the suitability of any product upgrade

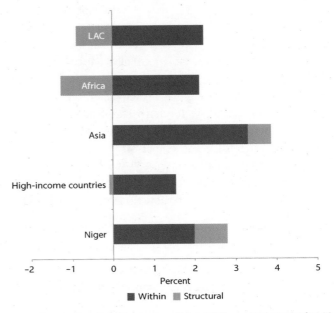

FIGURE O.4

Decomposition of labor productivity growth in Niger, 1990–2015, and other world regions, 1990–2005

Sources: Niger: National accounts and labor statistics; regional averages for LAC, Africa, Asia and high-income countries: Daki and López-Cálix (2017), based on McMillan, Rodrik and Verduzco (2014).
Note: LAC = Latin America and the Caribbean.

option based on its competitive endowment in terms of technology or skills and on its proximity to foreign markets for products with similar production capabilities.

The short-term focus should be on the very few products in which each country already has a strong comparative advantage and features dynamic exports. Not surprisingly, in general, few MCNG products are competitive, and their position in the product space is highly limited as well as peripheral, which does little to favor diversification or find new markets. However, success in making strategic bets relies on being highly selective. In this case, with the exception of extractives (oil and mineral), MCNG countries' competitiveness arises mainly from fruit and vegetable, meat, and cotton products. Hence, the short-term strategy should prioritize promoting those few products in which these countries have a strong competitive advantage as well as strong job-creation potential as a result of their rural location. For example, Niger is said to be the largest exporter of some agricultural products to neighboring Economic Community of West African States (ECOWAS) countries, including sorghum, millet, and onions. In addition, its livestock trade flows with Nigeria are on par with those from Chad and Mali. Mali's export competitiveness lies not only in cotton but also in sesame seed, tropical fruits (such as mangoes), and vegetable oils. Although Chad's exports are the least product-diversified, it has positive RCAs in gum arabic, sesame seed, maize (corn) flour, raw cotton, and derived fabrics and fibers. In contrast, Guinea has a much richer export supply nor only in vegetables and fruits but also in fish. Interestingly, in all four countries, the processed food industry is still young and growing.

Regarding new markets, beyond Asian ones, a concerted and comprehensive effort should be made by MCNG countries to ensure that ECOWAS provisions with Nigeria are applied. As the largest market in the ECOWAS region, Nigeria alone could be the engine of MCNG countries' export growth. The focus should be on reducing transaction costs, complementing investments in regional transportation and energy infrastructure, and improving logistics services. Vietnam and Gulf Cooperation Council (GCC) countries also have market potential. To initiate this strategic move, the first step should be to assess the mutual benefits that would derive to MNCG countries and Nigeria from mutually lowering both tariffs and nontariff barriers (NTBs) on key staple products, thus removing barriers to trade in agricultural and livestock products. These measures should be discussed as part of the ECOWAS forum as well as through bilateral channels. Greater joint efforts in security, including increased protection for populations, land, and livestock along the MNCG countries' long borders with Nigeria are also needed if they are to expand access to productive territory. Finally, these efforts should include guaranteed access to the Lake Chad shores in order to promote the fishing sector.

The medium-term focus should be on gradually stepping up efforts to promote more sophisticated (higher-value-added) export products, mostly in agribusiness goods and textiles, as well as in information and communications technology (ICT) and transportation services. The most critical challenge lies in acquiring a sufficiently large pool of local industrial skills and capabilities since these cannot be imported or developed in a short period of time. MCNG countries therefore need to encourage the upgrading and expansion of small and medium enterprises (SMEs), which currently provide only low-quality products to the domestic (or at best regional) market, into global markets with the support of foreign firms. Given common production patterns, the focus of possible pilot products might be on: (i) *Textiles*: Given the availability of the productive knowledge and skills required to manufacture these products, there is clear potential for domestic firms to increase their share of the domestic and global clothing markets, especially as their low labor cost advantage offers MCNG countries the opportunity to expand their textile industry into high-quality fabrics and garments such as woven fabrics; and (ii) *Agribusiness and livestock products* such as rice, pasta, fruits juices, vegetable oils, leather, dairy products, and frozen meat. Here, carefully selected FDI may stimulate an increase in agricultural productivity as well as enhanced storage, packaging, and transportation facilities in tandem with gradually expanding these countries' knowledge base with a view to manufacturing more sophisticated agribusiness products. Finally, ICT and travel and transportation services have also potential. However, close ongoing consultation with the private sector is fundamental in making the final selection.

Overall, and especially at the pilot stage, the government should not forcefully promote all identified priority sectors simultaneously. Rather, a stepwise selection combining a short-term with a medium-term approach with sound implementation and monitoring mechanisms is highly advisable.

In Steps 3 and 4, success requires a GVC 2.0 cluster-based approach

Selecting a few strategic bets (or alternatively choosing from an open menu of about a dozen emerging products) is only the initial step. Making new GVC development a national priority and developing GVC potential is a much bigger challenge. In this respect, a shared national vision would provide clear goalposts for the export strategy in terms of both the few agribusinesses selected and the macro diversification targets (openness ratios, export growth rates, jobs created, etc.) Developing GVC potential also requires learning from experience. In fact, many projects supported by the World Bank Group for GVC development in MCNG countries have identified a number of pitfalls, resulting from their almost unidimensional approach centered on single products and lack of dedicated efforts to upgrade producers' organizations, adopt international health and technical product standards, attract foreign firms, and foster participation by the private sector. While MCNG countries reinvigorate their agribusinesses exports by initially promoting the lower-value-added products in which they have a comparative advantage in a given GVC (step 1) and reaching new markets (step 2), both horizontal and vertical policies are needed to help them develop a comparative advantage in higher-value-added products.

Given limited financing resources in these countries, the policy framework should carefully ponder the scope of application, the types of instruments to be used, and their period of application. In terms of scope, policies can be vertical (applicable to selected products or sectors) or horizontal (applicable to all sectors).[3] As regards the types of policy instrument, these may take the form of public input useful to private production or a market intervention that affects the behavior of particular firms. In addition, policy interventions should be temporary and carefully weighed against options and available resources. The matrix below presents a typology of the mix of a number of possible export diversification policies (both horizontal and vertical) for MCNG countries (table O.1). Please note that this list is not exhaustive and has been customized and detailed in each country study. The aim here is to give a broad summary of the main policy areas to consider.

This GVC 2.0 cluster-based approach emphasizes that what matters to success is the need to deal with the integrality of the value chain and not just with isolated parts of it. Hence, it is possible to summarize a carefully selected set of key complementary policies that would provide the fundamentals for private-sector-driven export diversification in MCNG countries. These are grouped in four components (pillars) of complementary micro and macro diversification-prone policies that compose the logical chain of the desired reform (table O.2):

i. *Effective, well-coordinated government interventions aiming at upgrading selected strategic bets* in terms of the development of regional value chains (RVCs) and GVCs for products and services. Key interventions should concentrate on: (i) improving the production, yields, and quality of the strategic bets; (ii) developing the capacity and organization of the chains actors; (iii) complying with international certifications and traceability standards; and (iv) attracting FDI in greenfield projects by lead regional and international firms.

ii. Given the highly limited fiscal and external borrowing space prevailing in MCNG countries, *spatially targeted investments in trade infrastructure (including*

TABLE O.1 Cluster-based typology of export diversification policies

	HORIZONTAL POLICIES	VERTICAL POLICIES
Public inputs	• Business climate improvement reforms • Investment in infrastructure (spatially located on export production regions and key logistics corridors)	• Quality, phytosanitary, and packing standards and controls • Matching grants to export-dedicated SMEs • Specialized training programs for production
Market interventions	• Trade policy, customs, and logistics reforms • Access to digital finance and competition policies • Research and development fund • Job skills programs	• Farm management upgrade support to SMEs with export growth potential • Temporary tax exemptions for investment in export-oriented GVCs • Land access concessions

Note: GVCs = global value chains; SMEs = small and medium enterprises.

TABLE O.2 Revamped main export diversification policies in Mali, Chad, Niger, and Guinea ("game changers")

MAIN CHALLENGES	KEY POLICIES AND MARKET INTERVENTIONS	MAIN OUTPUTS AND OUTCOMES	
Component 1: Upgrading strategic GVCs			
• Low process and product upgrading (participation in low-value chain segments such as livestock and raw products, producers' organizations at a nascent stage, poor quality and lack of certification and control standards, deforestation)	• Introduce productivity and animal health enhancements (vaccine, fertilizer, certified seed, storage, sanitation, environment standards) [step 1] • Strengthen producers' organizations and management [step 1] • Training on quality certification, control, and lab testing [step 1] • Financial support to produce higher-value products: e.g., frozen meat, sesame oil, soap [step 1] • Digitization of agricultural financial transactions [steps 1–3] • Create risk-sharing facility for start-up exporters [steps 1–3]	• Process and product upgrades (with productivity enhancements) of selected GVCs • Improved farming techniques and producers' skills • Increased number of export products complying with quality standards • Eligible exporters access to prefinancing	• Increased output and exports of selected products • Gradual diversification of export supply toward higher-value-added goods and services
• Low market upgrading and global links (lack of market information, unskilled producers and workers)	• Develop information systems on foreign markets [step 2] • Consider lighter and better packaging and branding [step 2] • Financial support for exploring new (niche) markets [step 2]	• Market information upgraded • New brands developed for higher-value-added products	• Increased exports to new markets abroad
Component 2: Targeting investments in trade infrastructure and main corridors			
• Infrastructure gaps in power, water, irrigation and roads • Nonorganized domestic transportation • Logistics corridors in poor condition and trucking subject to road harassment • Cumbersome and corruption-prone customs and logistic procedures	• Financial support to off-grid solar panel power solutions and new irrigation techniques (pumps, drips) [steps 3, 4] • Rehabilitating and maintaining 5 key corridors: Bamako-Dakar; Bamako-Abidjan; N'Djamena-Douala; Niamey-Cotonou, and Niamey-Lomé [steps 3, 4] • Reduce road checks [step 1] • Introduce single window for customs supported by risk-based postaudit and e-payments [steps 3, 4]	• Increased access rates to power and water by populations • Lower transportation costs • Lower transit time and customs costs • Reduce the number of corruption-prone transactions	• More conducive environment for GVC export development
Component 3: Revamped trade and access to finance policies			
• High anti-export bias with tariff exemptions and escalation (despite move to CET • Distortionary and corruption-prone use of NTBs	• Reduce CET to four bands (0, 5, 10, and 20) [step 1] • Redefine or phase out inefficient tariff exemptions [steps 1, 2] • Eliminate cross-border barriers and illegal paratariffs [step 1, 2]	• Lower the cost of imports and elimination of illicit customs fees	• Increased trade openness • Increased access to foreign markets • Financial inclusion • Reduced informality • Increased access to land • Lower cost and time lags thanks to modern and more efficient trading
• Farmers' low access to formal banking • Lack of awareness on digital finance • Lack of access to foreign markets for farmers	• Digitize farmers' land registry and payments of public inputs (seed, fertilizer) using mobile phones [steps 1, 2] • Digitize payments by farmers' organizations [step 3]	• Increased use of mobile money, digital money, and e-commerce • Better access to finance for farmers	

continued

TABLE O.2, *continued*

MAIN CHALLENGES	KEY POLICIES AND MARKET INTERVENTIONS	MAIN OUTPUTS AND OUTCOMES
Component 4: Facilitating a business-friendly investment climate		
• Cumbersome procedures for SME creation	• Lower the cost of registration to a flat fee and reduce or eliminate capital requirements [step 1] • Finalize computerization of registry of firms [step 3]	• Reduced cost and time needed for registration
• Slow and corruption-prone granting of land permits	• Lower the cost of concessions to a flat fee [step 1] • Reduce procedures and time needed to obtain concessions [step 3] • Create a website for granting concessions [step 3]	• Reduced cost and time needed to obtain land concessions
• Outdated trade ICT systems	• Full implementation of SYDONIA WORLD in customs [step 2] • Update mapping of import and export procedures followed by electronic submission [step 3]	• Reduced cost and time needed for import/export transactions

Note: Each policy action has a suitable sequence of intervention (shown in brackets as steps) on the export diversification ladder. Steps 1–2: short term; steps 3–4: medium term. CET = common external tariff; GVS = global value chain; ICT = information and communications technology; NTBs = nontariff barriers; SME = small and medium enterprise.

access to power and water) and rehabilitation and maintenance of key road corridors with a view to increasing agricultural productivity and reducing transportation costs. It is crucial to develop five regional economic corridors to serve already prioritized RVCs or GVCs. These investments should be accompanied by a thorough review of customs and Conakry port transit procedures.

iii. *A strong policy commitment to reduce trade and logistics costs and become globally competitive.* Trade policy should remove any bias against exporting and ensure effective competition in markets for products and in key services such as transportation, energy, and communication. Free trade agreements (FTAs) should foster exchanges with key commercial partners in the strategic bets. Digital technologies can lead to steep declines in transportation and communication costs and create substantial opportunities to export services such as back-office processing. E-trade can also widen the range of mechanisms through which small producers in developing countries can grow through exporting, create jobs, and enhance their productivity.

iv. *A clear, transparent, predictable business-friendly investment climate* that would facilitate adequate incentives for domestic and foreign private investors. Having a modern investment code is not enough to attract foreign and domestic private investment. Rather, key policies and market interventions should aim to reduce the cost of registration of business start-ups, simplify tax payments, speed up the issuance of land and construction permits, especially those for sites located in key producing areas, encourage access to credit and digital financial inclusion, improve court management and corporate governance, and develop the framework for an effective competition policy and public-private partnerships (PPP).

In general, for agricultural sellers, upgrading strategic bets in MCNG GVCs requires densification and economic upgrading to higher-value-added activities. Densification is about engaging more local actors (firms and workers) in the agricultural GVC network. This contributes to the overall goal of increasing a country's value added as it creates spillovers across sectors and resilience to external shocks, which are likely to increase with greater export orientation, other things being equal. In turn, economic upgrading is about gaining competitiveness in higher-value-added products, tasks, and sectors. Three types of economic upgrading exist: (i) moving into more sophisticated products; (ii) increasing value-added shares in existing GVC tasks through technology; and (iii) moving into new value chains with higher-value-added shares. Policy makers and entrepreneurs need to decide on the type of economic upgrading desired.

Lessons learned from GVC upgrading experiences worldwide show that single-policy moves and stepwise strategies tend to fail and that successful global (and regional) value chains rely instead on a mix of several key ingredients: (i) The development of agricultural hubs under a cluster-based approach, that is, a multidimensional GVC upgrading strategy with simultaneous programs involving producers' organizations, comprehensive and flexible GVC-specific marketing policies and foreign investment; (ii) adopting a new farm management approach focused on improvements in product quality and standards implementation across the chain and aimed at developing producers' collective action so as to raise farmers' output and incomes; (iii) specialized foreign investment from dedicated multinational firms that are both proven global champions in upgrading product-specific value chains with the active participation of producers and processors and in exploring trajectories linking raw agricultural commodities to higher-value-added industries; and (iv) agricultural policy support aligning producers' need to avoid social, environmental, or economic failure with requirements from global and regional markets, that is, a new productive industrial development policy that fosters agribusinesses GVCs with renewed private sector participation.

An effective and comprehensive cluster-based approach should also address the numerous infrastructure gaps that affect production (power and water) or plague trade transit along the key corridors linking its economy to the ports of Dakar and Abidjan (Mali), Cotonou and Lomé (Niger), and Douala (Chad) as well as to Nigeria's markets. Road and logistics infrastructure are poor. The management of dry ports in neighboring countries (such as Dosso for the Cotonou corridor and Niamey Rive Droite for the Lomé, Tema, and Abidjan corridors) needs to be reviewed as these countries have potential for concessionary management by the private sector. Another priority government initiative should be the construction of a 49-hectare parking area in Maradi for trucks en route to Nigeria. Finally, governance along corridors is a major issue given significant illegal payments and associated road harassment on transit routes. Finally, cross-border trade remains expensive and inefficient, to a great extent due to difficulty in obtaining import and export licenses.

High customs tariffs resulting from regional trade arrangements and NTBs ensure that MCNG economies remain highly protected. All MCNG countries (except Guinea) have little independent control over the two traditional instruments of trade policy: the exchange rate, and tariffs. Since 1960, Mali, Niger, and Chad have shared a common currency, the CFA franc, whose value is linked to that of the euro. As member countries of the West African Economic and Monetary Union (WAEMU), Economic and Monetary Community for Central Africa (CEMAC), or ECOWAS, these states have also agreed to adopt a common external tariff (CET), which has been in effect since the end of the 1990s. While the recent depreciation of the CFA franc has favored Niger's export competitiveness, high tariffs, numerous exceptions, and high tariff escalation make diversification harder. Despite ongoing nominal tariff reductions agreed under regional arrangements, Mali, Niger, and Chad's applied tariffs remain not only higher than those of most regions, but their projected level of protection under the CET will not decrease significantly at the end of the transition period. To make matters worse, tariffs are subject to considerable distortions arising from either a multiplicity of ad hoc border taxes and fees or NTBs such as misapplication of rules of origin or health and sanitary standards, which encourages informal trade and corruption. Renegotiating the CET in regional forums, eliminating inefficient exemptions, and removing parafiscal taxes and fees and NTBs are obvious policy priorities.

The trade facilitation agenda would also need to include significant streamlining of customs. Procedures should be put in place to reduce opportunities for corruption arising from opaque and antiquated administrative practices and lack of modern systems. Current reforms are being implemented only slowly. After many years, the full adoption of ASYCUDA (Automated System for Customs Data) World is expected to be completed and operational in most customs offices by end-2019. Work on a national single window for customs, which will expedite the harmonization of import and export documents, is in its early stages. There is also a need to introduce regulations enabling customs automation as this also reduces opportunities for corruption and to revise the Customs Code so as to integrate e-payments. Other desirable initiatives include a harmonized application of the World Trade Organization (WTO) Trade Facilitation Agreement (TFA).

A predictable business-friendly investment climate requires tackling the major constraints to private investment in MCNG countries. Firms surveyed by a World Bank enterprise survey in all four countries identified political instability, corruption, informality, poor regulatory oversight, energy gaps, and low access to finance as major constraints. Exporters in particular consider customs and trade regulations as well as access to finance higher constraints than do nonexporters. Given current trends, the subregion runs the risk of widening its competitiveness gap with regional and global comparators. However, among the four countries, Niger has recently recorded promising and steady improvements in its Doing Business ranking. Mali is a prime example of a country that has initiated but has not been able to sustain systematic reform. Guinea and Chad are at preliminary stages in undertaking a holistic reform effort addressing investment climate issues. Furthermore, complementary firms' productivity analysis shows that Mali's, Niger's, and Guinea's labor productivity appears to be at about the level expected given their per capita income level. However, labor productivity among Guinean firms shows about twice that found in Mali and Niger. Exporters are also more productive than nonexporters in the three countries in this study. Median exporters in these three countries produce about twice as much per worker as median nonexporters. However, this difference is not due to higher capital intensity or skills but rather to a higher presence of foreign firms with their good technological and organizational skills. Finally, Nigerien firms appear less likely to export than Guinean and Malian ones. Overall, perhaps excepting Niger, the single most important factor underlining these poor results is these countries' chronic lack of a sustained and comprehensive reform drives as governments keep acting on isolated aspects of the investment climate with little significant long-lasting impact on firms' productivity. Hence, the need to make this aspect part of the cluster-based approach.

The importance of the International Finance Corporation (IFC) in attracting FDI to the development of the GVC 2.0 cluster-based approach cannot be overstated. On the one hand, the vast number of SMEs currently producing for consumption in the domestic market or selling their raw products in foreign markets have few linkages with the modern, mostly foreign-owned companies trading in the international markets and involved in vertically integrated trading. These SMEs have no or little access to modern technology or knowledge. Despite the market incentives granted to foreign-owned and domestic firms as well as to SOEs and designed to foster a level playing field, experience indicates that these incentives are neither the best strategy for attracting FDI nor the only policies that matter to them (World Bank 2014, 2018). On the other hand, in practice, studies of successful cases conducted in Africa strongly advocate the key role played by international firms as well as the supporting role played by IFC. This role has been redefined under the Maximizing Finance for Development (MFD) framework, which leverages private investments and optimizes the use of public funding. The MFD framework is represented by a Cascade approach, which prioritizes private sector solutions (whenever possible), gradually introducing public interventions only to deal with market failures and risks, and favoring PPPs as needed. In practice, the GVC 2.0 cluster-based approach is already being piloted in Mali. Since 2017, a mango project has been supported under the World Bank Group's Joint Implementation Plan (JIP). The project supports four actors: producers, transporters, processors, and traders. The division of labor has the Bank tackling infrastructure and logistics and institutional bottlenecks, IFC supporting SMEs with agrifinance, the financing of the Africa Leasing Facility, and investment in an African fruit processing company, and Multilateral Investment Guarantee Agency (MIGA) providing a political risk guarantee.

NOTES

1. In addition, if a commodity price windfall were to occur, for the most part, only the owners of the natural resource in question and high-skilled workers would benefit from such terms-of-trade improvement.
2. Other possible shifts are change in the sectoral composition of outputs (often toward the manufacturing and services subsectors), rising urbanization (creation of productive mid-sized cities), and an upgrade in the quality of jobs and demographic transition from high to low birth rates (World Bank 2019).
3. A recent (2018) World Bank analytical tool, the Country Private Sector Diagnostic, aims to identify priority sector-specific constraints and links to private sector opportunities. Guinea is in the process of completing such a study.

REFERENCES

Daki, S., and J. R. López-Cálix. 2017. "Structural Change in Niger." Background paper, *Niger: Leveraging Export Diversification to Foster Growth*, World Bank, Washington, DC.

Delarue, J., and H. Cochet. 2013. "Systemic Impact Evaluation: A Methodology for Complex Agricultural Development Projects: The Case of a Contract Farming Project in Guinea." *European Journal of Development Research* 25: 778–96.

Fund for Peace. 2016. Fragile States Index, Washington, DC, https://fundforpeace.org/wp-content /uploads/2018/08/fragilestatesindex-2016.pdf.

McMillan, M., D. Rodrik, and Í. Verduzco-Gallo. 2014. "Globalization, Structural Change, and Productivity Growth, with an Update on Africa." *World Development* 63: 11–32.

World Bank. 2014. "World Bank Group: A New Approach to Country Engagement." World Bank, Washington, DC.

——. 2017. "Niger: Leveraging Export Diversification to Foster Growth." Report No. 120306-NE, World Bank, Washington, DC.

——. 2018. *Global Investment Competitiveness Report 2017/2018: Foreign Investor Perspectives and Policy Implications*. Washington, DC: World Bank. doi:10.1596/978-1-4648-1175-3.

——. 2019. "On the IDA-18 Special Themes: Jobs and Structural Transformation." Unpublished paper, World Bank, Washington, DC.

1 Development Context for Export Diversification in Mali, Chad, Niger, and Guinea

ABSTRACT

- *Mali, Chad, Niger, and Guinea (MCNG) face adverse geography in their effort to develop exports.*

- *Three structural challenges have prevented them from diversifying: poor connectivity conditions, continuous security threats in fragile environments, and low human capital.*

- *The spatial dimension also matters to export diversification in fragility contexts.*

- *All MCNG countries feature varying degrees of the "Dutch disease," arising from high export concentration in natural resources commodities in a small number of foreign markets, thus preventing the development of their nonresource economies and perpetuating conflicts arising from state appropriation.*

- *Low insertion into global value chains is accompanied by foreign direct investment (FDI) inflows concentrated in extractive industries, and only recently for some countries in services.*

- *To date, MCNG countries have received no FDI either in agriculture or in efficiency-seeking projects commonly associated with export diversification.*

CHALLENGES IN THE QUEST OF EXPORT DIVERSIFICATION

Exploring the potential for export diversification in the economies of Central and West Africa and especially in Mali, Chad, Niger, and Guinea (MCNG) should initially consider their geospatial configuration, which presents a unique mix of adverse features for emerging products. First, three of the countries—Niger, Mali, and Chad—are landlocked, which contributes to their isolation from external markets. Second, low population densities pose further challenges to market opportunities (map 1.1). For example, the Communauté Économique et Financière d'Afrique Centrale (Economic and Monetary Community for Central Africa; CEMAC) region, represents a market

MAP 1.1

Market potential of West African agglomerates

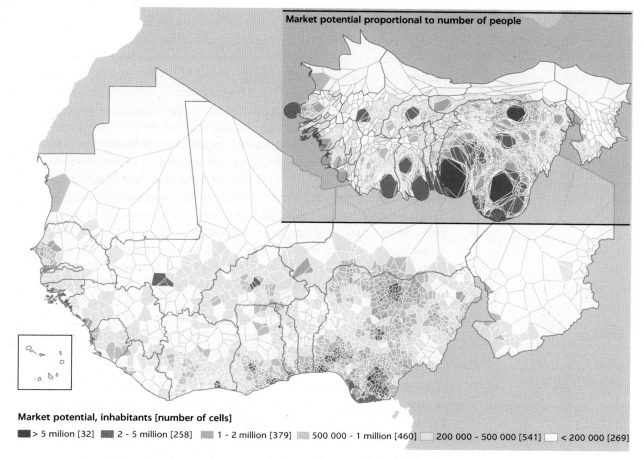

Market potential proportional to number of people

Market potential, inhabitants [number of cells]

■ > 5 milion [32] ■ 2 - 5 million [258] ▨ 1 - 2 million [379] ▨ 500 000 - 1 million [460] ▨ 200 000 - 500 000 [541] □ < 200 000 [269]

of 42.5 million people spread over more than 3 million km², while the total population of the West African Economic and Monetary Union (WAEMU) region, numbering 119 million in 2017, is spread over a slightly larger region (3.5 million km²). Niger and Chad have domestic territories twice the size of France but with smaller populations (one-third to one-fourth, respectively) thinly spread in local clusters across the vast landscape. Thus low population densities and isolation reduce the market potential given the lack of market interactions and the higher per capita costs of service delivery, including key market infrastructure and facilities. In the Sahel region, except for Nigeria (Lagos and Abuja clusters) and Mali's border with Guinea, the capital cities of Chad, Niger, and Mali display only small agglomerations. Third, small population clusters (less than 2,000,000) are located close to border regions, which explains in part the predominance of informal trade between neighboring countries. Finally, these small, isolated economies display a number of common characteristics, including thin markets, subsistence agriculture, and low purchasing power, which contribute to poor integration while enabling informal trade, including smuggling and local cross-border trade.

Landlocked geography also introduces other adverse challenges to export diversification, particularly the unfavorable transit environment encountered by exporters, which raises their transaction costs and impacts regional and global trade prospects. Since Niger, Chad, and Mali are landlocked, they are entirely dependent on their neighbors' infrastructure and administrative procedures for transporting goods by sea, the most expedient channel for international commerce.

In 2014, approximately 92 percent of their trade used land routes, 8 percent used rail, and barely 0.2 percent used air transport.[1] Niger primarily relies on Cotonou port in Benin and dry ports in Burkina Faso. The N'Djamena to Douala port route is currently the primary coastal access for Chad, while Dakar and Abidjan are widely used by Mali. Finally, Conakry (Guinea) is not only fed by a long, incomplete, and poorly maintained trucking route, but its port, which is often seen as a feeder or exit door for Malian trade, is poorly managed. MCNG connectivity to markets therefore needs to be understood from a broader perspective. While some policies and measures aiming to support export diversification and regional integration are within these countries' domestic spheres, others, such as regional trade policies and the development of efficient logistics and transit corridors, require them to strongly coordinate with their neighbors and to a lesser extent with their respective regional economic corridors (RECOs).

Continuous security threats in fragile environments also hamper trading opportunities for the poor and for women. All four MCNG countries are considered fragile (see chapter 2). While reliance on natural (mostly mining) resources offers significant opportunities, it also comes with major shortcomings that hit particularly hard in countries engaged in conflict-prone situations either out of greed (where the benefits derived from resource-based growth justify the opportunity cost of fighting) or grievance (with resources appropriated by narrow elites). In this regard, important security-related risks have come to the forefront, in particular associated with Boko Haram's increased activities in northern Chad, Niger, and Nigeria but also with other instances of violence in northern Mali. Such developments not only pose serious fiscal risks, but if exacerbated, also directly impact growth, especially in agriculture, cloud the political climate, and deter domestic and foreign investors. Such security risks also impact women traders disproportionately, an outcome with significant social consequences. In sum, security-related risks affect production of certain noncommodity exports in specific areas.

The spatial dimension has also other implications in fragile contexts. All MCNG countries except Guinea face major difficulties in accessing certain areas of the country affected by violent conflict. As increased military outlays shrink the fiscal space for filling infrastructure gaps (roads, energy, irrigation, etc.), this also implies that selectivity is essential to rehabilitating and maintaining safe logistics corridors and provide water and electricity in productive areas. For example, as shown in map 1.2, Mali's key export corridors for sesame and cashew are those linking Bamako and Dakar,[2] followed by Bamako-Abidjan (cashew) and Bamako-Tema (sesame seed). In the same vein, potentially alternative corridors, especially those located in the conflict-prone northern area close to Gao, are less conducive to transportation and trade facilitation due to security concerns in addition to local trade-related services being unreliable.

All four MCNG countries rank at the bottom of Human Capital Index, which affects their productivity and competitiveness (figure 1.1).[3] In addition, fragile, resource-abundant countries such as the MCNG countries, where about 60 percent of the population live below the poverty line, have higher poverty rates on average than nonfragile countries.

Not surprisingly, all four MCNG countries rely on unproductive subsistence agriculture. However, given its major contribution to both gross domestic product (GDP) and employment, the sector has potential to modernize. In Niger, agriculture contributes about 46 percent of GDP and represents about 80 percent of total employment, but also features the lowest labor productivity (World Bank 2017). Similar characteristics are found in Mali, whose agriculture export potential is also underdeveloped, being essentially centered on cotton and exposed to weather-related

MAP 1.2

Mali: Main logistics corridors for cashew and sesame in the south of the country away from the conflict-prone north

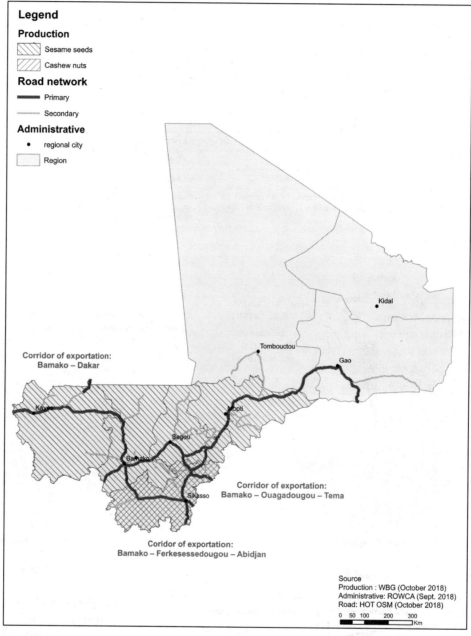

Source: FCV Global Themes/GEMS Team, Nelly Bachelot, nbachelotworldbank.org.
Note: Km = kilometers.

as well as security shocks. Cotton exports tend to register wide variations due to rainfall conditions. The potential of commercial farming in Mali (and the need for complementarities between domestic and export-oriented agriculture) is reflected in the fact that the two most dynamic subsectors in the past 35 years have been export agriculture (cotton) and subsistence farming (World Bank 2018a). In contrast, the agriculture sector in Chad shows a lack of dynamism, with its average sectoral growth rate (3 percent) the lowest among all sectors. Moreover, its labor productivity is also lowest, and its contribution to GDP (around 27 percent) is almost equivalent to that of its entire oil industry in the last decade (World Bank 2018b).

All four MCNG economies are nondiversified, that is, they depend on their natural resources for a very high share of GDP or exports, and countries with

FIGURE 1.1

Human Capital Index in Sub-Saharan Africa (low-income countries only)

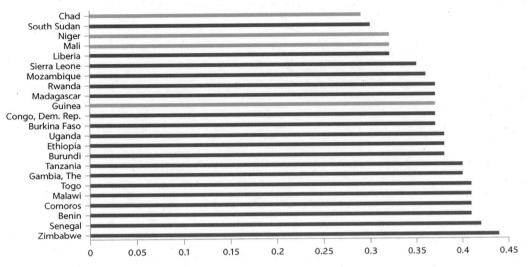

Source: Human Capital Index (database), World Bank, Washington, DC, http://www.worldbank.org/en/publication/human-capital.

FIGURE 1.2

Degree of export diversification, 2015

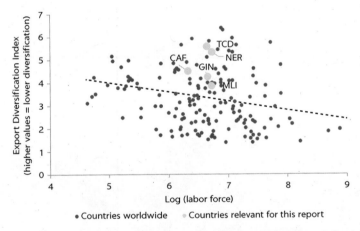

Sources: Diversification Index (database), IMF, Washington, DC, https://www.imf.org/external /np/res/dfidimf/diversification.htm; World Development Indicators labor (database), World Bank, Washington, DC, https://databank.worldbank.org/source/world-development-indicators. *Note:* CAF = Central African Republic; GIN = Guinea; MLI = Mali; NER = Niger; TCD = Chad.

an output structure that is heavily reliant on the production of one or few commodities tend to be prone to conflict. In fact, all MCNG countries rank among economies with low export diversification, as compared to the rest of Africa or worldwide. Figure 1.2 shows that with respect to the size of their labor force (a proxy for country size), MCNG economies rank among the least diversified (with higher values above the trend line indicating lower levels of export diversification). According to the "greed hypothesis," in countries featuring these characteristics, the presence of natural resources encourages certain groups to capture some of the commodity wealth and perpetuates contemporary conflicts.[4]

Export concentration is accompanied by high levels of market concentration: oil in Chad, gold and cotton in Mali, uranium in Niger, and bauxite in Guinea (table 1.1). Chad's export concentration in one product is by far the highest as 94 percent of its exports consists of oil (figure 1.3). In addition, export markets for the very few export products these countries rely on are heavily concentrated on a few countries located mainly in three or

TABLE 1.1 Export diversification share in total exports of MCNG countries, 2015

COUNTRY	MAIN EXPORT PRODUCTS		TOP 3 EXPORT DESTINATIONS	
	Product	*Percent of total*	*Country*	*Percent of total*
Chad	Oil	94	United States	61
	Vegetables	2.5	India	17
	Textiles	1.6	Japan	12
Guinea	Bauxite	66	India	26
	Precious metal (gold)	20	Ghana	14
	Foodstuffs	3	Spain	6.4
Mali	Gold	59	Switzerland	50
	Raw cotton	20	India	16
	Oil seeds	7.2	China	9
Niger	Oil/chemical products	46	France	44
	Uranium	31	China	11
	Vegetables	6.8	United States	11

Sources: UNCTAD Trade Database, UNCTAD, Geneva, https://unctad.org/en/Pages/DITC/Trade-Analysis/TAB-Data-and-Statistics.aspx, and Observatory of Economic Complexity (database), https://oec.world/en/; except for Guinea: Khebede 2017b.

FIGURE 1.3

Exports, by product, 2015

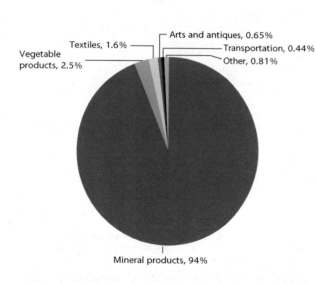

a. Chad

Textiles, 1.6%
Vegetable products, 2.5%
Arts and antiques, 0.65%
Transportation, 0.44%
Other, 0.81%
Mineral products, 94%

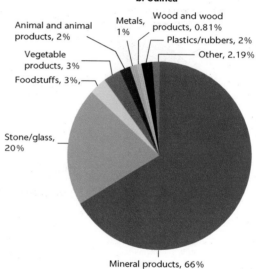

b. Guinea

Animal and animal products, 2%
Metals, 1%
Wood and wood products, 0.81%
Plastics/rubbers, 2%
Vegetable products, 3%
Foodstuffs, 3%
Other, 2.19%
Stone/glass, 20%
Mineral products, 66%

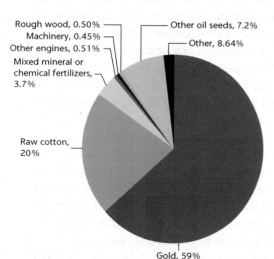

c. Mali

Rough wood, 0.50%
Machinery, 0.45%
Other engines, 0.51%
Mixed mineral or chemical fertilizers, 3.7%
Other oil seeds, 7.2%
Other, 8.64%
Raw cotton, 20%
Gold, 59%

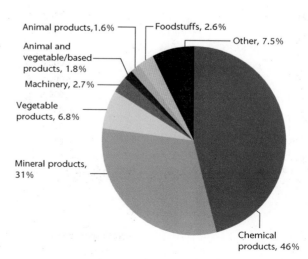

d. Niger

Animal products, 1.6%
Animal and vegetable/based products, 1.8%
Machinery, 2.7%
Vegetable products, 6.8%
Foodstuffs, 2.6%
Other, 7.5%
Mineral products, 31%
Chemical products, 46%

Sources: Khebede 2017a, 2017b, 2018a, 2018b.

FIGURE 1.4

Exports destinations, 2015

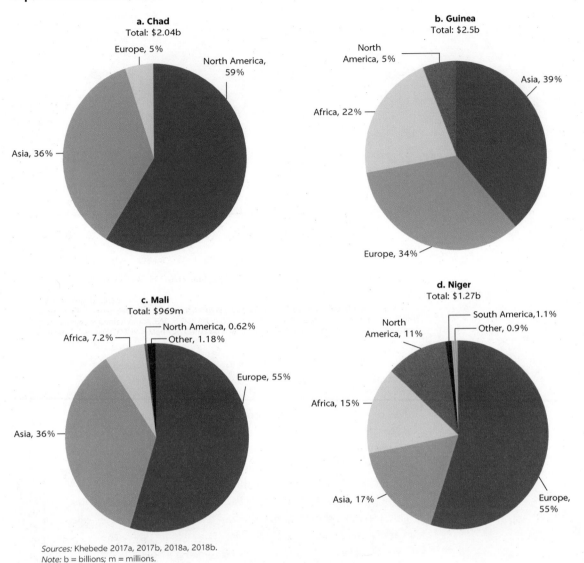

Sources: Khebede 2017a, 2017b, 2018a, 2018b.
Note: b = billions; m = millions.

four regions (figure 1.4). However, new products and less traditional markets are emerging, as all countries have identified a dozen potential agribusinesses, with emerging markets concentrated in China, India, and Middle East countries.

Reliance on natural resources also perpetuates a dearth of nonresource exports, thus entailing large spillovers into the nontradable economy. The pervasive effect of reliance on a single commodity can be further illustrated by MCNG's export performance. For instance, over the last 15 years, Chad has benefited from substantial investments in the oil sector and now draws most of its revenues from oil exports. Over the same period, the ensuing "Dutch disease" of booms and busts associated with low competitiveness in sectors other than extractives has hindered the development of alternative sectors, particularly agriculture, which has remained stagnant (figure 1.5). Only in Guinea (figure 1.6) and to a lesser extent in Niger has resource-based activity not deterred mild but steady growth in nonresource exports.

FIGURE 1.5

Growth in oil vs. non-oil exports in Chad

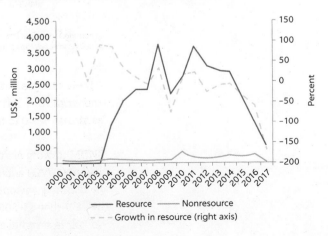

Source: Pitigala 2018b.

FIGURE 1.6

Nonresource export growth in Guinea, Niger, and Mali

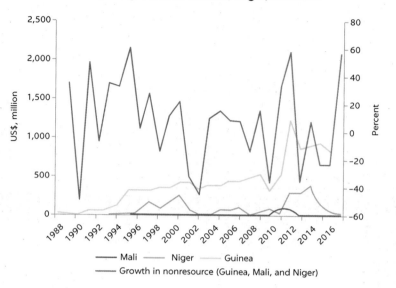

Source: Pitigala 2018a.

Reliance on natural resources in MCNG countries is deeply rooted in the political economy that surrounds the discovery of natural resources and biases incentives against private investment. It should come as no surprise that the number of exporters in these four countries is rather small. Perhaps the most extreme example of how the political economy modified the entire economic landscape of the productive basis of the country is the discovery of oil in Chad in 2002, an event that led past attempts at economic diversification to fail. As Chad's economy (and exports) became almost exclusively centered on the oil industry, economic incentives turned against the production of other tradable goods. This bias against "anything but oil" production not only prevented private investment from developing, but it let infrastructure deteriorate and disrupted trade. Public support to agriculture (other than cotton) was phased down, and traditional exports such as gum arabic were allowed to deteriorate. The ensuing downsizing of government intervention in the agriculture sector bottomed out about 4 percent of GDP over the 2003–12 period, among the lowest ratios in Sub-Saharan Africa, with a marked impact on already low agricultural productivity and limited involvement of the private sector in the Chadian agriculture. About 15 years later, the authorities realized that oil-boosted growth is short-lived and insufficient to sustaining high growth and that taking this economic route was leading the country to miss substantial opportunities to translate oil windfalls into public investment in support of export diversification.

Overall, the three wider regions incorporating MCNG countries—CEMAC, WAEMU, and ECOWAS—have also performed poorly in terms of both regional and global export shares. These three regions are among the least integrated worldwide, with none reaching 1 percent of world trade (figure 1.7). Their cumulative share only exceeded 1 percent in 2010 and reached a peak of 1.2 percent in 2012 but declined to 0.9 percent in 2016, largely following the collapse in world commodity prices, including oil. As far as regional integration is concerned, Economic Community of West African States (ECOWAS) has experienced a remarkable increase in intraregional exports in recent years, but it remains short of its historic highs of the early 2000 (figure 1.8).

FIGURE 1.7

World export shares of selected regions, 2002–06

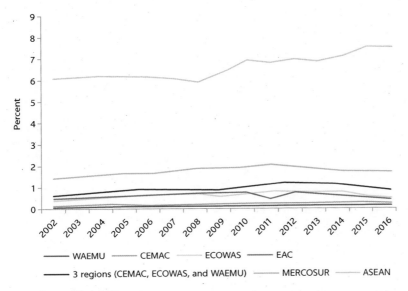

Source: Pitigala 2018a.
Note: ASEAN = Association of Southeast Asian Nations; CEMAC = Economic and Monetary
Community for Central Africa; EAC = East Asian countries; ECOWAS = Economic Community of West
African States; MERCOSUR = Mercado Comun de Suramerica; WAEMU = West African Economic and
Monetary Union.

FIGURE 1.8

Regional exports of selected regions

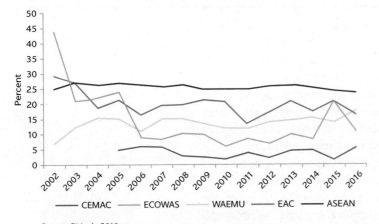

Source: Pitigala 2018a.
Note: ASEAN = Association of Southeast Asian Nations; CEMAC = Economic and Monetary Community
for Central Africa; EAC = East Asian countries; ECOWAS = Economic Community of West African States;
WAEMU = West African Economic and Monetary Union.

Similarly, WAEMU's and especially CEMAC's intraregional exports are low
when compared to other customs unions around the world, with intracom-
munity exports in CEMAC accounting for only 5.1 percent of these countries'
total in 2010.

Beyond lagging export diversification and low regional trade growth, MCNG
countries are also poorly integrated into global value chains (GVCs), which
prevents them from accessing the critical channels of technology, productivity
growth, and markets. When comparing their average for 2008–12 with 1991–95,
oil exporters in the Sahel are the least integrated into GVCs in terms of the foreign value-added content of their exports (figure 1.9). While diversification away

FIGURE 1.9

Share of foreign value added in exports, 2008–12

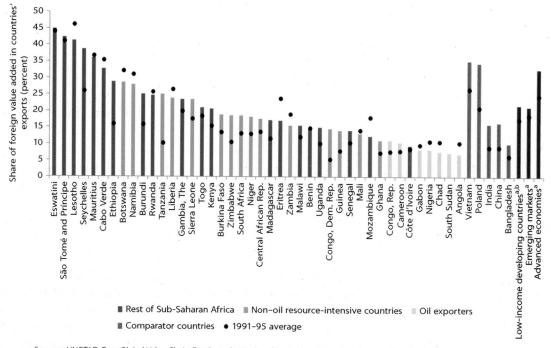

Sources: UNCTAD-Eora Global Value Chain Database, https://worldmrio.com/unctadgvc/; and IMF staff calculations.
a. See the lists of country groups under https://www.imf.org/external/pubs/ft/weo/2018/02/weodata/weoselagr.aspx.
b. Excluding Sub-Saharan African countries.

FIGURE 1.10

Sub-Saharan Africa: Depth of integration into global value chains, average 1991–95 vs. 2008–12

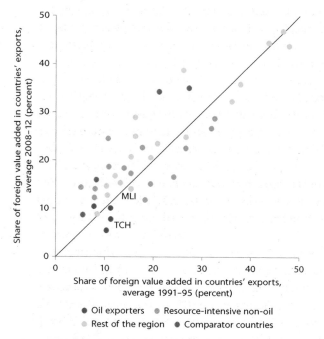

Sources: UNCTAD-Eora Global Value Chain Database, https://worldmrio.com/unctadgvc/; and IMF staff calculations.
Note: MLI = Mali; TCH = Chad.

from natural resources has reversed or stagnated in Chad and Mali, it has slightly improved in Niger and Guinea along the lines of the rest of the Sub-Saharan Africa region. In fact, a majority of Sub-Saharan Africa countries (24 out of 35) have made progress, albeit from a low starting point (figure 1.10). This improvement is most widespread among non-oil exporters, including Burkina Faso, the Central African Republic, the Democratic Republic of Congo, Ghana, Guinea, Niger, Sierra Leone, and Zimbabwe. This suggests that integration into value chains can take place even in countries where nonnatural-resource commodities play a role. For countries with a limited manufacturing or service export base and a large pool of labor, such as many in Sub-Saharan Africa, this development can provide an opportunity for structural transformation.

Low GVC integration should come as no surprise as over the last decade (2007–16), three of the four MCNG countries experienced a decreasing trend in their foreign direct investment (FDI) inflows. Andersen (2018) shows that Niger experienced the highest inward flows (as a share of GDP) and saw the most dramatic rise in FDI inflows across time, with inflows rising sharply

FIGURE 1.11

Inward FDI flows over time for MCNG countries, 2007–16

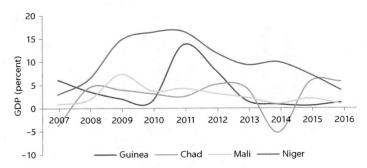

Source: UNCTAD Trade Database, several years, UNCTAD, Geneva, https://unctad.org/en/Pages
/DITC/Trade-Analysis/TAB-Data-and-Statistics.aspx.
Note: FDI flows are on a net basis (capital transactions' credits less debits between direct
investors and their foreign affiliates). FDI = foreign direct investment; GDP = gross domestic
product; MCNG countries = Mali, Chad, Niger, and Guinea.

upward from 2008 onward. Of the remaining AFCW3 (World Bank's administrative regions comprising Mali, Chad, Niger, and Guinea) countries, Chad
exhibited the second highest inflows and is the only MCNG country to feature
a rising trend in FDI inflows (as a share of GDP) in recent years. Guinea and
Mali have both seen relatively stable FDI inflows since 2013 (figure 1.11). Based
on the FDI performance index, (i) Chad and Mali have been attracting roughly
the amount of FDI expected of economies of their size; (ii) Niger appears to
have attracted a greater share of global FDI inflows than its share of global
GDP would predict; and (iii) Guinea's FDI performance spiked in 2012 and has
fallen below parity since 2014.

Not surprisingly, foreign investment flows in MCNG countries have followed
the same pattern of product and market concentration in extractive sectors,
but on a declining trend. Between 2007 and 2016, all of Chad's projects were
in natural resources, while Guinea saw about 90 percent of its projects in natural resources, Mali 80 percent, and Niger 60 percent. The top sources of FDI
projects vary per country, though all received FDI from either the United States,
the United Kingdom, or both. Both Chad's and Niger's top source of FDI was
India; Guinea's top investors were from the United Kingdom; and Canadian and
French investors comprised the top sources of FDI in Mali. Meanwhile, China
was the source country investing the greatest amounts over the period in Chad
and Niger. Interestingly, over the same period, none of the MCNG countries received any greenfield investment in agriculture, while in the most recent years
(2012–16), all MCNG countries received most new FDI projects in services,
seeing their share of FDI in extractives decline over time. The only exception,
Mali, was the outlier in the group as its investments in extractives rose again in
recent years (Andersen 2018).

Importantly, none of the MCNG countries received any efficiency-seeking
FDI in the last five years. Based on a typology that classifies FDI into natural
resources, domestic markets, efficiency, and strategic assets-seeking investments,[5] efficiency-seeking FDI is export-oriented and contributes the most to
diversifying the economy away from extractive sectors. Andersen (2018) also
found that most recent FDI projects in MCNG countries were either domestic
market-seeking investments in services or natural resource-seeking FDI in
mining, which still accounts for about 30 percent of investments in Mali and

FIGURE 1.12

FDI typology: Share of Mali's greenfield FDI by type, 2012–16

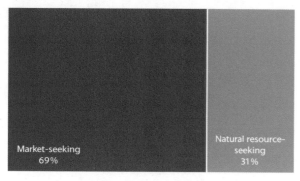

Sources: Andersen 2018. Computation based on UN COMTRADE Database, United Nations, https://comtrade.un.org/, and UNCTAD-Eora Global Value Chain Database, https://worldmrio.com/unctadgvc/.
Note: Data based on the sum of announced greenfield projects over the period. Mali received a total of 13 greenfield projects from 2012 to 2016. FDI = foreign direct investment.

FIGURE 1.13

FDI typology: Share of Mali's greenfield FDI by type and sector, 2012–16

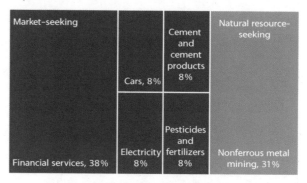

Sources: Andersen 2018. Computation based on UN COMTRADE Database, United Nations, https://comtrade.un.org/, and UNCTAD-Eora Global Value Chain Database, https://worldmrio.com/unctadgvc/.
Note: Data based on the sum of announced greenfield projects over the period. Mali received a total of 13 greenfield projects from 2012 to 2016. FDI = foreign direct investment.

FIGURE 1.14

FDI typology: Share of Guinea's greenfield FDI by type, 2012–16

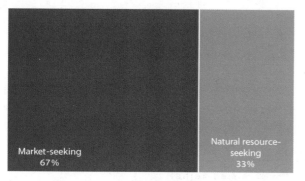

Sources: Andersen 2018. Computation based on UN COMTRADE Database, United Nations, https://comtrade.un.org/, and UNCTAD-Eora Global Value Chain Database, https://worldmrio.com/unctadgvc/.
Note: Data based on the sum of announced greenfield projects over the period. Guinea received a total of 12 greenfield projects from 2012 to 2016. FDI = foreign direct investment.

FIGURE 1.15

FDI typology: Share of Guinea's greenfield FDI by type and sector, 2012–16

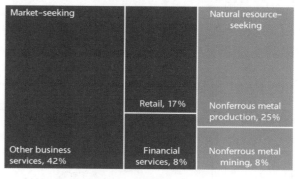

Sources: Andersen 2018. Computation based on UN COMTRADE Database, United Nations, https://comtrade.un.org/, and UNCTAD-Eora Global Value Chain Database, https://worldmrio.com/unctadgvc/.
Note: Data based on the sum of announced greenfield projects over the period. Guinea received a total of 12 greenfield projects from 2012 to 2016. FDI = foreign direct investment.

Guinea (figures 1.12–15). Sub-Saharan Africa comparators show that MCNG countries diverge from the high shares of efficiency-seeking FDI received by countries such as Senegal (34 percent of projects), Ghana (32 percent), and Namibia (28 percent), with most efficiency-seeking projects focused on business services rather than agribusiness. This finding should come as no surprise as export-oriented FDI relies on its capacity to move across borders in a timely and cost-efficient fashion, and agribusiness logistics are more vulnerable to conflict than investments that focus exclusively on natural resources or mainly serve the domestic economy. Hence, a more dedicated effort by MCNG countries to attract experienced FDI, used to face security risks, in fragile countries has become a necessity.

ANNEX 1A

MAP 1A.1

Niger: Meat and onion value chain (October 2018)

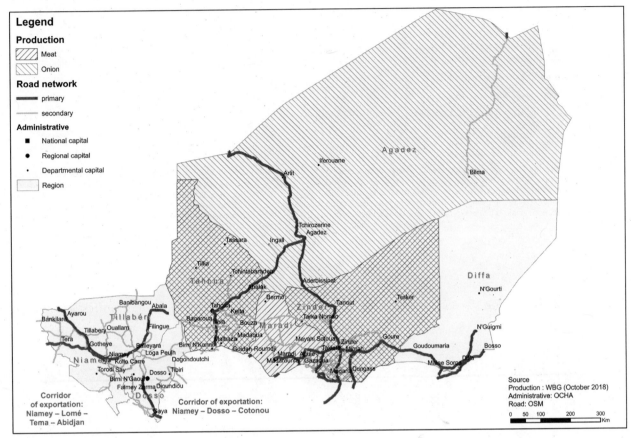

Source: FCV Global Themes/GEMS Team, Nelly Bachelot, nbachelotworldbank.org.
Note: Km = kilometers.

MAP 1A.2

Chad: Arabic gum and sesame seeds value chain (October 2018)

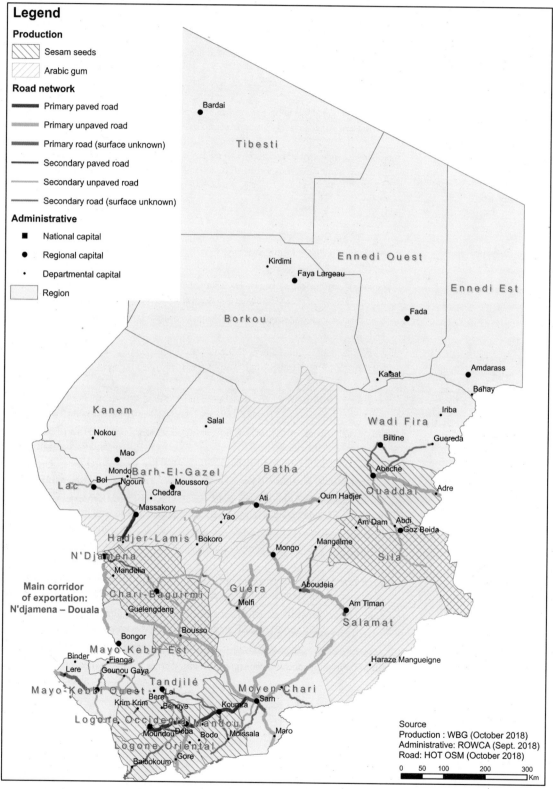

Legend

Production
- Sesam seeds
- Arabic gum

Road network
- Primary paved road
- Primary unpaved road
- Primary road (surface unknown)
- Secondary paved road
- Secondary unpaved road
- Secondary road (surface unknown)

Administrative
- ■ National capital
- ● Regional capital
- · Departmental capital
- Region

Main corridor
of exportation:
N'djamena – Douala

Source
Production : WBG (October 2018)
Administrative: ROWCA (Sept. 2018)
Road: HOT OSM (October 2018)

0   50   100   200   300
                              Km

Source: FCV Global Themes/GEMS Team, Nelly Bachelot, nbachelotworldbank.org.
Note: Km = kilometers.

NOTES

1. The importance of the ongoing Single African Air Transport Market spearheaded by the African Union through the African Civil Aviation Commission to integrate the fragmented West African market cannot be emphasized enough.
2. Similar maps for meat and onions in Niger and gum arabic and sesame in Chad are available in Annex 1A of this chapter.
3. The Human Capital Index relies on three dimensions: survival, health, and education of a child born today (World Bank 2018c).
4. The greed hypothesis argues that benefits from economic growth influence the opportunity cost of fighting, and raises gains from state appropriation, and the state's capacity for bargaining with or fighting insurgencies (World Bank 2019).
5. The FDI typology methodology used in this analysis was developed by Erik von Uexkull and José Ramón Perea, Senior Economists with the Global Investment and Competition Unit in the Macroeconomics, Trade, and Investment Global Practice.

REFERENCES

Andersen, M. R. 2018. "FDI Snapshot: Mali, Chad, Niger and Guinea." Background paper, World Bank, Washington, DC.

Khebede, E. 2017a. "The Product Space of Niger." Unpublished background paper, *Niger: Leveraging Export Diversification to Foster Growth*, World Bank, Washington, DC.

———. 2017b. "The Product Space of Guinea." Unpublished background paper, World Bank, Washington, DC.

———. 2018a. "Exploring Chad's Opportunities for Export Diversification." Unpublished background paper, *Chad: Leveraging Export Diversification to Foster Growth*, World Bank, Washington, DC.

———. 2018b. "The Product Space of Mali." Unpublished background paper, *Niger: Leveraging Export Diversification to Foster Growth*, World Bank, Washington, DC.

Pitigala, N. 2018a. "Trade Policy Options for Export Diversification of MCNG Economies." Background paper, World Bank, Washington, DC.

Pitigala, N. 2018b. "Trade Diagnostics and Policy Assessment of Chad." Unpublished background paper, *Chad: Leveraging Export Diversification to Foster Growth*, World Bank, Washington, DC.

Prieto Curiel, R., P. Heinrigs, and I. Heo. 2017. "Cities and Spatial Interactions in West Africa: A Clustering Analysis of the Local Interactions of Urban Agglomerations." West African Papers 05, OECD Publishing, Paris.

World Bank. 2017. "Niger: Leveraging Export Diversification to Foster Growth." Report No. 120306-NE, World Bank, Washington, DC.

———. 2018a. "Mali: Leveraging Export Diversification to Foster Growth." World Bank, Washington, DC. https://openknowledge.worldbank.org/handle/10986/31829.

———. 2018b. "Chad: Leveraging Export Diversification to Foster Growth." World Bank, Washington, DC. https://openknowledge.worldbank.org/handle/10986/31839.

———. 2018c. *The Human Capital Project*. Washington, DC: World Bank.

———. 2019. "Africa's Pulse, No. 19: An Analysis of Issues Shaping Africa's Economic Future." (April), World Bank, Washington, DC.

2 Why Export Diversification Matters to MCNG Countries

ABSTRACT

- In the last decade, there is conclusive evidence that fragile, resource-based Sub-Saharan Africa countries had worse growth performance than nonfragile, diversified (nonresource-based) countries.

- Past diversification efforts in Mali, Chad, Niger, and Guinea (MCNG) countries have failed for at least one of three major reasons: (i) high frequency of violent conflicts that not only prevented private investment but also destroyed infrastructure, disrupted trade, and shifted government consumption toward military expenditure; (ii) short-lived commodity booms that did not translate into sustained medium-term growth; and (iii) excessive reliance on natural resources that made MCNG economies less competitive and more vulnerable to shocks.

- MCNG countries have also three important reasons for diversifying its exports: (i) sustaining accelerated growth and reducing fiscal volatility; (ii) creating jobs in the agriculture sector, with higher population and poverty rates and untapped job creation potential; and (iii) fostering private investment and expanded insertion in global markets as their domestic markets are too small to attract the foreign direct investment (FDI) required to catch up with technology change and productivity enhancements.

- Ultimately, export diversification is good for accelerating sustained and inclusive growth. A simulation shows that increased trade openness, a desirable outcome of export diversification, would indeed be growth-enhancing. Macro scenarios from computable general equilibrium (CGE) modeling also support this finding.

WHY PAST DIVERSIFICATION EFFORTS FAILED

To understand why export diversification matters to Mali, Chad, Niger, and Guinea (MCNG) countries, it is critically important to first understand why past efforts have failed. Several reasons are proposed.

- First, the high frequency of political instability and violent conflicts prevented private investment, destroyed infrastructure, and disrupted trade. The 2016 Fragile States Index, which combines political and socioeconomic indicators such as fractionalized elites, group grievances, the presence of refugees and internally displaced populations (IDPs), uneven development, demographic pressure, and poverty (among others) resulted in these countries being ranked in the "Alert" category (figure 2.1). In addition, there is a strong, positive, endogenous relationship between fragility and high population growth, which, despite these countries' best efforts, makes it likely that the demographic dividend will turn out to be a demographic misfortune (Goldstone et al. 2010).

- Second, there is conclusive empirical evidence of the poor economic performance by fragile and resource-abundant African countries when compared to their peers between 2008 and 2017 (World Bank 2019). First, average economic growth in fragile countries remains lower than in nonfragile countries (2.4 versus 2.7 percent). Second, per capita growth in nonresource-abundant countries is higher than that in resource-abundant countries regardless of their condition of fragility, which supports the case for diversification. Third, the growth of fragile, nonresource-abundant countries (2.3 percent) remains lower than in nonfragile, nonresource-abundant countries (3.2 percent), which shows the positives of coming out of fragility status. Finally, in 1998–2007 and 2008–17, growth decelerated in nonfragile, resource-abundant countries (from 3.4 to 2.2 percent) while it accelerated in fragile, resource-abundant countries (from 1.0 to 2.4 percent). In the latter, however, according to the grievance hypothesis, the likelihood of conflict may still increase if additional resources are appropriated by narrow elites.[1]

- Third, episodes of growth being boosted by natural resources have been short-lived and did not lead their growth rates to converge with those of average middle-income and Sub-Saharan African economies. MCNG countries thus missed major opportunities to translate mining or oil revenue windfalls into more investment into human capital and infrastructure. Thus, in 1990–2014, Niger's, Chad's, and to a lesser extent Mali's per capita gross domestic product (GDP) incomes have broadly stagnated (except for 2002, when oil discoveries in Chad arose abruptly, only to increase mildly later) (figure 2.2). Low and decreasing per capita GDP ratios have also diverged from trends seen in Sub-Saharan Africa and middle-income economies, as Guinea's case illustrates. In 2016, Guinea's per capita GDP income was equal to 11 and 35 percent, respectively, of the 1994 level for average middle-income and Sub-Saharan Africa economies (World Bank 2018c).

FIGURE 2.1

Since 2016, Mali, Chad, Niger, and Guinea have been classified in the "Alert" category in the Fragile States Index

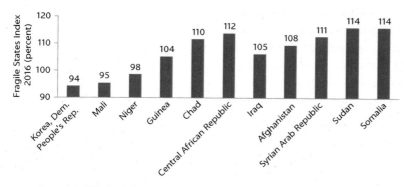

Sources: World Bank calculations based on Fund for Peace 2016.

- Fourth, these countries' "Dutch disease" dynamics shifted resources toward nontradable sectors and unproductive (low-skilled) services and military expenditure while damaging external competitiveness in tradable sectors and biasing government intervention against diversification-prone agricultural sectors. To make matters worse, economic rents (abnormal profits) from natural resources are larger among fragile countries compared to nonfragile countries (World Bank 2019). On the other hand, security-related expenses alone in MCNG countries oscillate between 3 and 5 percent of GDP (World Bank 2017,

FIGURE 2.2

Niger, Mali, and Chad per capita GDP income levels have broadly stagnated over 35 years

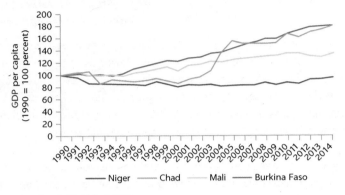

Source: World Bank 2017.
Note: GDP = gross domestic product.

2018a, 2018b). Such levels are almost identical to, for instance, Chad's budget for agriculture, which averaged about 4 percent of GDP over the 2003–12 period, among the lowest in Sub-Saharan Africa. Similar budget under allocations have contributed to low agricultural productivity and limited involvement of the private sector in the key agricultural sector of these countries.

Despite these difficulties, all MCNG governments concur that economic diversification is key for their sustained accelerated growth ambitions, and this report provides a solid rationale for this position.

- Mali's Vision 2025 identifies economic diversification as a priority for reaching sustained and faster growth (Government of Mali 1999). To do so, it proposes four strategic pillars: (i) capitalizing on Mali's agropastoral potential; (ii) strengthening the basic infrastructure investment program; (iii) promoting the private sector; and (iv) investing in human resources. These pillars guide the implementation of the Strategic Framework for Economic Recovery and Sustainable Development (CREDD 2016), which emphasizes the necessity to diversify exports from gold and cotton by developing other sectors, attract private sector investment into the agribusiness industry, and promote external and domestic trade. CREDD also aims to improve the governance and transparency of its extractive industries.

- Chad's Vision 2030 aims for an emergent economy driven by diversified and sustainable sources of growth. Its goal is to triple average per capita GDP from US$ 730 in 2014 to US$ 2,300 in 2030 at current prices while drastically reducing the poverty rate from 46.7 percent in 2011 to 8 percent over the same period. This would be made possible by the effective implementation of three consecutive five-year national development plans (2017–21; 2022–26; 2027–30), the country's operationalization instrument. Today, the drastic recent fall in oil prices and the decline in oil reserves makes export diversification even more pressing as Chad's estimated oil reserves are projected to be depleted within the next 17 years.[2] Not surprisingly, the first five-year National Development Plan (2017–21) sees Chad's economic diversification centered on its comparative advantages away from oil and focused instead on developing outward-oriented value chains in agriculture and livestock.

- Niger's Vision 2035 is to make it a prosperous country by 2035. This means not only a country whose economic growth is well above its population growth rate, that is, on or above 6 percent, but is also inclusive, with benefits reaching most of the population. The Economic Orientation Document (EOD) 2016–19 is embodied in Niger's Vision 2035, which acknowledges that the country has little choice but to make a competitive and diversified economy the cornerstone of the EOD. The document also sees Niger's economic diversification, which is centered on shifting exports away from natural resources, as a central foundation for industrialization and employment creation. Exports diversification also appears pressing as over the next few years, Niger's traditional export backbones (oil and minerals production) are projected to stagnate or improve only marginally.[3] This should convert exports diversification into a long due risk mitigation development strategy.

- Guinea's Vision 2040 sets the path for the country's sustainable development. The Vision translates into the 2016–20 National Plan for Economic and Social Development, which is structured around four strategic pillars[4] that rely on three drivers: (i) catalytic investments and good governance in the mining sector; (ii) productivity increases in the agropastoral and fishery sectors; and (iii) nonmining industrial diversification linked to regional agro-value chains and openness to trade and foreign capital.

With the approaching deadlines less than a few years away, all MCNG governments are currently at a crossroad. They can continue along their current commodity-based trajectory, which is paved with more boulders than stepping stones, or they can start diversifying from exports of unprocessed mining or oil to become middle-income, exporting, competitive countries. Neither path is easy, but global experience shows a strong correlation between export diversification and growth acceleration, the latter option being quite feasible as it has worked well for African countries with similar characteristics, and this seems to be the option chosen. In addition to acting as an entrepreneurship and private investment booster, export diversification attracts foreign investment and fosters domestic private investment. As the domestic market in these countries is too small and underdeveloped, it is unattractive to foreign investment or to an incipient private sector dominated by small and medium enterprises (SMEs). For instance, over 90 percent of Guinea's private sector consists of informal micro or small enterprises working in agriculture, trading, or service jobs with low salaries and skills (AfDB 2018).

RATIONALE FOR EXPORT DIVERSIFICATION

Despite past failures, these countries have a solid rationale for diversifying their exports. These are discussed next.

- *Strengthening macroeconomic stability.* High export concentration is akin to high fiscal and external volatility, which prevents steady, sustained growth accelerations. Even in countries such as Chad, with rapid initial gains in per capita GDP and poverty reduction since the discovery of oil in the early 2000s, episodes of oil price collapse have led to unprecedented fiscal adjustments, with severe negative spillovers for growth and employment (figure 2.3). Weather shocks related to rainfall have also affected Mali's and Niger's economies (figure 2.4).

- *Unfolding jobs creation potential.* Export diversification creates jobs, including among young people and women. Mining and oil activities are highly capital-intensive, and their well-known impact on domestic employment is small, which makes them unable to absorb the staggering demographic boom featured in these economies. In exchange, agribusiness-based exports hold untapped potential for creating both skilled and unskilled jobs.

FIGURE 2.3

Oil price slumps have dramatically deteriorated Chad's fiscal position

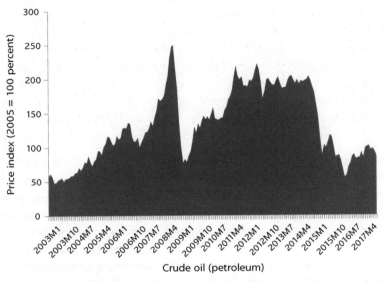

Sources: World Bank 2017, 2018a.
Note: M = month x of the year.

FIGURE 2.4

Rainfall and GDP growth: Niger's growth has featured wide booms and busts, due largely to the fact that the economy relies on rainfall and the price of uranium

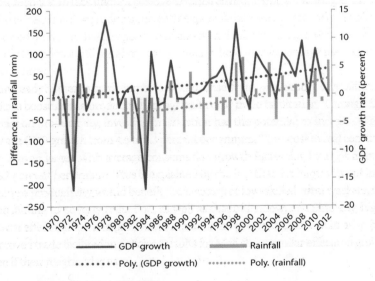

Sources: World Bank 2017, 2018a.
Note: GDP = gross domestic product; mm = millimeters; Poly. = Political Economy proxy variable.

- *Fostering the positive links between export diversification, economic growth, and foreign direct investment (FDI).* At least three channels are worth mentioning: (i) exposure to international trade, which allows for an efficient reallocation of factors of production from low-productivity to high-productivity firms, thereby increasing aggregate productivity. (ii) entry of multinational enterprises, which increases competition in inputs and output markets in the host economy; and (iii) presence of foreign firms, which supports the transmission of knowledge and technology to domestic firms and in turn increases their productivity.

Moreover, perhaps the most important reason why MCNG countries should opt for diversification is its impact on accelerating sustained inclusive growth. Simulations conducted on the four economies show that increased trade openness, a direct outcome of export diversification, would be growth-enhancing as it would generate significant growth gains for these countries (table 2.1).

Based on a familiar cross-country regression model developed to explain long-term growth, it is possible to make a quantitative assessment of the potential impact of trade reforms on economic growth in MCNG countries.[5] Specifically, these countries were benchmarked against other Sub-Saharan Africa countries identified as their peers and other aspirational peers. Scenarios were then simulated in which the gap in trade openness (as proxied by trade-to-GDP ratios) vis-à-vis a benchmark country is closed.[6] MCNG's Sub-Saharan Africa peers are countries featuring similar structural characteristics, notably comparable geography, income levels, and development experience. Two such countries were included: Côte d'Ivoire, and Burkina Faso. Meanwhile, MCNG's aspirational peers comprised two Asian countries with development trajectories worth emulating: Vietnam, and Malaysia. However, to avoid setting unrealistic or unattainable targets, MCNG values for the period 2010–16 were compared with average values for aspirational peers at the same stage of development as MCNG countries. This is more relevant than relying on policy gaps for the most recent period, namely 2016. Results are detailed next (table 2.2).

- If Niger became as open to international trade (that is, had the same trade-to-GDP ratio) as Burkina Faso and Côte d'Ivoire, its growth rate in per capita GDP would increase by 0.26 and 1.32 percentage points (ppts), respectively. The trade-to-GDP ratio of Niger would surpass those of East African countries such as Uganda, Tanzania, and Ethiopia. This reflects closer trade integration within West Africa, which is supported by a monetary union, compared to East Africa. If Niger's trade ratio were on a par with Vietnam and Malaysia, its growth in per capita GDP would increase by roughly 1.8 ppts and 0.9 ppts, respectively.

- Similarly, if Mali closed gaps in trade-to-GDP ratio with Burkina Faso and Côte d'Ivoire, its per capita GDP growth rate would accelerate by 1.0 and 2.1 ppts,

TABLE 2.1 **Average values of trade-to-GDP ratio**

Percent

CHAD	GUINEA	BURKINA FASO	MALI	CÔTE D'IVOIRE	NIGER	VIETNAM	MALAYSIA
			2010–16			1990s	1960s
75.2	78.1	64.3	54.8	76.3	61.2	82.9	71.2

Source: Estimates based on Haile 2016.
Note: GDP = gross domestic product.

TABLE 2.2 **Potential impact on the per capita GDP growth of Chad, Mali, and Niger**

Percent

	BURKINA FASO	CÔTE D'IVOIRE	VIETNAM	MALAYSIA
Chad	−1.29	0.43	0.71	1.17
Mali	0.99	2.06	2.57	1.63
Niger	0.26	1.32	1.83	0.89

Source: Estimates based on Haile 2016.
Note: GDP = gross domestic product.

respectively, while if Mali's trade ratio were on a par with Vietnam's or Malaysia's, its per capita GDP growth would increase by roughly 2.6 and 1.6 ppts, respectively.

- Finally, if Chad became as open to international trade as its peer Côte d'Ivoire, its annual per capita GDP growth rate would increase by about 0.43 ppts. Notice that the trade-to-GDP ratio of Chad already surpasses those of many Sub-Saharan Africa peer countries, most likely because of its high oil export component. If Chad's trade-to-GDP ratio was on par with Vietnam's or Malaysia's, two Asian economies Chad might aspire to emulate, its per capita GDP growth would increase by roughly 0.7 and 1.2 ppts, respectively. The benefits of openness are well known: well supported by structural reforms, it brings diversified assets and investment, better institutions, competition, and less oil-rents capture.

However, the findings of this simulation should be interpreted with a caveat in mind, even though they are confirmed by more sophisticated modeling. The benchmarking approach throws light on the potential increase in trade openness resulting from export diversification. As a result, the simulation is somewhat mechanistic and only shows how growth performance would fare if the country's openness closed its gap with the benchmark country.

Yet, complementary, more comprehensive macro scenarios based on computable general equilibrium (CGE) modeling applied to Niger and Mali find highly positive growth impacts from export diversification policies (World Bank 2017, 2018b). The model first shows that without export diversification, Niger's and Mali's economies would be expected to grow at average annual rates of 4.6 and 4.7 percent, respectively, until 2025, modest rates at best in per capita GDP terms given the very high population growth rates. Moreover, this conclusion is unaffected by a positive terms-of-trade shock. In fact, under a positive external environment, simulating an increase in the price of mining products currently exported (or even a decrease in the price of imported products, that is, a positive terms-of-trade shock), the growth effect would be only temporary and not alter fundamentally these modest average medium-term growth rates.[7]

Instead, higher growth impacts would arise from pro-export diversification policies boosting the productivity of agriculture or trade facilitation. Through their impact on productivity, investing in irrigation has the potential to increase Niger's average GDP growth from 4.6 to 5.3 percent per annum. The boost to real consumption is even larger, with average consumption growth increasing by 1 ppt from 4.6 to 5.7 percent per annum. This is explained by the fact that the improvement in agriculture productivity would benefit the incomes of low-skilled rural workers, thus contributing to poverty reduction, as well as that of landowners. Similarly, higher growth effects, albeit less pronounced than in the previous case, would arise from improved trade facilitation policies. Results for Mali show similar effects on growth, even if their magnitudes vary.

NOTES

1. The "grievance hypothesis" suggest that greater availability of resources as a result of economic growth may reduce (or increase) the likelihood of conflict depending on how these resources are distributed or appropriated by narrow elites.
2. Chad has about 1.5 billion barrels of proven reserves, or about 145 barrels per capita. This amount is modest when compared to 502 barrels for Angola and 243 barrels for Nigeria. With annual extraction rates of about 8 percent, oil reserves are expected to be depleted by around 2035. Eventual output from other fields do not significantly alter this outcome.

3. While the large Imouraren uranium project is temporarily on hold, prospects for oil and gold output expansion are favorable but limited to existing fields. Gold exports expect declining prices in the medium term.

4. These pillars are: (i) promoting good governance for sustainable development; (ii) sustainable and inclusive economic transformation; (iii) inclusive development of human capital; and (iv) sustainable management of natural capital.

5. The analysis mainly uses the cross-country growth regression model in Brueckner (2014). See Araujo et al. (2016), Moller and Wacker (2015), and Haile (2016) for applications in the context of Latin America, Tanzania, and Ethiopia, respectively.

6. This simulation assumes that the trade openness ratio increases with export diversification, not only by lowering tariffs (since some African countries have similar external tariffs) but by lowering trade costs, nontariff barriers (NTBs), levies, etc. However, export diversification cannot be the only reason for such eventual increase as it might be a result of higher export concentration.

7. This result confirms that these countries' current mining-based growth model has reached its limits and that under conditions of a commodity price windfall, only owners of the commodity and highly skilled workers would benefit from such terms-of-trade improvement.

REFERENCES

AfDB (African Development Bank). 2018. "Guinea Economic Outlook." AfDB, Abidjan.

Araujo, J. T., E. Vostroknutova, M. Brueckner, M. Clavijo, and K. M. Wacker. 2014. *Beyond Commodities: The Growth Challenge of Latin America and the Caribbean.* Latin American Development Forum. Washington, DC: World Bank.

Brueckner, J. K. 2014. "National Income and Its Distribution." IMF Working Paper WP/14/101, IMF, Washington, DC.

CREDD 2016–2018. 2016. "Strategic Framework for Economic Recovery and Sustainable Development." Government of Mali, Bamako.

Fund for Peace. 2016. Fragile States Index, Washington, DC, https://fundforpeace.org/wp-content /uploads/2018/08/fragilestatesindex-2016.pdf.

Goldstone, J. A., R. H. Bates, D. L. Epstein, T. R. Gurr, M. B. Lustik, M. G. Marshall, J. Ulfelder, and M. Woodward. 2010. "A Global Model For Forecasting Political instability." *American Journal of Political Science* 54 (1): 190–208.

Government of Mali. 1999. "Mali's Vision." Government of Mali, Bamako.

Haile, F. 2016. "Global Shocks and Their Impact on the Tanzanian Economy." Discussion Paper 2016–47, Kiel Institute for the World Economy, Kiel.

Moller, L. C., and K. M. Wacker. 2015. "Ethiopia's Growth Acceleration and How to Sustain It: Insights from a Cross-Country Regression Model." Policy Research Working Paper 7292, World Bank, Washington, DC.

World Bank. 2017. "Niger: Leveraging Export Diversification to Foster Growth." Report No. 120306-NE, World Bank, Washington, DC.

——. 2018a. "Chad: Leveraging Export Diversification to Foster Growth." World Bank, Washington, DC.

——. 2018b. "Mali: Leveraging Export Diversification to Foster Growth." World Bank, Washington, DC.

——. 2018c. "Country Partnership Framework for the Republic of Guinea for the Period FY2018–FY23." World Bank, Washington, DC. https://openknowledge.worldbank.org /handle/10986/29906.

——. 2019. "Africa's Pulse, No. 19: An Analysis of Issues Shaping Africa's Economic Future." (April), World Bank, Washington, DC.

3 Conceptual Approach
THE EXPORT DIVERSIFICATION LADDER AND STRUCTURAL TRANSFORMATION

ABSTRACT

- *Literature shows a strong correlation between export diversification and growth acceleration and confirms that reliance on natural resource exports does not achieve sustained growth, brings many shortcomings, and slows structural change, the mirror image of export diversification.*

- *Mali, Chad, Niger, and Guinea (MCNG) countries should consider climbing the four-step ladder of an export diversification strategy: (i) exporting more of the same; (ii) opening new foreign markets, both regional and global; (iii) identifying emerging and more sophisticated agri-export winners; and (iv) moving into full-fledged agribusiness.*

- *Export diversification will bring (among others) an acceleration in processes of structural change in MCNG countries.*

- *All MCNG economies show a positive, albeit slow, pattern of structural change, which differs from the dominantly negative trend for the average of Sub-Saharan Africa countries, which also feature de-industrialization. Thus, MCNG rural labor is moving toward productive urban sectors, including finance, construction, and public utilities, but proportionally less than toward sectors associated to informality.*

WHAT THEORY SAYS ABOUT EXPORT DIVERSIFICATION AND GROWTH

Theory concludes that reliance on natural resource-generated wealth hardly achieves sustained growth acceleration and that far from being a blessing, it brings many shortcomings, including:

- Tendency to grow beyond potential in booming times (overheating): In the initial phases of a commodity boom, domestic demand tends to grow too fast, and expansionary fiscal policy often has an inflationary impact. Additional spending affects both tradable and nontradable goods. Increased commodity production increases export supply, and through the use of foreign exchange thus generated, it serves to finance imports while nontradable goods also rise to satisfy excess domestic demand in the country. Hence, demand for nontradables generated by the commodity boom usually comes accompanied by larger than usual current account deficits, thus overheating the economy.

- High gross domestic product (GDP) growth volatility. Commodity prices are highly volatile, that is, they show high standard deviations (often above 30 percent per year). In addition, terms-of-trade shocks tend to be persistent, even structural, such as the last oil shock, with severe price slumps that create major contractions and uncertainty in the economy. This produces a highly volatile resource-based GDP growth boom and causes nonresource-based GDP to also follow such a pattern. This transmission mechanism is by itself a major obstacle to sustained growth acceleration.

- "Dutch disease" (and ensuing tendency for real exchange rate appreciation). Commodity booms allow the price of tradable goods to be pinned down by excess demand for imported goods or even decline due to an exchange rate appreciation that favors nontradable goods. The ensuing loss of competitiveness hits the tradable sectors, further hampering the potential for export diversification and making investment in nontradable sectors (for example, construction) more attractive.

- Biased budget priorities toward rent seeking and noncompetitive activities. Commodity-generated government revenues tend to be misallocated to nonpriority needs, following an often nontransparent political process favoring vested interests. Such discretionary policy favors unproductive public outlays in nontradable activities rather than in tradables with higher-value-added and favoring agricultural productivity.

Some of these undesirable effects may be mitigated by well-applied fiscal stabilization mechanisms (such as fiscal rules or stabilization funds). However, despite their apt design, national or regional fiscal institutions have not yet become institutionally strong enough in Mali, Chad, Niger, and Guinea (MCNG) countries to enforce these rules.[1] In fact, their fragility status is associated with weak institutions, especially with respect to the rule of law and political stability, and cannot guarantee macroeconomic stability or the ability to attract more investors and business activities.

Theory also supports the existence of a positive correlation at both cross-country and national levels between export diversification and higher growth. While correlation per se does not imply that diversification causes growth, abundant literature supports this positive relationship. There is strong evidence of how export diversification makes the economy less vulnerable to terms-of-trade shocks and reduces growth volatility, which in turn fosters growth in the long run (see Imbs and Wacziarg 2003; de Ferranti et al. 2002; Jansen 2004; Bachetta et al. 2007, and Lederman and Maloney 2012, among others, while comprehensive treatments of the topic are found in Newfarmer, Shaw, and Walkenhorst 2009 and Al-Marhubi 2000). The overall conclusion is that countries with more concentrated production and export structures typically have lower income levels compared to countries that are more diversified. More recently, McIntire et al. (2018) found that among small states, those with more diversified exports have lower output volatility and higher average growth rates than less diversified ones. For their part, Calderón and Cantu (2018) investigated the effects of trade openness, diversification, and the role of natural resources on growth in Communauté Économique et Financière d'Afrique Centrale (Economic and Monetary Community for Central Africa; CEMAC) countries, including Chad. Two important findings emerge from this analysis: (i) trade openness has a positive and significant causal relationship with growth; and (ii) conversely, export product concentration (and share of natural resource exports in total exports) has a negative and significant relationship with growth.

THE EXPORT DIVERSIFICATION LADDER

While there is no single export diversification recipe that will fit every country, many nonmutually exclusive options are open to MCNG. Based on the lessons from international experience, a simple typology of export diversification helps define what broad policy choices these countries face. Such typology should not be seen as a set recipe but as an organizational tool that will allow them to combine multiple export diversification pathways. Each government should consider each option as part of a customized policy mix leading to the design of its own strategy.

The proposed typology considers four steps, in order of the value-added content of the export bundle designed to climb the export diversification ladder (figure 3.1).

- In the first step, a country simply aims to export more volume of what it already produces as nonresource products, or growth in its intensive margin.

- In the second step, the country exports what it produces as nonresource exports to new markets, or growth in its extensive margin.

- In exchange, the third step sees a country moving to emerging, often pilot higher-value-added nonresource products. This is the case when countries target the promotion of a few nontraditional exports (or strategic bets), commonly agribusiness-based value chains in West Africa. This leads not only to less export concentration on a narrow basket of commodities but unleashes a learning-by-doing process in the medium term.

- Finally, in the fourth step, emerging new higher-value-added, nonresource export goods (and eventually services) lead to the recomposition of subsectoral GDP in favor of a higher share of nonresource-based, higher-value-added products, eventually achieving sectoral diversification of the economy.

Two important caveats should be kept in mind. First, steps 1 and 2 are best suited to MCNG countries featuring dynamic exports with low value added and complexity

FIGURE 3.1

Export diversification ladder

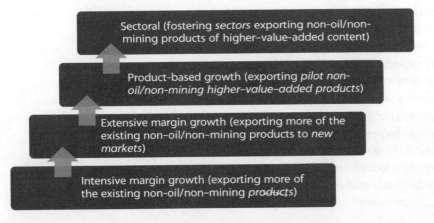

(the latter concept to be developed in chapters 4 and 5). At these stages, simple actions such as facilitating cross-border transactions or opening new markets may be of particular importance in a fragility context. In exchange, steps 3 and 4 require gradually moving into higher-value-added, more complex goods (or services). This implies the interaction of a more comprehensive set of policies addressing the key challenges or barriers found in the initial trade and business environment specific to each agribusiness value chain selected and later with broader reach. In addition, the last two steps should be accompanied by a mirror shift of the labor force moving from low- to high-productivity goods or sectors of the economy as part of a process known as "structural change," whose status is further explored below. " Second, even though each MCNG government is expected to customize the sequencing and prioritization of the list of policy actions contained at the end of each of the following chapters, this report also presents the key game changers for areas of intervention as well as their ideal location on the ladder (see table 8.5).

DIVERSIFICATION AND STRUCTURAL CHANGE DYNAMICS

As seen above, several Sub-Saharan Africa countries, including MCNG, have formulated plans with the goal of achieving middle-income status by 2030–35, which will require (among others) an acceleration of the process of structural change, the mirror image of export diversification. Structural change (or transformation) consists of the dynamic reallocation of labor from less productive sectors to those with higher productivity. Typically, structural change has been associated with the process of industrialization. However, the term has come under scrutiny as many Sub-Saharan Africa countries, including MCNG, still appear significantly underindustrialized (below an average of 10–12 percent of GDP in Sub-Saharan Africa countries) or even de-industrializing. However, some progress is being observed thanks to public investment in the construction of oil refineries and cement plants and the development of agrifood industries with structural change explaining a significantly positive share of MCNG labor productivity growth. Hence, contrary to a seemingly Sub-Saharan Africa regional pattern, structural change is indeed happening, albeit slowly, in MCNG economies.

Typically, industrialization and structural change are linked. Both processes tend to converge as countries that have managed to attain high levels of structural transformation have also been characterized by the reallocation of agricultural labor and other resources toward modern urban activities, often in manufacturing or services, which leads to a general increase in productivity and income levels. Typically, during the 1970s and 1980s, countries in East Asia successfully transformed their economies from agrarian to manufacturing. In contrast, Sub-Saharan Africa economies, such as those of MCNG countries, typically specialized in agriculture and natural-resource-led activities. As a result, their expected structural transformation, which should emphasize the generation of economies of scale, the adoption of new technologies, and the development of capabilities centered on manufacturing or services, also occurred but at very slow speed. In fact, the speed at which structural transformation occurs is an important determinant of the success of the process (McMillan, Rodrik, and Verduzco 2014).

The pattern of structural change also tends to be associated with a bell-shaped curve for manufacturing output (as a fraction of GDP), in a phenomenon referred to as "premature de-industrialization." In general, the turning point seems to occur at much lower levels of income for developing countries, such that their decline in manufacturing begins at levels of income that are a fraction of those at which advanced economies start to de-industrialize. Thus, in principle, developing countries should transition into service economies earlier than developed ones. This appears to be the case for Sub-Saharan Africa countries, which experienced a major decline in manufacturing's share of GDP from 15 percent in the 1980s to about 11 percent in 2015, with parallels decreases in both employment and real value added. As a familiar policy response aiming to prevent premature de-industrialization, a familiar argument has been that their prospects for diversification still depend critically on fostering new manufacturing industries (Rodrik 2016). In the case of MCNG countries, this argument would require refining as the potential for accelerating structural change may rather lie in fostering agribusiness and related services.

Finding a common pattern for structural change in Africa is linked to the fragility factor. Recent research (World Bank 2019) for the 2008–17 period found that: (i) there still is a very large share of workers employed in agriculture in fragile countries; (ii) the share of employment in services in fragile countries is significantly smaller than in nonfragile countries; (iii) the reduction in the share of agricultural employment is faster in nonfragile countries than in fragile countries; (iv) the increase in the share of employment in services over the same period is faster in nonfragile countries; and (v) there are no marked differences in the share of industrial employment between fragile and nonfragile economies.

In this regard, traditional industrialization anchored in high protectionism in MCNG countries is replete of cases of failure. The case of Chad's stagnant industrialization is illustrative. Centered on its state-owned enterprises (SOEs), whose financial sustainability is highly questionable, Chad's manufacturing share of GDP steadily increased from 2005 to 2012, reaching the Sub-Saharan Africa average, before breaking the trend and declining, with minor fluctuations between 2013 and 2015 (figure 3.2). The discovery of oil in the early 2000s was initially followed by the creation or expansion of SOEs in oil refining, cement manufacturing, tractor assembly, ironmaking, bicycle assembly, fruit juice production, and the revival of the textile and leather industries. Cofinanced by the government through its own budget and loans from China and India, these investments initially had significant positive impacts on job creation and economic diversification. However, their profitability became affected not only by poor management and an unfavorable business climate but also by declining subsidies following price slumps.[2] An International Monetary Fund (IMF) study (IMF 2017) noted that state-owned enterprise subsidies were widespread and had increased to 4.8 percent of non-oil GDP in 2012, which represented a major drain on the budget. For its part, Niger's industrialization is no exception: its share to GDP has stagnated around 6 percent of GDP since the early 1990s, with only a slight increase in the mid-2010s. In the same vein, the average share of manufacturing to GDP in Mali has stagnated at around 10–11 percent for more than three decades. Meanwhile, its growth in all subsectors has been volatile and lackluster during the period (figure 3.3). Finally, Guinea's manufacturing is also small, stagnating below 9 percent of GDP and mainly concentrated in Conakry (World Bank 2017).

FIGURE 3.2

Manufacturing value added in Chad vs. Sub-Saharan Africa

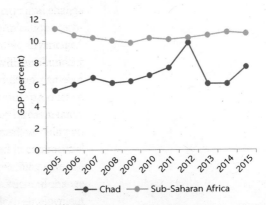

Sources: World Development Indicators (database), World Bank, Washington, DC, https://datacatalog.worldbank.org/dataset/world-development-indicators; Chadian authorities.
Note: GDP = gross domestic product.

FIGURE 3.3

Mali's industrialization is stagnating

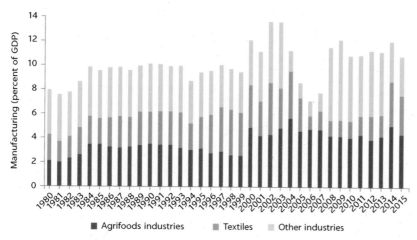

Source: Government of Mali 2017.
Note: GDP = gross domestic product.

The rest of this section assesses the pace and type of structural change in MCNG countries over the period 1990–2015.[3] In all these countries, previous analyses show that while the agriculture sector has the lowest level of labor productivity, it has the highest share of employment and contribution to GDP, albeit declining. Thus, a valid question is whether there is a flow of labor from the low-productivity agriculture sector to high-productivity sectors. As regarding pace, focusing on this period is relevant for two reasons: (i) this is the most recent period for which data are available and during which important changes occurred; and (ii), this is the period covered by a larger sample of developing countries available in the Groningen Growth and Development Centers—Africa Sector database. Regarding its type, findings below confirm that the more productive extractive or mining sectors have not created abundant jobs, thus reflecting low complementarity and weak spillovers between the mining and nonmining economies.[4] More importantly, the analysis finds a common positive pattern of structural change for all MCNG countries across various periods, which differs from predominantly declining regional patterns worldwide, including those seen in Sub-Saharan Africa economies.[5]

- Guinea's positive structural transformation was accompanied by labor flows not only from agriculture to high-productivity sectors but also to low-productivity ones. As shown in figure 3.4, the path of structural transformation locates agriculture (characterized by low productivity and declining labor shares) in the lower-left quadrant, and the more dynamic sectors, such as mining and quarrying, public utilities, construction, and manufacturing (characterized by high productivity and a very small, albeit rising, labor share) in the upper-right quadrant. Interestingly, although Guinea's labor force left agriculture, it predominantly moved into other low-productivity sectors, such as community and government services and wholesale and retail trades. In addition, there has been a nonnegligible flow of labor to relatively high-productivity sectors, such as finance, transportation, and telecommunications, a dynamic that is encouraging as it facilitates structural change.

- Niger also features positive structural change accompanied by labor flows from agriculture to high-productivity sectors but also to low-productivity ones. The path of structural change in Niger also locates agriculture and wholesale trade (characterized by low productivity and a declining labor share) in the lower-left quadrant and the relatively more dynamic sectors, including government services and mining and quarrying (characterized by high productivity and a rising labor share), in the upper-right quadrant (figure 3.5). Niger's labor force has left agriculture and predominantly moved into community services (mostly education and healthcare) and to a lesser extent manufacturing and transportation services, which saw small improvements in productivity. Though small, the latest shifts are positive. Needless to say, the impact of these shifts on overall productivity (and ultimately growth) would have been much stronger if labor had relocated to more productive sectors, which for various reasons (lack of fiscal space, low private investment due to a poor business climate, and commodity price slumps) seemed to have reached a ceiling in terms of their potential for job creation.

• For its part, Chad featured modest but positive structural change. Figure 3.5 shows that the path of structural change for Chad also locates agriculture (characterized by low productivity and a declining labor share) in the lower-left quadrant and the relatively more dynamic sector, including mining and quarrying and financial services (characterized by high productivity and a rising labor share) in the upper-right quadrant, but with little job creation. Hence, when Chad's labor force left agriculture, it predominantly moved into less productive manufacturing and wholesale and retail (informal) trade as well as hotel and restaurant services.

Thus the pattern of positive, though slow, structural change in MCNG countries differs from the dominant one for the average of Sub-Saharan Africa countries. When results based on regional averages for four groups of countries—Latin America and the Caribbean, High Income, Sub-Saharan Africa, and Asia—are presented, it is possible to corroborate that MCNG's labor productivity decomposition into a within-sector component due to technological change, capital accumulation, and reduced misallocations and structural change differs from the dominant one seen in other Sub-Saharan Africa countries. Figure 3.6 shows that structural change accounted for about 35 percent of labor productivity growth in Chad over the entire period 2005–15. Figure 3.7 shows that Niger's structural change accounted for about 30 percent of labor productivity growth over the entire period 1990–2015. Mijiyawa (2018) also found that structural change accounted for about 40 percent of labor productivity growth during 2006–15. These shares are nonnegligible, even when compared to those for Asia, the region where the contribution of structural change had been the largest.[6]

Finally, two important caveats are that prioritizing agriculture does not mean discounting the potential of expanding services and that having a large surplus of workers in agriculture should not be considered a handicap for structural change per se. On the former, as seen later, some information and communications technology (ICT) and travel services have revealed positive comparative advantages. On the latter, countries that start the process of structural change with an abundant and available labor force, such as MCNG, have a common initial condition, namely a large number of unskilled workers prepared to move into relatively more productive activities than the subsistence activities that can be developed in rural areas, namely agribusiness industrialization or supporting services. In this regard, working on the complementarities between agribusiness value chains engaged in commercial farming initially oriented toward the domestic market and later reaching external markets is a natural initial step. In the end, what really matters for structural change is the capacity of the rural economy to generate abundant and modern employment through the development of more productive, competitive, export-oriented agribusiness value chain activities.

FIGURE 3.4

Guinea: Correlation between sectoral productivity and changes in employment share, 2006–15

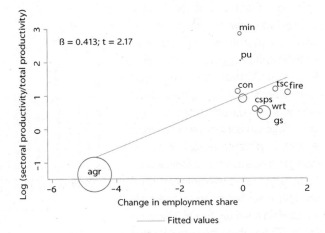

Source: Mijiyawa's (2018) calculations based on data from Institut National de la Statistique (National Statistical Institute; INS).

Note: Circle size represents employment share in 2006. agr = agriculture; con = construction; csps = community, social, and personal services; fire = finance, insurance, and real estate; gs = government services; min = mining and quarrying; pu = public utilities; β = coefficient of independent variable in regression; t = t-statistic, standard testing of the significance of the beta estimated; tsc = transport and telecommunications; wrt = wholesale and retail trade, hotels, and restaurants. Ln (p/P) = α + βΔ employment share.

FIGURE 3.5

Niger and Chad's correlation sector productivity and changes in employment, 1990–2015 and 2005–15

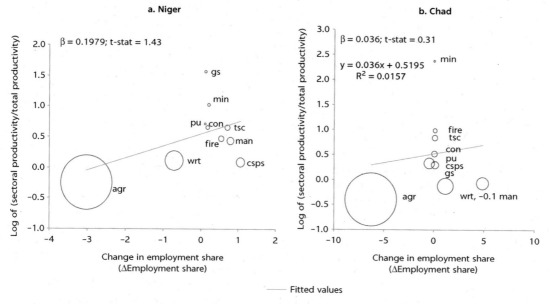

Source: Daki and López-Cálix 2017.
Note: Circle size represents employment share in initial year. agr = agriculture; con = construction; csps = community, social and personal services; fire = finance, insurance, and real estate; gs = government services; man = manufacturing; min = mining and quarrying; pu = public utilities; β = coefficient of independent variable in regression; t = t-statistic, standard testing of the significance of the beta estimated; tsc = transport and telecommunications; wrt = wholesale and retail trade, hotels, and restaurants. Ln (p/P) = α + βΔ employment share.

FIGURE 3.6

Chad: Decomposition of labor productivity growth, 2005–15

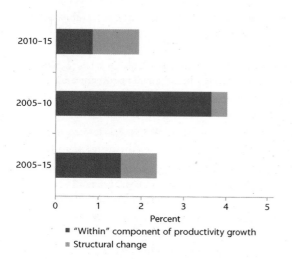

Source: Original estimates based on Daki and López-Cálix 2017.

FIGURE 3.7

Decomposition of labor productivity growth between Niger, 1990–2015, and world regions, 1990–2005

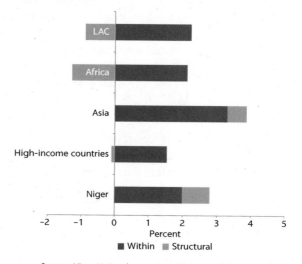

Sources: Niger: National accounts and Labor statistics; regional averages for LAC, Africa, Asia and high-income countries: Daki and López-Cálix (2017), based on McMillan, Rodrik and Verduzco (2014).
Note: LAC = Latin America and the Caribbean.

NOTES

1. In the early 2010s, Chad designed a fiscal rule, but its Parliament did not approve it. Following many unsuccessful attempts, West African Economic and Monetary Union (WAEMU) and CEMAC countries agreed to an improved multilateral monitoring framework, including the commitment to reach a fiscal deficit of 3 percent of GDP (basic, including grants) by 2019. López-Cálix (2017) reviews the past implementation of these measures.

2. In the cases of the cement plants and oil refinery, these subsidies were necessary because the Government imposed a ceiling on the selling prices of their products in order to make them more affordable. The refinery, inaugurated in June 2011, was shut down in January 2012 as a result of the Chinese company's refusal to deliver the fuel at prices below the cost of production.

3. All countries except Mali, for which disaggregated sectoral labor data are not available. Chad has labor data available from 2005 only. This section is based on Daki and López-Cálix (2017).

4. Despite this finding, getting mining right (that is, improving its governance) remains a priority as it is probably easier and faster than developing new agribusiness exports. Moreover, some countries have managed to strengthen the spillovers between both economies. A good example is Botswana's industry moving from diamonds to beef.

5. There is little evidence that significant structural change has underpinned Africa's recent growth as previous studies found no structural change taking place in Sub-Saharan Africa countries. McMillan, Rodrik, and Verduzco (2014) covers the period 1990–2005, which saw a labor shift from sectors with above-average productivity into sectors with below-average productivity in Sub-Saharan Africa.

6. The results for MCNG countries are not exactly comparable to those of other regions due to data shortcomings, a different base period, and the per capita data applied when computing the decomposition used in McMillan, Rodrik, and Verduzco (2014).

REFERENCES

Al-Marhubi, F. 2000. "Export Diversification and Growth." *Applied Economics Letter* 7 (9): 559–62.

Bachetta, M., M. Jansen, C. Lennon, and R. Piermartini. 2007. "Exposure to External Shocks and the Geographical Distribution of Exports." In *Breaking Into New Markets: Emerging Lessons for Export Diversification*, edited by Richard Newfarmer, William Shaw, and Peter Walkenhorst, 81–100. Washington, DC: World Bank.

Calderon, C., and C. Cantu. 2018. "Foreign Trade and Growth in CEMAC: Intensity and Concentration." Unpublished background paper, *CEMAC: Country Economic Memorandum*. World Bank, Washington, DC.

Daki, S., and J. R. López-Cálix. 2017. "Structural Change in Niger." Background paper, *Niger: Leveraging Export Diversification to Foster Growth*, World Bank, Washington, DC.

De Ferranti, D., G. E. Perry, D. Lederman, W. F. Maloney. 2002. *From Natural Resources to the Knowledge Economy: Trade and Job Quality*. Washington, DC: World Bank.

Government of Mali. 2017. *National Accounts 2017*. Bamako: The Institute of National Statistics.

Imbs, J., and R. Wacziarg. 2003. "Stages of Diversification." *American Economic Review* 93 (1): 63–86.

IMF (International Monetary Fund). 2017. "Chad: Request for a Three-Year Arrangement Under the Extended Credit Facility and Cancellation of the Current Arrangement." Country Report 17/246, IMF, Washington, DC.

Jansen, M. 2004. *Income Volatility in Small and Developing Economies: Export Concentration Matters*. Geneva: World Trade Organization.

Lederman, D., and W. F. Maloney. 2012. *Does What you Export Matters? In Search of Empirical Guidance for Industrial Policies*. Washington, DC: World Bank.

López-Cálix, J. R. 2017. "Fiscal Rules in CEMAC Countries." Background paper to the Biannual Meeting of Finance Ministers, French Treasury, Paris, April, 13.

McIntire, A., M. Xin-Li, K. Wang, and H. Yun. 2018. "The Economic Benefits of Export Diversification." IMF Working Paper IMF WP 18/86, IMF, Washington, DC.

McMillan, M., D. Rodrik, and Í. Verduzco-Gallo. 2014. "Globalization, Structural Change, and Productivity Growth, with an Update on Africa." *World Development* 63: 11–32.

Mijiyawa, A. 2018. "Structural Change in Guinea." Unpublished background paper, World Bank, Washington, DC.

Newfarmer, R., W. Shaw, P. Walkenhorst, eds. 2009. *Breaking Into New Markets: Emerging Lessons for Export Diversification*. Washington, DC: World Bank.

Rodrik, D. 2016. "Premature Desindustrialization." *Journal of Economic Growth* 21: 1–33.

World Bank. 2017. "Guinea: Systematic Country Diagnostic." World Bank, Washington, DC.

———. 2019. "Africa's Pulse, No. 19: An Analysis of Issues Shaping Africa's Economic Future." (April), World Bank, Washington, DC.

4 Micro Foundations (1)
IDENTIFYING OPPORTUNITIES FOR EXPORT DIVERSIFICATION

ABSTRACT

- At the microlevel, an export diversification strategy initially requires identifying potential non-oil goods (or services) opportunities.

- Opportunities are scarce in Mali, Chad, Niger, and Guinea (MCNG) as these countries feature among the least product-diversified and most market-concentrated export ratios in Sub-Saharan Africa; in a few cases, such ratios are even deteriorating.

- Two parametric approaches measuring product competitiveness—revealed comparative advantage (RCA) and five-year growth rates—allow for the identification of emerging goods.

- Two complementary approaches—product space, and complexity—determine the suitability of any product upgrade option based on its competitive endowment in technology and skills and its proximity to markets abroad for products with similar capabilities for production.

- In general, the position of most competitive MCNG products in the product space—mineral, vegetable, and textile—is highly sparse, peripheral, and scattered, which does little to favor their diversification.

- However, the success of placing strategic bets still relies on being highly selective and on providing the missing public inputs for removing obstacles to their development.

- Hence, the short-term strategy (steps 1 and 2 on the ladder) should focus on the very few products where each country already has a strong comparative advantage and already features dynamic exports.

- The medium-term strategy (steps 3 and 4 on the ladder, which are associated with structural change) should gradually increase efforts toward more sophisticated (higher-value-added) export products, mostly in agribusiness goods and textiles, and supporting information and communications technology (ICT) and transportation services.

PREVIOUS EFFORTS AT IDENTIFYING NEW EXPORTS

Chad, Guinea, Mali and Niger are some of the countries with the highest export concentration ratios in the world, which limits their potential to grow faster. As seen above, in 2015, over 80 percent on average of these countries' export revenues came from just one or two primary goods, and that trend has not changed since the 1970s. This makes their export earnings highly volatile as they are influenced largely by global demand and prices. To offset this disadvantage, multiple initial efforts toward export diversification have been made.

All Mali, Chad, Niger, and Guinea (MCNG) countries already engage actively in identifying potential export winners.

- In *Niger*, the Nigerien Export Promotion Agency (ANIPEX) produced a report that examines the country's export potential (ANIPEX 2016). The report provides ample information on potential production capacity and key constraints to export growth. According to the report, Niger has high export potential in 8 products: cowpeas, gum arabic, handicrafts, hides and skins, livestock and meat, onions, sesame seed, and nutsedge (souchet).

- In *Mali*, the International Trade Centre (ITC) prepared a report for the Export Promotion Agency that examines Mali's export potential (ITC 2014). More recently, the Ministry of Agriculture laid out a strategic profile for the development of Mali's Agricultural Competitiveness and Diversification Program (PCDA). Both reports identified 11 products in which Mali has high export potential: cotton, fertilizer, fish, green beans, gum arabic, karite, mango, potato, rice, sesame seed, and sugar.

- ANIPEX in *Chad* and Agence Guinéenne de Promotion des Exportations (Guinean Export Promotion Agency) in Guinea have completed similar analyses. Their findings are valuable as they present countries with a valid starting point. Each analysis, which is based largely on each country's comparative advantage and its current knowledge base, nor only filters those findings but also shows that MCNG countries have additional opportunities to diversify their export portfolio, not only in goods but also in services, as initially explored by these agencies. Based on these findings, a selective approach to targeting emerging products is proposed.

APPLYING REVEALED COMPARATIVE ADVANTAGE ANALYSIS

The two sequential analyses presented below (a country's export potential and product space) are based on the concept of hidden capabilities. The first method applies an indicator to estimate the country's ability to compete globally known as revealed comparative advantage (RCA). RCA measures countries' relative competitiveness in exporting different goods (Annex 4A). The commodity pattern of trade reflects intercountry differences in relative costs as well as in nonprice factors (Balassa 1986). The advantage of using the RCA index is that it is consistent with changes in the economy's relative factor endowment and productivity.[1] The disadvantage is that the reliability and robustness of its findings is questionable in the presence of import barriers and export constraints (French 2017). To take this handicap into account, complementary indicators are needed. Ideally, in such cases, RCAs should be estimated based on bilateral trade flows. However, the poor quality of official statistics on bilateral flows in MCNG countries—given their high share of unrecorded trade—minimizes the presumed gains in reliability of such an approach. Instead, a more pragmatic alternative approach (applied here) is to also estimate past average export growth over five years, an approach often used as a proxy for identifying export discoveries. Although such estimates are not always consistent with RCA findings, as table 4.2 shows, the approach allows for expanding the number of commodities with export potential while detecting those that have recently been declining. Below are the main findings from the RCA analysis (further details can be found in each Country Report).[2]

Initially, broad sector-level product-specific RCAs are estimated in order to assess the sectoral competitiveness of these countries (table 4.1). The analysis focuses on export commodities with values up to US$ 1.9 billion in 2015. Interestingly, all of them appear to have a strong comparative advantage (RCA > 1) in vegetable products. In fact, Chad's and Guinea's highest comparative advantages are in vegetable products, while Mali's highest relative comparative advantage is in hide and skins. In contrast, Niger's relative comparative advantages were not as strong in any of its exports as for the other three countries. In fact, Niger's highest RCA is only 1.9 in vegetables.[3]

As a second step, product-specific RCAs reveal competitiveness in just a handful of products. Grouped results for all competitive MCNG products are presented in table 4.2 along with their five-year average export growth. The list is not extensive and somewhat selective. The country with the highest number of competitive products is Niger (including its traditional exports). This suggests that while countries could be exporting dozens of products, most of them may have very low export potential. For instance, in 2015, Chad exported just over 120 commodities (with values ranging from US$ 1,000 to 1.9 billion), with a relative comparative advantage in only 11 of them. This means that Chad's share of world exports in these 11 commodities is larger than what would be expected from the size of its export value and from the size of the world market for such products. Moreover, this list does not increase much when taking into account products whose export growth has been positive (preferably in double digits) over the past five years.[4] Hence, Chad's highest comparative advantages are in vegetable products, especially gum arabic, sesame seed, cotton, and maize (corn) flour. Other highly competitive agri-based exports are in animal leather, hides and skins, and manufactured textiles products.[5]

Specific services have also made important strides into emerging MCNG exports. Two industries in particular—information and communications technology (ICT) and travel—feature positive RCAs. In Niger and Mali, the ICT industry has grown at an average rate of 33 and 12.5 percent, respectively. The travel industry is another sector

TABLE 4.1 Average revealed comparative advantage by sector in Chad, Guinea, Mali, and Niger, 2015

	CHAD	GUINEA	MALI	NIGER
	2015	2015	2014	2014
Vegetable products	63.8	100.22	64.4	1.9
Metals	31.9	13.79	n.a.	0.1
Mineral products	2.1	7.83	n.a.	0.4
Animal and animal products	1.6	4.17	3.5	1.3
Textiles	1.4	3.18	8	0.3
Raw hides, skins, leather, and furs	0.6	2.89	175.5	0.8
Wood and wood products	0.1	1.76	n.a.	0.1
Stones and glass	0.1	0.38	28.8	0.1
Plastics and rubber	0.04	0.36	1.7	0.03
Chemicals and allied industries	0.02	0.34	20.8	0.04
Foodstuffs	0.01	0.16	n.a.	0.5
Footwear and headgear	0.001	0.02	1.7	0.1

Sources: Observatory of Economic Complexity (database), https://oec.world/en/; Khebede 2018a, 2018b.
Note: Normalized data. n.a. = not available.

TABLE 4.2 Summary of selected products with higher potential for export diversification

CHAD			GUINEA			MALI			NIGER		
Product description	RCA 2015	5-year CGR (percent)	Product description	RCA 2015	5-year CGR (percent)	Product description	RCA 2015	5-year CGR (percent)	Product description	RCA 2015	5-year CGR (percent)
Maize (corn) flour	17.4	100	Aluminum ore and concentrate	1,152	n.a.	Goat or kid skin leather (excluding further preparation)	592	−37.0	Uranium ore and concentrates	875.9	n.a.
Sesame seed	57.1	7,051	New stamps, stamp-impressed paper, banknotes	324	n.a.	Sheep or lamb skin leather (excluding further preparation)	395	10.4	Natural uranium and compounds	622.7	n.a.
Natural gum arabic	625.7	83.5	Fresh or chilled *Salmonidae* (excluding HS-0302.11)	104	440.9	Sesame seed	379	27.2	Sesame seed	78.7	231
Petroleum oil and oil from bituminous	19.7	−9.4	Other natural rubber (in primary forms or in plastic)	100	99.7	Cotton (not carded or combed)	278	2.1	Live goats	72.5	−30
Reptile hides and skins (fresh or preserved)	2.7	−32.9	Cashew nuts (fresh or dried)	80	3.4	Natural gum, resin, gum-resin, and balsam	123	69.7	Printed plain cotton weave (>85% cotton)	48.3	48.3
Reptile leather	1.1	674	Frozen flat fish (excluding halibut, plaice, and sole)	57	13.8	Natural gum arabic	91	33.0	Husked (brown) rice	27.8	27.8
Cotton (not carded or combed)	22.0	3.1	Nickel ores and concentrates	45	n.a.	Mineral or chemical fertilizers (with nitrogen)	86	n.a.	Second-hand clothing and other articles	25.9	n.a.
Dyed woven fabrics (<85% synthetic fibers and cotton)	3.8	3,800	Gold in semimanufactured form (nonmonetary)	37	n.a.	Guava, mango, and mangosteen (fresh or dried)	86	−3.0	Vegetable fats and oils and their fractions	22.1	2.6
Artificial fiber wadding (articles)	1.8	37.9	Cocoa beans (whole or broken, raw or roasted)	29	28.9	Sheep or lamb skins (without wool, not picked)	48	30.4	Potatoes (frozen)	20.1	2.2
			Frozen *Salmonidae* (excluding Pacific, Atlantic)	28	5.9	Gold in unwrought forms (nonmonetary)	35	n.a.	Other mineral substances	19.5	n.a.
			Beeswax, other insect waxes, and spermaceti	25	−33.7	Woven fabrics (<85% synthetic staple fibers)	30	150.3	Vegetables used mainly for human conservation	16.6	9.7
			Frozen fish	19	19.5	Cotton yarn (excluding sewing)	22	31.8	Onions and shallots (fresh or chilled)	15.5	−9
			Gold in unwrought form (nonmonetary)	17	n.a.	Other fruit, prepared or preserved	17	25.9	Roots and tubers with high starch content (fresh)	15.5	n.a.
			Dried fish (not smoked, excluding cod)	16	16.2	Wood (rough, excluding treated)	15	n.a.	Live horses (other than pure-bred)	11.9	−10
						Other jams, fruit jellies, marmalades	13	321			

Source: BACI international trade database based on HS-6 digit data, http://www.cepii.fr/CEPII/en/publications/wp/abstract.asp?NoDoc=2726.

Note: A RCA value above 1 indicates export potential. This table should be interpreted cautiously due to poor data quality as well as the role of smuggling and re-exports. MCNG countries import rather than export second-hand clothing. Mali may not produce or export yarn. Niger's oil exports as well as its exports of printed plain cotton weave and second-hand clothing may in fact be re-exports. CGR = compounded growth rates; HS = harmonized system code; MCNG = Mali, Chad, Niger, and Guinea; n.a. = not available; RCA = revealed comparative advantage.

in which these countries have a relative comparative advantage. Moreover, looking beyond ICT and travel and assuming that security concerns will ease in the medium term, reviving the tourism sector would provide another opportunity for diversification. Finally, all MCNG countries could benefit from the expansion of their transportation services, an industry with low complexity. Complementary transportation infrastructure development is also crucial to supporting export activities, as highlighted below.

APPLYING PRODUCT SPACE ANALYSIS: A COMPLEMENTARY APPROACH

Product space analysis determines the degree of difficulty applying to different diversification and product upgrade options. The product space approach uses economic output as a proxy for a country's endowments (that is, its capability set). If a country can compete globally with other suppliers, it must have the skills necessary to produce a given product. The method employs a single metric, known as "density," a measure of proximity in the worldwide product space. Density allows us to determine the relatedness of a potential new industry to a country's existing capability stock (that is, the goods a country already exports competitively). In essence, this measure captures visually the feasibility for a country of expanding into offering a new product or service. The underlying idea is that the process of accumulating productive knowledge is not random but rather path-dependent based on existing capabilities. That is, those products a country produces today define what it may be able to develop in the near future. Hence, a country can easily develop a new product if it already possesses all or most of the capabilities required for that production. If the required technology and skills are not yet present in the country, it will be much more difficult to set up the industry locally. In simple terms, it is easier for a country to move from producing chairs to producing sofas than from producing chairs to producing cars.

Figure 4.1, panel a–d, shows the visual representation of the four countries' product space using export trade data for 2014–15. The colored nodes in the figures represent products the MCNG countries exported with RCA (>1) in 2014–15. The pale nodes represent products in which the countries did not have a significant presence (RCA < 1) in 2014–15. Two products are connected by links based on their probability of being co-exported by the country. These links define the structure of the product space. In turn, this structure is what affects the ability of countries to move into new products. Products that are close together share a significant amount of the requisite capabilities and knowhow, making it relatively easy for these countries to move to nearby products.

MCNG goods position in the product space is highly sparse, peripheral, and scattered. These countries export very few products with RCA, and their current position in the product space is highly handicapped. In all cases, mineral products account for a larger share of their exports by value, yet they have only peripheral location in the product space, which does little to facilitate diversification into other products. Of the four countries, Chad is the least diversified, with a scattered product space consisting of vegetable products, sesame seed, and natural gum arabic. As for Guinea, aluminum ore and gold products, the country's largest export sectors by value, have a peripheral location in the product space (far left and around lower right), which does little to facilitate diversification into other products. Fish and wood sectors also provide strong potential for diversification in Guinea. With regard to Mali, its staple exports of sesame seed, guava, mango, and mangosteen as well as other vegetables and fruits are also relatively peripheral, being scattered near the center of the graph. At the very top are a few processed, nonperishable vegetable products (dried legume, vegetable oil, tropical fruit, jams and jellies, dried fruit, and pasta) as well as a few animal products

FIGURE 4.1

Product space for Chad, Guinea, Mali, and Niger, 2014–15

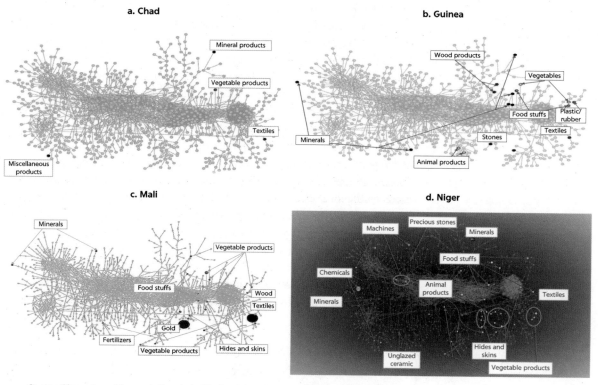

Sources: Observatory of Economic Complexity (database), https://oec.world/en/, and original analysis.

(live sheep and goats and skins and hides). Exports of animal products and processed foodstuffs (pasta, jams and jellies, fruit juices, etc.) also suggest opportunities for diversification in these sectors. Like the other three countries, Niger's product space is dominated by primary commodity exports. However, as seen above, it has strong potential to expand its agroprocessing and textiles.

APPLYING THE FITNESS APPROACH: ANOTHER COMPLEMENTARY APPROACH

The economic fitness approach is also based on the concept of hidden capabilities. Widely used by the International Finance Corporation (IFC) of the World Bank Group and relying in the previous concept of complexity, economic fitness also uses economic output as a proxy for a country's endowments (that is, its capability set). A product is complex if only few and generally more advanced countries can produce it. Economic fitness represents the country's complexity-weighted export products diversity. The assumption is that if a country is to compete globally with other suppliers of a given product, it must have the skills necessary to produce it. Also using RCA to assess the degree of competitiveness of a given product, product complexity captures the level of capabilities required to produce it. In the same vein, economic fitness measures the development of the country's stock of capabilities by examining the diversity of goods a country can produce and how complex those goods are. A country is said to have high complexity and fitness if it can produce a single good (or a bundle of many different goods) that are exclusive, that is, only few other countries possess the capabilities needed to be competitive in producing such a good (Tacchella et al. 2013). In general, while product space and fitness are closely related concepts, the economic fitness measure is considered preferable to product space thanks to its quantified parameters.

MCNG's fitness in MCNG countries shows no major surprises during the period 2012–17 except that well-known export-oriented sectors seem to have lost some ground (figure 4.2). Mali's fitness in fabricated metals (gold) and animal products (meat and livestock) improved, while its fitness in agricultural crops (cotton), which was very high in 2012, decreased. Similarly, Chad's fitness in forestry (wood), agricultural crops, and oil and gas improved, in contrast to leather, where it decreased significantly. For its part, Niger's fitness decreased in its most competitive sectors (animal production, meat, and livestock, mining (uranium), agricultural crops, and machinery, while, consistent with recent discoveries, it improved in the oil and gas sectors. Overall, the three countries seem to be wavering, or losing fitness, in important sectors with previous export potential. Unless reversed by fostering some of the individual emerging products identified above, their sectoral patterns suggest a declining stock of capabilities as well as increasing difficulty in diversifying exports and in upgrading to more complex products in the future. Ultimately, a country can easily develop a new product if it already possesses all (or most) of the capabilities required for its production, that is, such a move has high feasibility (and low complexity). However, if the required technology and skills are not yet present in the country, it will be much more difficult to set up the industry locally.

OPPORTUNITIES FOR EXPORT DIVERSIFICATION

While controversy surrounds the pros and cons of alternative export diversification approaches centered on either picking winners or on an open menu, the extremely limited list of products with export potential in MCNG countries—a few dozen per country—makes such a debate almost irrelevant. In theory, from a public sector's viewpoint, picking winners allows for explicitly prioritizing policies and scarce fiscal resources toward a limited number of carefully identified products. This is particularly suited to fragile countries, such as the MCNG economies, which carry a heavy budgeting burden to meet their military and security needs. In contrast, from a private sector's viewpoint, an open menu of options is preferable because it leaves more space for the private sector, including small and medium enterprises (SMEs) and farmers' organizations, to respond to market opportunities. This is particularly valid when start-up products, which barely show in the statistics, such as fonio in Guinea or shea in Niger, enjoy not only domestic capacity for increasing production but also demand from external (frequently regional) markets for their eventual export.

In response, the short-term focus should be on expanding existing competitive products and finding new markets for them (that is, steps 1 and 2 on the export diversification ladder). As seen above, with the exception of extractives (oil and mineral), MCNG countries' competitiveness arises mainly from certain agricultural and livestock products. Hence, the short-term strategy should prioritize promoting the handful of products where countries have a strong competitive advantage, and because of their rural location, also have strong job-creation potential. Given that the previous analysis suggests prioritizing about a dozen products per country, the following agricultural products are identified for more than one country: cashew, sesame seed, maize (corn) flour, natural gum arabic; mango, onion, bovine meat, and existing textile products such as raw cotton, dyed woven fabrics, and artificial fiber wadding. Note that this list is not substantially different from what governments on their own had previously

FIGURE 4.2

Mali, Chad, and Niger's economic fitness, 2012–17

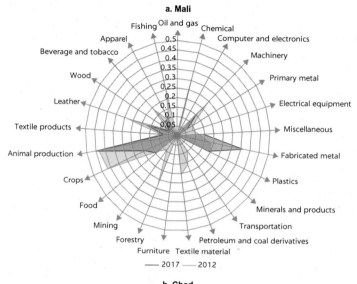

a. Mali

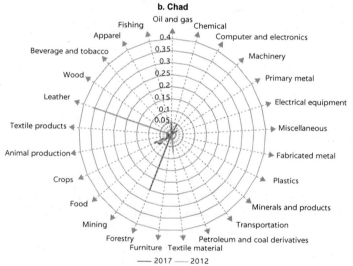

b. Chad

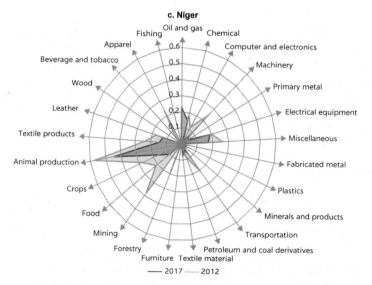

c. Niger

Source: Original calculations based on Cader 2019.
Note: Values in figure are normalized sector values from 0 to 1.

identified. For instance, the ITC already identified a list of key products for Mali, including mango, gum arabic, sesame seed, *green beans, potato, rice, karite, sugar,* and *fish* (with italics indicating those products identified in the previous analysis). This also applies to Niger, for which an ANIPEX report identified the following products: sesame seed, gum arabic, hides and skins, livestock and bovine meat, *cowpea, onion, nutsedge, hides and skins,* and *handicrafts.* Finally, in the case of Guinea, the government has also identified fonio, rice, pineapple, cocoa, cashew, and fish (Khebede 2017; World Bank 2017, 2018a, 2018b). For all of these products, larger export volumes should also naturally lead to a more active search for new (regional and global) markets.

Learning from best practices, MCNG countries should gradually step up their export diversification efforts in the medium term from pilot to mainstreaming by targeting a few more sophisticated products (steps 3 and 4). In this regard, the most critical challenge is acquiring a sufficiently large pool of local industrial skills and capabilities, which cannot be imported or developed in a short period of time. Therefore, countries need to encourage the upgrading and expansion of currently small-scale, low-productivity enterprises, mainly providing low-complexity products to the domestic (or at best regional) market. Initially (step 3), certain industries will pilot entry points and capabilities for certain products. At a more advanced stage, some industries may acquire sufficient knowledge and develop capital intensive industries to be able to provide reasonable incentives to foreign firms to make investments locally (step 4). Given common production patterns, two types of low-complexity product focus may be:

- *Textile products.* Assuming that countries acquire the productive knowledge and skills required to manufacture garments (such as woven fabrics), there is clear potential for domestic firms to raise their intervention in global textile markets. A significant low labor cost advantage offers MCNG countries the opportunity to upgrade their clothing industry into high-quality fabrics.

- *Agribusiness products.* So far, developing MCNG agri-value chains to export higher-value-added products (for example, pasta, fruit juice, and vegetable oil) has been impeded by the inability to produce or process agro-industrial commodities, thus limiting the scope for industrialization. Selectively attracted foreign direct investment (FDI) may stimulate those agro-industries, first by increasing agricultural productivity as well as by minimizing postharvest losses resulting from inadequate storage, packaging, and transportation facilities, and second by gradually expanding their knowledge base in order to manufacture more sophisticated agribusiness products. More specific global value chains (GVCs) are considered in chapter 5.

ANNEX 4A: TECHNICAL DEFINITIONS

Revealed Comparative Advantage

The index for country *c* and good *i* is calculated as follows:

$$RCA(c,i) = \frac{x(c,i) \Big/ \sum_i x(c,i)}{\sum_c x(c,i) \Big/ \sum_{i,c} x(c,i)}$$

where $x(c,i)$ is the value of the exports of country c in the *i*'th good. The index of revealed comparative advantage (*RCAic*) has a relatively simple interpretation. If it shows a value greater than unity, the country has an RCA in that product. Conversely, when $RCA(c,i) < 1$, that country is not a competitive exporter of that product (Balassa 1986).

Product Space Density

Density represents the average proximity of a new potential product j to a country's current competitive export (Hidalgo et al. 2007):

$$\omega_j^k = \frac{\sum_i x_i \phi_{ij}}{\sum_i \phi_{ij}}$$

where ω_j^k is the density of good j for country k. ϕ_{ij} is the proximity between good i and good j, where proximity is defined as the minimum pairwise conditional probability of a country exporting good i given that it exports good j.

Fitness and Complexity

Fitness of countries and complexity of products are specified as a dynamical system, as follows (Tacchella et al. 2013):

$$\tilde{F}_c^{(n)} = \sum_p M_{cp} Q_p^{(n-1)}$$

$$\tilde{Q}_p^{(n)} = \frac{1}{\sum_c M_{cp} \dfrac{1}{F_c^{(n-1)}}}$$

where $F_c^{(n)}$ is the fitness of country c at the n'th iteration of the algorithm. Conversely, $Q_p^{(n)}$ is the n'th iteration of the complexity of product p. M_{cp} represents the matrix of binary RCA values, which indicates whether country c is a competitive exporter of product p. At each step, F and Q are normalized.

Starting conditions for the algorithm are $F_c = 1$ and $Q_p = 1$.

NOTES

1. A comparative advantage is revealed if RCA > 1. If RCA < 1, the country is said to have a comparative disadvantage in that product or industry. Alternatively, RCA is often conveniently presented in binary form depending on whether the country's RCA is higher or lower than 1, thus indicating whether the country is a competitive exporter (RCA = 1) or not (RCA = 0) in that product.

2. The full list of export products with past five-year average export growth (compounded) and their RCAs is included in each of the country reports for Mali, Chad, and Niger and in Khebede (2017) for Guinea and are also available from the authors upon request. Notice also that some country reports include other indicators, including attractiveness (complexity) (see the Chad, Guinea, and Niger Country Reports).

3. Using sector-level RCAs, it was also possible to confirm that some countries have lost competitiveness in the last two decades across a number of key sectors. These include Chad, where the largest decline is observed in the textiles and raw hides and skins sectors, with only the metals and mineral sectors showing marginal gains in competitiveness.

4. See World Bank (2018). Notice that this list does not include products such as livestock, where informal trade is substantial and carries high potential. In addition, some agri-exports exist in combination, including rice and palm oil or sorghum and cotton.

5. Estimated RCAs for the full list of exports per country are included in each individual country's reports, whose analyses also include two other parameters: product complexity, and latest five-year compounded export growth rates.

REFERENCES

ANIPEX (Agence Nigérienne de Promotion des Exportations). 2016. "Étude sur les potentialités des exportations du Niger." Ministry of Commerce, Government of Niger, Niamey.

Balassa, B. 1986. "Comparative Advantage in Manufactured Goods: A Reappraisal." *Review of Economic and Statistics* 68 (2): 315–19.

Cader, M. 2019. "Economic Fitness for Mali, Chad, and Niger." Unpublished paper, World Bank, Washington, DC.

French, S. 2017. "Revealed Comparative Advantage: What is Good for?" *Journal of International Economics* 106 (C): 83–103.

Hidalgo, C. A., B. Klinger, A.-L. Barabási, and R. Hausmann. 2007. "The Product Space Conditions the Development of Nations." *Science* 317 (5837): 482–87.

ITC (International Trade Centre). 2014. "Mali Country Report." UNCTAD, Geneva.

Khebede, E. 2017. "The Product Space of Guinea." Unpublished background paper, World Bank, Washington, DC.

——. 2018a. "Exploring Chad's Opportunities for Export Diversification." Unpublished background paper, *Chad: Leveraging Export Diversification to Foster Growth*, World Bank, Washington, DC.

——. 2018b. "The Product Space of Mali." Unpublished background paper, *Niger: Leveraging Export Diversification to Foster Growth*, World Bank, Washington, DC.

Tacchella, A., M. Cristelli, G. Caldarelli, A. Gabrielli, and L. Pietronero. 2013. "Economic Complexity: Conceptual Grounding of a New Metrics for Global Competitiveness." *Journal of Economic Dynamics and Control* 37 (8): 1683–91.

World Bank. 2017. "Niger: Leveraging Export Diversification to Foster Growth." Report No. 120306-NE, World Bank, Washington, DC.

——. 2018a. "Chad: Leveraging Export Diversification to Foster Growth." World Bank, Washington, DC. https://openknowledge.worldbank.org/handle/10986/31839.

——. 2018b. "Mali: Leveraging Export Diversification to Foster Growth." World Bank, Washington, DC. https://openknowledge.worldbank.org/handle/10986/31829.

5 Micro Foundations (2)
UPGRADING AGRICULTURAL VALUE CHAINS

ABSTRACT

Lessons learned from global value chain (GVC) upgrading experience worldwide show that single policy move and stepwise strategies tend to fail. Rather, successful global (and regional) value chains rely on the mix of several key ingredients:

- *Develop agricultural hubs under a cluster-based approach, that is, a multidimensional GVC upgrading strategy with simultaneous programs involving producer organizations, comprehensive and flexible GVC-specific policies focusing on marketing, and foreign investment.*

- *Adopt a new farm management approach focused on improvements in product quality and standards implementation across the chain and on developing producers' collective action so as to raise farmers' output and incomes.*

- *Seek specialized foreign investment from dedicated multinational firms that are proven global champions in upgrading product-specific value chains with the active participation of producers and processors and in exploring trajectories linking raw agricultural commodities to higher-value-added industries.*

- *Implement agricultural policy support aligning producers' needs with rectifying social, environmental, and economic failures in line with requirements from global and regional markets, that is, a revamped productive industrial development policy that fosters GVCs in agribusinesses with renewed private sector participation.*

Based on the analysis, six broad policy recommendations are as follows:

- *Develop stronger stakeholders in industry and farmers' organizations as well as coordination.*

- *Build product reliability by increasing both quantity and quality, the latter by providing intensive training and implementing standards required by regional and global demand.*

- *Explore increased external demand for crops by foreign firms and improve the infrastructure required to strengthen their market links.*

- *Ensure focused policy interventions to achieve lower production costs and monitor timely linkages between various projects being upgraded.*

- *Raise value chain efficiency, integrity, and reliability by shifting industry decisions and coordination as much as possible to the farm level.*

- *Provide extension services that support GVC development, such as research and development and education and training programs.*

INTRODUCTION

This chapter determines possible upgrading trajectories for Mali, Chad, Niger, and to a lesser extent, Guinea so as to increase their participation in global (and regional) value chains and improve their growth and economic diversification prospects[1] in partnership with government officials and other country-level stakeholders and based on previous analyses, the following priority industries were identified: bovine (Niger), cashew (Mali), gum arabic (Chad), onion (Niger), and sesame seed (Chad and Mali). Work should aim to understand global value chain (GVC) trends in gum arabic, oilseed, nuts, livestock, and horticulture in order to identify lead firms, governance structure, and market dynamics. In addition, key regional competitors and value chain footprints and obstacles should be identified to optimize the development strategy for the agriculture sectors. Lessons from successful cases are also extracted.

Following a GVC benchmarking-based methodology (box 5.1), five questions are addressed:

BOX 5.1

Benchmarking-based methodology for classifying global value chains

GVCs refer to the sequence of value-added activities that include the creation, delivery, and end-use of economic subsectors, products, or services. Applied to the agrifood sector, the framework examines actors, activities, policies, and transformations in global and local agriculture networks and their effects on food security outcomes (Ahmed et al. 2017). Governance is a centerpiece of the analysis and explores how authority and power relations shape the distribution of profits and risks in an industry and identifies the actors who exercise such power (Gereffi 2014). Seven types of upgrading trajectories are considered (De Marchi, Di Maria, and Micelli 2013; Humphrey and Schmitz 2002; Barrientos, Gereffi, and Rossi 2012):

- *Process upgrading,* by improving the efficiency of the production process through the reorganization of productive activities, technology adoption, and workforce development.

- *Product upgrading,* by developing more sophisticated, higher-value products through certification and product development as certified organic products are higher in value than noncertified products.

- *Functional upgrading,* by investing in human and technological capital to enter new activities and provide a unique, higher-value product or service; activities in research and development, branding, and distribution are examples of this type of upgrading.

continued

Box 5.1, *continued*

- *Chain or intersectoral upgrading,* by entering new industries that are often not related, for example, moving from agriculture production to developing a transportation and logistics network.

- *Market upgrading,* by developing new markets and distribution channels, for example, going from village-level markets to regional-level markets.

- *Social upgrading,* by improving workers' well-being in the value chain. This is achieved through education, healthcare, training, and other services that improve workers' knowledge, pay, and quality of life.

- *Environmental upgrading,* by reducing the environmental damage footprint. Water savings, land management, agrochemical reduction, management, and reforestation are examples of environmental upgrading.

Using primary and secondary data collected between January 2017 and April 2018, a total of 13 agricultural industries were assessed in 13 countries in Africa, with a focus on Chad, Mali, and Niger. Over 60 structured and semistructured industry interviews were conducted in those three countries and with global buyers. These were compared to findings from country cases for Côte d'Ivoire, the Arab Republic of Egypt, Ethiopia, Mozambique, Namibia, Nigeria, Senegal, Tanzania, and Sudan, which also assessed regional participation in GVCs. Firms and industry stakeholders were identified through online research, industry reports, referral sampling, industry databases, and reports. With respect to global trade, production and policy data and multiple country-level and international databases were consulted, included those of the World Bank, the International Monetary Fund (IMF), the Food and Agriculture Organization (FAO), and the United Nations' Comtrade. Finally, a standard GVC analysis framework was used to conduct industry-specific diagnostic and identify upgrading trajectories. This was complemented with the use of Wry et al.'s (2013) risk management analysis and Neilson, Pritchard, and Wai-Chung Yeung's (2014) and Pfeffer and Salancik's (1978) studies of firms' influence to understand dependencies on global buyers.

- What is the position of Mali, Chad, Niger, and Guinea in the typology of GVCs?

- How are GVCs in the key agriculture sector organized with a focus on gum, oilseed, nuts, livestock, and horticulture? What are the key trends that influence trade?

- How do value chains differ in each country? What are the affected products? How do end-markets differ?

- Who are the relevant actors at the national and regional levels? How do lead firms govern the chain? How are production and trade coordinated?

- Given major economic, social, and environmental barriers to upgrading, what are specific strategies that will help Mali, Chad, Niger, and Guinea (MCNG) upgrade in the selected GVCs?

THE POSITION OF MALI, CHAD, NIGER, AND GUINEA IN THE TYPOLOGY OF GLOBAL VALUE CHAINS

Most countries in Sub-Saharan Africa engage weakly in regional value chains (RVCs), and MCNG are no different in this regard. Sub-Saharan African countries tend to export products that are upstream, that is, remote from the final

TABLE 5.1 Population, incomes, and value-added shares, 2000 vs. 2015: Mali, Niger, Chad, Guinea, and comparator countries

COUNTRY	POPULATION	GDP PER CAPITA (US$)	VALUE-ADDED SHARES 2015					VALUE-ADDED SHARES 2000				
	2015	2015	AGR.	COMM.	IND.	MFG.	SERV.	AGR.	COMM.	IND.	MFG.	SERV.
Burkina Faso	18,105,570	631	32.9	15.7	21.9	6.2	45.2	32.8	8.4	21.5	13.2	45.7
Cameroon	23,344,179	1,309	23.9	14.5	27.8	13.4	48.2	22.1	15.2	36.0	20.8	41.8
Chad	14,037,472	952	52.4	11.3	14.2	2.9	33.4	42.3	2.4	11.3	8.9	46.3
Côte d'Ivoire	22,701,556	1,492	23.7	8.9	21.5	12.5	55.5	25.0	4.3	21.5	17.2	53.5
Ethiopia	99,390,750	486	41.0	12.2	16.3	4.1	42.8	47.8	6.2	12.2	6.0	40.0
Guinea	12,608,590	417	20.2	30.2	37.0	6.7	42.9	22.4	29.4	33.5	4.0	44.2
Malaysia	30,331,007	10,877	8.4	16.3	39.1	22.8	44.3	8.6	17.5	48.3	30.9	43.1
Mali	17,599,694	903	41.0	n.a.	19.3	n.a.	39.8	35.9	n.a.	23.5	n.a.	40.6
Niger	19,899,120	384	36.4	11.9	17.6	5.7	37.3	37.8	11.0	17.8	6.8	44.4
Uganda	39,032,383	673	24.7	11.7	20.4	8.7	54.9	29.4	15.3	22.9	7.6	47.7
Vietnam	91,703,800	1,685	17.0	19.6	33.3	13.7	39.7	22.7	17.1	34.2	17.1	43.1

Sources: Taglioni 2018; World Development Indicators, World Bank, Washington, DC, https://databank.worldbank.org/source/world-development-indicators.
Note: Green = high value; orange = medium value; red = low value. AGR. = agriculture; COMM. = commerce; GDP = gross domestic product; IND. = industry; MFG. = manufacture; n.a. = not available; SERV. = services.

consumer, due to their specialization in agricultural products or commodities that require little domestic value-added creation. In 2015, agriculture represented a large share in the value added in Chad (52 percent), Niger (26 percent), and Mali (41 percent) and a medium share in Guinea (20 percent) (table 5.1). At the same time, manufacturing contributed less than an average 7 percent to overall value added in these countries. By contrast, Vietnam showed a manufacturing value-added share of over 13 percent despite its relatively high reliance on agriculture value added (17 percent).

GVC participation, especially on the buying side, helps these countries benefit from global knowledge and productivity spillovers. One important transmission channel for learning about and upgrading GVCs is to engage with global buyers and producers. Being a supplier to brands that sell on the global markets requires firms to import foreign technology, skills, and intermediate inputs to meet the high quality standards required to serve these markets. Such spillovers can accelerate countries' economic and social development (Taglioni and Winkler 2016).

However, the bulk of production and exports in MCNG does not appear to have made use of this transmission channel. The low percentage of foreign value added embodied in these countries' gross exports shows their low integration on the buying side, ranging from only 6 percent in Chad to 11 percent in Guinea and Mali and 17 percent in Niger in 2011. In Vietnam, by contrast, the foreign value-added share in total exports (foreign value added by exports) exceeded 43 percent, pointing to a very strong integration as a buyer. Ethiopia is also classified as a GVC buyer despite its relatively high agricultural value-added share (41 percent) (table 5.2).

At the same time, a large portion of domestic value added in Chad, Guinea, Niger, and Mali is embodied in third-country exports, pointing to a medium to high integration of these countries as sellers. Its percentage in exports (herein called as DVA3X) is extremely high in Guinea, reaching almost 70 percent in 2011, while the share exceeds one third of exports in Niger and Chad and represents

TABLE 5.2 **Global value chain share as buyer and seller, 2000 vs. 2011: Mali, Niger, Chad, Guinea, and comparator countries**

COUNTRY	GVC TYPE 2011	FVAX (PERCENT OF EXPORTS)		DVA3X (PERCENT OF EXPORTS)	
		2000	2011	2000	2011
Burkina Faso	seller_agr	7.2	24.3	30.1	24.6
Cameroon	seller_agr_mfg	8.6	8.5	41.0	49.5
Chad	**seller_agr**	9.4	6.2	32.2	35.5
Côte d'Ivoire	seller_agr_mfg	7.4	8.3	31.4	36.4
Ethiopia	buyer_agr_mfg	54.3	46.1	12.7	20.2
Guinea	**seller_agr**	6.5	11.4	63.3	69.6
Malaysia	buyer_mfg	40.3	37.8	23.1	28.6
Mali	**seller_agr**	13.5	11.1	26.7	26.8
Niger	**seller_agr**	10.2	17.0	37.1	34.6
Uganda	seller_agr	10.6	14.2	26.2	26.9
Vietnam	buyer_agr_mfg	23.7	43.6	21.4	18.7

Sources: Taglioni 2018; UNCTAD-Eora Global Value Chain Database, https://worldmrio.com/unctadgvc/.
Note: Green = high value; orange = medium value; red = low value. agr = agriculture; DVA3X = domestic value added embodied in third-country exports; FVAX = foreign value added by exports; GVC = global value chain; mfg = manufacture.

slightly more than a quarter of exports in Mali (table 5.2). By contrast, Vietnam or Ethiopia show the lowest share of domestic value added embodied in third-country exports. These contrasting statistics and the latter countries' success in achieving high growth are proof that integration into international markets is a superior strategy to import substitution, particularly for low-development countries with a relatively shallow and small domestic private sector.

The pattern described above is confirmed by the average distance (upstreamness) of exports and imports to the final consumer. Mali, Niger, Chad, and Guinea specialize in the production and exports of resource-intensive products that require little domestic processing. Such countries tend to show high distance to final demand (upstreamness) in their average export basket, in fact the highest upstreamness level of their average exports across the sample (table 5.3).

On the other hand, these countries tend to show much shorter distance to final demand of imports, reflecting their dependency on final goods imports, including consumption and capital goods. This is confirmed by the data, which suggest that the average import basket in Chad, Guinea, Mali, and Niger shows the shortest distance to the final consumer (table 5.3). The gap between the upstreamness of imports and exports can thus give an indication of the potential for a country's transformation and value-added capture. Countries that buy imported inputs, components, and machinery and export further downstream tend to show a positive gap (for example, Vietnam), while countries that buy final goods and export commodities show a negative gap. The latter is the case for our four West African countries of interest, especially Chad.

Drawing on the three types of measures described above, a new GVC taxonomy classifies a country's integration into GVCs from a macroeconomic perspective (Taglioni and Winkler 2016). The GVC taxonomy classifies 132 countries into four broad GVC groups: agricultural sellers, commodity sellers, other sellers, and buyers. This is based on a country's degree of GVC participation on the buying and

TABLE 5.3 Upstreamness of imports and exports and gap, 2000 vs. 2014: Mali, Niger, Chad, Guinea, and comparator countries

COUNTRY	UPSTREAMNESS OF IMPORTS		UPSTREAMNESS OF EXPORTS		GAP	
	2000	2014	2000	2014	2000	2014
Burkina Faso	2.06	2.18	3.26	2.44	−1.21	−0.25
Cameroon	2.38	2.34	3.03	2.91	−0.65	−0.57
Chad	1.82	1.94	3.76	3.35	−1.94	−1.41
Côte d'Ivoire	2.50	2.37	2.07	2.13	0.43	0.24
Ethiopia	2.23	2.23	1.87	2.18	0.36	0.05
Guinea	2.07	2.10	2.96	2.89	−0.89	−0.79
Malaysia	2.50	2.50	2.32	2.54	0.18	−0.04
Mali	2.17	2.08	2.89	3.02	−0.72	−0.94
Niger	1.98	2.01	3.03	2.89	−1.05	−0.88
Uganda	2.13	2.17	1.93	2.07	0.20	0.09
Vietnam	2.37	2.41	2.07	1.80	0.30	0.61

Sources: Taglioni 2018. Data: Antràs and Chor 2018; UN COMTRADE Database, United Nations, https://comtrade.un.org/.

Note: Upstreamness means the average distance from final use in terms of the production stages a particular product goes through. Green = high value; orange = medium value; red = low value. GAP = upstreamness of imports minus upstreamness of exports.

selling side, average distance of its import and export baskets to the final consumer, and its economic structure in value-added terms.

The four GVC groups consist of several GVC subtypes and are characterized as follows:

- *Agricultural sellers* are countries that participate via agribusiness and agroprocessing (manufacturing), including Chad, Guinea, Mali, and Niger and most of Sub-Saharan Africa.

- *Commodity sellers* are countries that participate as pure commodity-selling economies or via a combination of commodity value added plus manufacturing, commodity value added plus services, or commodity value added plus manufacturing and services.

- *Other sellers* are countries that participate via manufacturing plus services (for example, Europe, the Republic of Korea), including the hubs formed by Germany, Japan, the United States, and more recently China.

- Finally, *buyers* include countries that participate primarily as buyers in value chains for agribusiness and manufactures, buyers focusing more strongly on manufactures (for example, Eastern Europe and East Asia), or buyers for manufactures or services.

By understanding the structural transformation of different economies over time, the taxonomy allows for identifying past and future upgrading trajectories, informing country and sector diagnostics, and identifying suitable policies for different country contexts. Typical upgrading trajectories between 2000 and 2011 were found to be: (i) agricultural sellers with manufacturing activity becoming various types of manufacturing buyers; (ii) concentrated commodity sellers diversifying into manufacturing; (iii) more diversified commodity sellers becoming manufacturing buyers with a stronger services sector; and (iv) manufacturing buyers diversifying into services but mainly remaining buyers.

In the past, MCNG were classified as agricultural sellers 2000 and 2011, suggesting that they did not fully seize opportunities to benefit from buying in GVCs. Chad and Mali, in particular, saw their foreign value-added share in exports decline over the period, while Guinea and Niger expanded their foreign value-added share (table 5.2). On the selling side, Guinea expanded its huge share of domestic value added embodied in third-country exports further over the period, while Chad and Mali showed smaller increases and Niger a small decline (table 5.1). This is also reflected in the countries' upstreamness of imports and exports over time. Chad, Guinea, and Niger managed to reduce their negative gap between 2000 and 2014, in particular by reducing the upstreamness of their exports. At the same time, the distance of their respective import baskets moved further away from the final consumer. Only Mali increased its negative gap due to a larger upstreamness of exports and shorter distance to the final consumer of imports.

HOW ARE GLOBAL VALUE CHAINS IN THE KEY AGRICULTURE SECTOR ORGANIZED?

The global agriculture sector is worth over US$ 5 trillion, with lead international firms active in high value segments. Vertical integration and deeper globalization by firms such as Cargill (grains and other commodities), Olam (grains, oilseeds, nuts, and spices), and Nexira (gum arabic) is a strategic choice. This may involve these firms in upgrading to higher-value segments such as branded products or diversified markets. The landscape of top global buyers is expanding to include firms from Asia (for example, China Oil and Foodstuffs Corporation [COFCO]), India (Rallis),[2] Turkey (Ülker), and Saudi Arabia (Savola Group). Agriculture markets are highly competitive, forcing global firms to invest in innovation, supply chain risk, resource management, data analytics, and technology in order to maintain a competitive edge. Consumer trends such as healthier foods, clean labeling, and fair trade drives demand requirements for global processors, including organic and halal certifications. The key characteristics of the selected GVCs are summarized in table 5.4.

Global firms have asymmetric power in the chain as they are lead buyers and their supply chain arrangements in Africa do not necessarily lead to upgrading. These firms develop complex intermediate products and have relational and captive relationships with limited information exchange with exporters from Chad, Mali, and Niger. On the other hand, global processors engage in a knowledge-intensive, captive, and relational transactions with food brand manufacturers such as Kellogg, which stimulates their upgrading and keeps higher-value know-how in developed and emerging markets. Their powerful position in the chain is an outcome of investments in markets, product and technology development, and data analytics, which makes them price givers. On the other hand, exporters from West Africa are wholesalers, which facilitate trading, are more opportunistic and unorganized and sell agriculture commodities in spot markets. Exporters in Chad, Mali, and Niger are price takers and operate in volatile markets with little or no investment in upgrading. Nor do they adopt a proactive approach to secure and improve their market position, which exposes them to high volatility and market shifts. One example is the salmonella outbreak in sesame seed, which resulted in trade bans on African sesame exports. Figure 5.1 provides an overview of chain governance in the selected GVCs in these countries.

TABLE 5.4 **Characteristics of selected global value chains**

VARIABLE	BOVINES (LIVE)	CASHEW NUTS (IN SHELL OR DRIED)	GUM ARABIC	ONIONS (FRESH OR CHILLED)	SESAME SEEDS
Trade*	US$7.7b	US$2.3b	US$361m	US$3.3b	US$2.6b
Growth rate*	Mixed (-16% to +616%)	2.3%	1.1%	Mixed (-21% to +15%)	3.6%
Top exporters*	France, Australia, Canada, Mexico, Germany	Ghana, Côte d'Ivoire, Tanzania, Guinea-Bissau, Burkina Faso	Sudan, France, Chad, United Kingdom, United States	Netherlands; China; India; Mexico; Egypt, Arab Rep.	Ethiopia, India, Sudan, Nigeria, Tanzania
Top importers*	United States, Italy, Turkey, Indonesia, Spain	India, Vietnam, Singapore, Brazil, Togo	France, United States, India, Germany, United Kingdom	United States, Vietnam, United Kingdom, Germany, Malaysia	China; Turkey; Japan; Korea, Rep.; Vietnam
Regional leaders*	Ethiopia, Sudan, Namibia	Ghana, Côte d'Ivoire, Tanzania	Sudan, Chad, Mali	Egypt, Arab Rep.; South Africa; Sudan	Ethiopia, Sudan, Nigeria
Lead firms	Tyson, Cargill, JBS, BRF	Olam, Mondelēz International, Planters, Silk, Ülker, Kellogg	Nexira, Alland & Robert, TIC Gums, Kerry	Olam, McCain Foods, Nestlé, Pepsico	Olam, Wilmar, COFCO, Ülker
African lead firms	Meatco (Namibia), Allana Group (Indian firm in Ethiopia)	Olam (Côte d'Ivoire, Tanzania, Mozambique)	Gum Arabic Co., Dal Food, Coca-Cola Bottling Co. (Sudan)	Olam (Egypt, Arab Rep.), Brefoots of Botley (United Kingdom investor in Senegal)	Olam (Ethiopia, Tanzania), Wilmar (Ethiopia)
Location of higher value chain segments	North America, European Union	United States, Canada, European Union, Brazil, India, Vietnam	European Union, North America	North America, Europe, Asia	Japan, China, Singapore, United States, Canada
Critical factors for upgrading	Human capital, technology, certifications and standards, traceability, quality, economies of scale, private sector, infrastructure, brands				

Source: Ahmed 2018.
Note: b = billions; m = millions.
* 2016 Data from Chatham House 2018 retrieved from https://resourcetrade.earth/.

FIGURE 5.1

Governance in agricultural commodities value chains in Chad, Mali, Niger, and Guinea

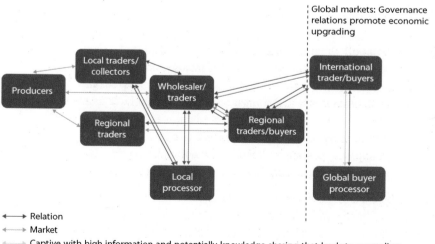

→ Relation
→ Market
→ Captive with high information and potentially knowledge sharing that leads to upgrading
→ Captive with low information sharing

Source: Ahmed 2018.

HOW DO THE VALUE CHAINS DIFFER IN EACH COUNTRY?

Selected value chains in these countries can play a significant role in their export diversification strategies as well as poverty alleviation. Chad and Mali are already players in raw cotton commodity markets, but they could leverage their advantage in other strategic commodities. Both countries are emerging players in gum arabic and sesame seed. Gum arabic is unique to the African belt, with growing demand from European and North American buyers. Sesame complements the production of other products such as cotton and peanuts while providing inputs for oil processing and animal feed. In Niger, the bovine industry is an opportunity to emerge as a regional supplier and meet local and regional demand for milk that currently depends on imports. Niger's onions, of the Violet de Galmi type, is a preferred variety by regional consumers. The selected value chains are a source of employment, with women making up the majority of the workforce in certain segments such as artisanal processing and sorting and bagging activities for export. Table 5.5 provides an overview of the importance of selected value chains.

The selected value chains are underdeveloped, and their trading is in low-value segments. Table 5.6 shows key factors for Chad, Mali, and Niger, and

TABLE 5.5 **Importance of selected value chains in Chad, Mali, and Niger**

VARIABLE	CHAD		MALI		NIGER	
Importance of GVCs	**Gum arabic**	**Sesame seed**	**Cashew nuts**	**Sesame seed**	**Livestock (bovines)**	**Onions**
As % of agriculture exports (2016)	29%	30%	0.8%	7%	12%	2.3%
Global and regional demand	High	High	High	High	Medium to high	Medium to high
For economic diversification	• High value crop	• High value rotation crop • Input to animal feed and high protein edible oil and products	• High value cash crop	• High value rotation crop • Input to animal feed and high protein edible oil and products	• High value potential for meat exports, reduced dairy imports, and regional dairy exports • Potential for high value leather	• Potential for high value for export markets
Job-related activities for female workers	• Gum sorting and bagging for export	• Production of artisanal oils • Sorting and bagging for export	• Collection • Sorting and bagging for export • Artisanal jam	• Cultivation • Artisanal oils • Sorting and bagging for export	• Artisanal dairy	• Artisanal dried onions • Jute onion bags for exports
Employment potential	High	High	High	High	High	High
Food security implications	• Higher incomes	• Higher incomes • Can contribute to edible oils and animal feed	• Higher incomes	• Higher incomes • Can contribute to edible oils and animal feed	• Higher incomes • Meat and dairy for domestic consumption	• Higher incomes
Environmental considerations	High • Requires water • Reforestation opportunity	High • Requires water • Affects land use	High • Requires water • Land use	High • Requires water • Land use	High • Requires water • Land use • Deforestation risks	High • Requires water • Land use

Source: Ahmed 2018.
Note: Niger official livestock share is of total exports, while its livestock and onion shares exclude informal trade.

TABLE 5.6 **Characteristics of selected value chains and constraints**

VARIABLE	LIVESTOCK	ONIONS	SESAME SEEDS	CASHEW NUTS	GUM ARABIC
Primary orientation	Domestic and regional	Domestic and regional	Regional and global	Regional and global	Global
Country	Niger	Niger	Mali, Chad	Mali	Chad
Primary importer	Nigeria	Ghana	Mali, China, Chad, Turkey	Burkina Faso, India	United States, France
Value chain position	Low-value segments	Low-value segments	Low-value segments	Low-value segments	Low-value segments
Global links	None	None	Low	Low	Low
Value chain profile	• Large herds • Third largest export • Exports only live animals • Undeveloped meat processing, dairy, and leather	• Violet de Galmi variety • Largest exporter in West Africa • Falling exports and high waste • Undeveloped processing	• Rotation cash crop in Mali and Chad • Nascent chain in Mali and Chad • Mali: 450 cooperatives; Chad: 897+ cooperatives	• Infant chain • 12,000 small farms • Production increase: 11% annually • Nondeveloped processing	• Second largest export • Constrained supply • Unskilled gum workers • Nondeveloped chain
Powerful chain actors	Traders and high-volume butchers	Traders and cooperatives	Traders	Traders	Traders
Informality	High	High	High	High	High
Policy focus	Low	Low	Low	Low	Low
Standards, certifications	Low to none	Low to none	Low to none	Low to none	Low to none
Constraints	• Animal health • Low quality • Lack of market information • Low actors' organization • Lack of certifications • Infrastructure deficits • Lack of finance • Unskilled producers and workers	• Low quality • Lack of certification • Lack of market information • Low actors' organization • Infrastructure deficits • Lack of finance • Unskilled producers and workers	• Low quality • Lack of certification • Lack of market information • Low actors' organization • Infrastructure deficits • Lack of finance • Unskilled producers and workers	• Low quality • Lack of certification • Lack of market information • Low actors' organization • Infrastructure deficits • Lack of finance • Unskilled producers and workers	• Low quality • Lack of certification • Lack of market information • Low actors' organization • Deforestation • Infrastructure deficits • Lack of finance • Unskilled producers and workers

table 5.7 outlines their value chain characteristics. Countries enter the chain in the production segment but are not upgrading. All of them are lagging in adopting standards, improving quality, processes, and developing higher-value products. Trading is in low-value segments of raw commodities that are minimally processed, live animals, and fresh produce that lacks quality or certification requirements. The landlocked nature of the three countries implies that higher industry coordination while meeting quantity and quality requirements are critical to developing economies of scale and improving competitiveness.

• Gum arabic in Chad is a nontimber forest product destined mostly for exports in raw form. Gum exports are monopolized by a handful of traders and international firms. The industry is unorganized and faces a number of constraints, including deforestation and low-skilled labor. Sesame seeds in Chad are small, consumed domestically, and exported regionally. In Chad and Mali, expansion in sesame production is related to price volatility in cotton and peanuts, which forces farmers to explore other cash crops.

- In *Mali*, sesame seed and cashew nuts are in their infancy, but production is growing fast (at about 90 percent and 316 percent per year, respectively, in response to high demand from regional and international traders (FAO 2018). Neither Chad nor Mali had firms that upgraded by adopting international standards and by entering sophisticated primary or secondary processing. Only one processor in Mali, Promotion du Sésame au Mali (Sesame Promotion in Mali; PROSEMA), is in the process of upgrading its facilities and use mechanized cleaning and sorting of sesame and is seeking international certifications.

- In *Niger*, the bovine and onion value chains are largely regionally and domestically oriented, not maximizing value added and with derived products that are underdeveloped. The bovine industry is fraught with challenges related to the nonorganization of the sector, animal health, and powerful chains among larger herd owners and wholesalers. Conditions in both the live animals and meat segments of the chain are not conducive to increasing exports due to low animal health and sanitary conditions. Despite having extensive cattle herds, the country continues to depend on dairy imports due to low animal productivity and infrastructure constraints. The meat segment of the chain had only one modern and certified but nonoperational slaughterhouse. However, several firms have recently emerged in dairy. One firm has upgraded by adopting higher standards, implementing innovative measures to secure local supply, and supplementing it with imports to meet demand. Another firm has expanded into other products such as bottled water. The tannery segment of the bovine chain is artisanal and equally undeveloped.

- The onion value chain in Niger also suffers from low quality and lack of certification constraints, which excludes it from global markets. Intensifying competition from regional producers in Senegal and Ghana, while imports of Chinese and Dutch onions reduce Niger's regional exports. Compared to other selected value chains, the onion industry in Niger is organized into cooperatives and federations that are trying to improve the performance of the sector. The Onion Federation in Niger has developed a regional trading certificate in order to facilitate countrywide and cross-border transportation of onion exports.

WHAT ARE THE RELEVANT ACTORS AT NATIONAL AND REGIONAL LEVELS?

The selected chains are mostly informal, with large wholesale traders acting as lead players and power brokers in the chain (table 5.7). Global demand is driving exports from Chad, Mali, and Niger through a network of traders that use mostly informal channels to supply intermediaries of international firms and regional buyers. Wholesale traders are exporters operating from the capital cities and competing with regional informal traders for supplies. These actors have a network of trading intermediaries that source and transport agricultural commodities. Lead traders arrange cross-border transportation of goods, which go to regional ports on their way to international markets. Transactions in the chain are cash-based and opportunistic. Producers are not organized in the selected chains and depend on word of mouth for market information. Producers are price takers and have little power in the chain.

TABLE 5.7 **Value chain segments, lead actors, and chain governance**

COUNTRY	VALUE CHAIN	USE OF INPUTS	PRODUCTION	PROCESSING	LEAD FIRMS	SOURCE OF POWER
Niger	Livestock	Low	High but low quality	Low quality, artisanal	• Wholesale traders • Four public slaughterhouses and SONIPEV (not operational)	Access to herds
	Livestock dairy	Low	High but inaccessible	Depends on imports	Niger Lait, Solani, Laban	Scale
	Onion	Low	High	Low quality, artisanal	Cooperatives	• Scale • Trader- and buyer-driven
Mali	Sesame seeds	Low to none	Low	Undeveloped, primarily artisanal	Prodex	• Scale • Trader- and buyer-driven
	Cashew nuts	Low to none	Low	Undeveloped, primarily artisanal	CTARS (Project)	• Scale • Trader- and buyer-driven
Chad	Sesame seeds	Low to none	Low	Undeveloped, primarily artisanal	Seyal Chad, Afrimex, Africa Gums	• Scale • Trader- and buyer-driven
	Gum arabic	Low to none	Low yields	Undeveloped, primarily artisanal	SCCL, Africa Gum, SANIMEX	• Scale • Trader- and buyer-driven

Note: SCCL = Chadian Gum Arabic Corporation (*Société Commerciale du Chari et Logone*); SONIPEV = Nigerien Meat Production and Exportation Corporation (*Société Nigérienne de Production et d'Exportation de Viande*).

- Only recently did lead players such as PROSEMA (Mali, sesame) and Société Commerciale du Chari et Logone (Chadian Gum Arabic Corporation; SCCL) (Chad, gum arabic) start pursuing upgrading to improve their competitive advantage in global markets. Lead traders indicate an interest in adopting international standards and certifications but lack of investment by traders suggest a more passive approach to upgrading.

- The bovine value chain in Niger is highly informal and is controlled by large wholesale traders that supply slaughterhouses. These actors have little or no knowledge of regional or global buyer requirements and are powerful suppliers of slaughterhouses. The government owns and operates slaughterhouses that are currently in very poor condition. Investing in inputs such as animal breeding and animal health is very low. Société Nigérienne de Production et d'Exportation de Viande (Nigerien Meat Production and Exportation Corporation; SONIPEV), the only private and sanitary slaughterhouse in Niger, is currently not operational mainly due to lack of supply chain linkages.

- Lead players in the onion sector in Niger are farmer and trader organizations that are trying to address declining exports. These players have been successful in organizing and now compete with regional traders. However, their ability to influence upgrading is limited due to low awareness of markets and global standards and low adoption of improved seeds.

- Niger Lait in the dairy segment in Niger's bovine sector is the only lead firm that seems to be successfully upgrading. The company was founded by a female engineer educated in France and established a modern dairy International Organization for Standards certified facility. The firm is seeking to improve the well-being of its suppliers through training and fair wages. The company is engaged in process, product, chain, and social upgrading.

Lessons learned from comparative country cases reveal that economies of scale, quality improvements, private sector (domestic and foreign) investment, and policies required to support private sector growth and industry organization are critical to upgrading. In general, adopting early measures to create confidence in product quality through certification and traceability was key to enabling Meatco in Namibia to export meat to Europe and the United States. Strengthening industry associations and policies to increase production and private sector investments in sesame and livestock was a key component in Ethiopia's upgrading and becoming a lead exporter. Privatizing the gum arabic sector in Sudan and attracting Olam's investment in Ethiopia's sesame or Egypt's onion sector was a game changer for these countries in improving production and entering higher-value processing. Details of examples of best practices are found in box 5.2.

BOX 5.2

Learning from best practices worldwide for process and product upgrading

Ethiopia combines foreign direct investment (FDI) with active policies as a game changer in sesame upgrading into processing and improving standards. Olam is one of the largest buyers of Ethiopian coffee and sesame. The company is expanding its operations in coffee and sesame supply chains and imports key commodities such as fertilizer and wheat into Ethiopia. The company's forward integration strategies in Ethiopia has led to improving farmers' crop yields, quality, management, and crop traceability. Its involvement followed the establishment of the Agricultural Transformation Agency in 2010 to support change in the agriculture sector. Headed by a Council, the Agency's mission is to introduce new technologies and approaches that address systemic bottlenecks, facilitate the execution of policy priorities, and catalyze the transformation of the sector. Other global firms are Wilmar, the Asian agribusiness group, which entered into a joint investment agreement with: (i) Repi Soap and Detergent Co. in 2014 to upgrade an existing manufacturing facility to house an edible oil refinery and packing plant for specialty soft oils, soaps, detergents, and sesame seed processing; (ii) East Africa Holdings Ltd., a lead domestic and regional player in foodstuffs, cosmetics, soaps, and detergents; and (iii) the Impact Angel Network, which started operations in 2015 as a sesame company in Addis Ababa and now supports over 10,000 small farmers.

Gum arabic quality system and private sector development in Sudan. As one of the key countries in gum arabic production and marketing, Sudan has a well-established grading system for gum arabic. The grading system provides an important reference point to determine the value of the harvested gum and provides the basis for proper pricing. There are six main grades, and the most expensive grade is Grade 1, which is hand-picked and selected, with the cleanest, lightest in color, uniformly shaped, medium-sized nodules. There are now several private sector processors in Sudan. The Khartoum Gum Processing Company and several other small processors now produce spray-dried and kibbled gum.

More recently, the government announced investments by U.S. firms in the industry. In 2017, the largest gum drying facility opened and has the capacity to spray-dry 5,500 tons, worth US$ 37 million. The facility is affiliated with Dal Food Industry Group, Sudan's Coca-Cola Bottling Company, and the largest food and beverages manufacturer. The plant includes dried milk operation.

In India, the Indian Oilseeds and Produce Export Promotion Council (IOPEPC) is mandated to develop and promote exports of oilseeds, oils and oilcakes. Formally known as IOPEA, IOPEPC has been catering to the needs of exporters for last six decades. Beside focusing on exports, the Council also works toward strengthening domestic supply chains by encouraging farmers, shellers, processors, surveyors, and exporters to enhance the quality of oilseeds in India. Headed by its Chair, the Council places high emphasis on the development of oilseeds, edible oils, oilcakes, and other products under its purview. The Council works toward improving yields and the quality of oilseeds being produced in India to match requirements in global markets. Importing countries are

continued

Box 5.2, *continued*

permanently concerned about Aflatoxin (groundnuts), pesticide residues, and other chemical and microbiological contamination in the agricultural products being supplied by other countries. The Council conducts activities (workshops, distribution of pamphlets, etc.) to create awareness among farmers about controlling Aflatoxin and using safe and permissible pesticides.

In Ghana, AgroCenta was founded by two ex-Esoko employees, Francis Obirikorang and Michael K. Ocansey, in 2015 to improve the agricultural value chain in Ghana. Two critical problems within the value chain were the lack of access to market for smallholder farmers in rural areas, which subjected them to the activities of exploitative buying intermediaries and the lack of a coordinated truck delivery system to transport their output from farms to markets. Both issues of logistics and transportation were solved using AgroCenta's patent TrucKR solution, which allowed smallholder farmers in remote villages to receive offers from interested buyers and to access trucks at the click of a button, a development that could be called an "Uber service for trucks." AgroCenta has also increased the productivity of smallholder farmers by using technology to solve problems they encounter in agriculture.

SCOPE FOR DIVERSIFICATION: SPECIFIC UPGRADING STRATEGIES AND POLICY OPTIONS

To identify possible trajectories, it is initially relevant to explore what the current capabilities of Mali, Niger, and Chad in individual crops of interest look like and what they can expect based on the experience of peer countries that have managed to be in a good position in these particular crops.

- *Niger*. Niger's products of interest are bovine meat and live animals. The country is interested in producing frozen meat for export to Nigeria. However, Niger's capabilities in bovine products are limited. Official numbers of live bovine and other animal exports are difficult to determine due to the high informality of the sector, and the significant number of hoof transport of animals across borders, especially with Nigeria its main trade partner. In 2009, estimated export earnings reached about 20 percent of commodity exports, but only half of them were officially registered as exports (World Bank 2017). Goat, sheep, bovine, camel, equines and donkeys, in that order, are the main types of livestock. Traditionally, countries with capabilities in nonpure breed live bovines went on to develop a comparative advantage in pure-bred live bovines. If Niger succeeds in developing the infrastructure necessary to produce and export frozen meat, many more opportunities for diversification will open up. Product space analysis suggests that the bovine meat market is densely connected and provides many opportunities for developing other processing capabilities within as well as outside the meat sector, including in diary, animal feed, and agricultural machinery (figure 5.2). Experience from peer countries suggests that becoming competitive in the export of offal products may lead to diversification toward products with similar cooling processes (that is, that require freezing). Countries tend to become competitive first in general bovine offal and subsequently in specialized offal such as livers or tongues. Countries that specialized in frozen offal subsequently became competitive in animal fats and oils as well as machinery for tanning hides, skins, and leather. Other opportunities from frozen bovine meat include starting with frozen boneless bovine cuts before moving on to bone in cuts, then to carcasses and half carcasses, and

FIGURE 5.2

Typical product diversification path from live bovine meat for countries with Niger's capabilities

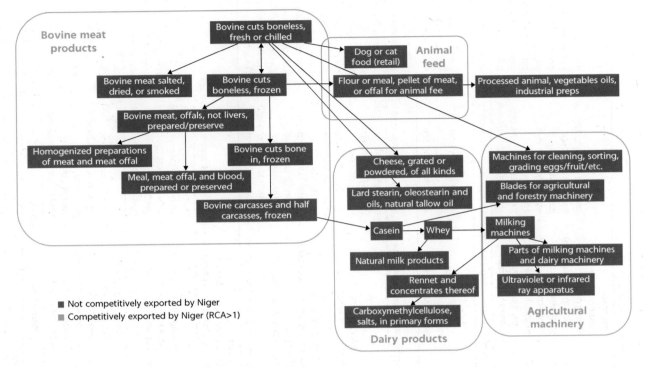

Source: Taglioni 2018.
Note: RCA = revealed comparative advantage.

from there to dairy products, and in particular processed products such as casein and whey.

- *Mali.* Mali is currently and increasingly a competitive producer and exporter of sesame seed. It already exports cashew (both in shell and shelled), but its comparative advantage in higher-value shelled cashew is low. The aspiration of Mali is to diversify into sesame oil, cashew oil, and packaged cashew nuts. The current capabilities in sesame production and the experience of peer countries suggest that Mali has a good chance of developing and becoming competitive in the export of sesame oil, partly due to the capabilities the country has already developed in gum arabic production (figure 5.3). The progression probability of becoming competitive in the production of shelled and packaged cashew is also high, building from the current low base of exports and reflecting experience by peer countries.

- *Chad.* Chad's objective is to develop a gum arabic export industry beyond European markets and to become competitive in the production and export of sesame oil (figure 5.4). The country is already a successful exporter of gum arabic and sesame seed, two products that require similar skills and capabilities. These endowments should facilitate an expansion of the country into sesame oil and gum arabic. These capabilities suggest that in future, Chad could diversify its range into other agribusiness products, including dried vegetables, cereal products, and other refined nut oils.

Lessons learned from GVCs' upgrading experiences worldwide show that single policy moves and stepwise strategies tend to fail. Instead, successful global (and regional) value chains rely on a mix of several key ingredients:

FIGURE 5.3

Typical product diversification path from sesame seed and shelled cashew for countries with Mali's capabilities

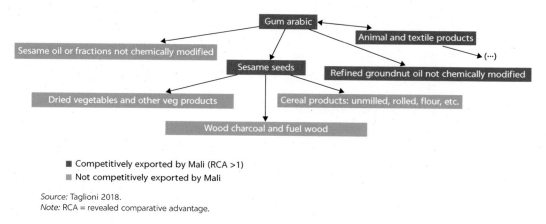

Source: Taglioni 2018.
Note: RCA = revealed comparative advantage.

FIGURE 5.4

Typical product diversification path from sesame seed and gum arabic for countries with Chad's capabilities

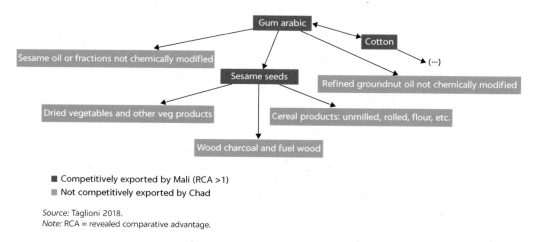

Source: Taglioni 2018.
Note: RCA = revealed comparative advantage.

- The development of agricultural hubs under a cluster-based approach, that is, a multidimensional GVC upgrading strategy with simultaneous programs involving producer organizations, comprehensive and flexible GVC-specific policies from design to marketing, and foreign investment.

- Adopting a new farm management approach focused on improvements in product quality and standards implementation across the chain and on developing producers' collective action so as to raise farmers' incomes. This approach is developed in table 5.8.

- Foreign investment from dedicated multinational firms that are both proven global champions in upgrading product-specific value chains with the active participation of producers and processors and in exploring trajectories linking raw agricultural commodities to higher-value-added industries.

- Finally, an agricultural policy support aligning producers' needs and social, environmental, and economic failures with requirements from global and regional markets, that is, a new productive industrial development policy that fosters GVCs in agribusinesses with renewed private sector participation. Such policy

TABLE 5.8 Upgrading components of the cluster approach and policy options

VARIABLE	CHAD		MALI		NIGER	
Value chain	Gum arabic	Sesame seed	Cashew nuts	Sesame seed	Bovine	Onions
Key policy elements for GVC upgrading	• Supply chain coordination • Economies of scale • Workforce development • Quality certification	• Supply chain coordination • Economies of scale • Workforce development • Quality certification	• Supply chain coordination • Scale economies • Workforce development • Quality certification	• Supply chain coordination • Economies of scale • Workforce development • Quality certification	• Supply chain coordination • Animal health and sanitation • Workforce development • Quality certification	• Supply chain coordination • Workforce development • Quality certification
Examples of upgrading observed	n. a.	n. a.	Natio-Cajou: vertically integrated nut processor	PROSEMA: trader and primary processor seeking globally certifications	ONIPEV: certified, modern slaughterhouse Niger Lait: certified vertically integrated dairy processor	Farmers' organization developed an export certificate
Economic upgrading	• Process and product upgrading into certified products such as organic and Halal. Build product reliability by improving data, traceability, and quality • Process and organizational upgrading to increase flows, reduce costs, and improve industry coordination • Process upgrading to facilitate stronger links between local, regional, and global buyers • Process upgrading. Develop the gum arabic, sesame seed, and cashew nut value chains' capacity to increase production and effectively manage the industry's growth • Process and product upgrading. Develop the value chain's efficiency, integrity, and reliability by shifting industry decisions and coordination to the farm level and attracting game-changing FDI • Process, product, and market upgrading into higher-value niche products and markets. Improve producers' and harvesters' incomes by increasing external demand for Chadian and Malian crops and diversifying markets • Process upgrading to intensify production. Improve linkages between gum arabic, sesame seed, and cashew nut projects with other local development projects addressing social, environmental, or economic failures				• Process and product upgrading by improving animal health and breeding practices • Process and product upgrading by privatizing slaughterhouses and developing milk and leather clusters • Market upgrading by diversifying export markets	• Process and product upgrading for certified seed, improving farm management, storage, and logistics, smaller packaging, and attracting game-changing FDI • Market upgrading by diversifying markets
Social upgrading	By creating farm level production and trading clusters that improve production, adopt certification, promote processing and trading, and encourage women's entrepreneurship				Milk clusters around Niamey	Train women in making smaller bags
Environmental upgrading	Training in tree harvesting, reforestation, and water and land use management	Water and land use management	Water and land use management	Water and land use management	• Water and land use management • Improve sanitation	• Water and land use management • Reduce waste
Policy instruments	In addition to a public-private dialogue, a continuous public-public dialogue is necessary to create coherent policies and a one-stop shop for agribusiness					
	• Industry taskforce • Extension services • Industry strategy and production targets • Explore regional block to attract FDI brand • Environmental standards	• Industry taskforce • Extension services • Industry strategy and production targets • Explore regional block to attract FDI in brand • Environmental standards	• Industry taskforce • Extension services • Industry strategy and production targets • Explore regional block to attract FDI in brand • Environmental standards	• Industry taskforce • Extension services • Industry strategy and production targets • Explore regional block to attract FDI in global brand • Environmental standards	• Privatize slaughterhouses • Extension and support services • Animal zoning and standards • Industry taskforce • Environmental standards	• Industry task force • Extension and support services • Branding • Export and investment facilitation

Note: FDI = foreign direct investment; GVC = global value chain; n.a. = not available; PROSEMA = Sesame Promotion in Mali (*Promotion du Sésame au Mali*).

also needs to tackle the macro fundamentals, especially trade and business environment policies. This is developed in the following chapters of this report.

Last but not least, the GVC analysis reveals that Chad, Mali, and Niger face similar production, quality, and market share threats. The weakest links in the chain are in production with direct impact on product quantity and quality in global and regional markets. The production segment is not connected to buyers' specifications or to global and regional dynamics. Producers face strong pressure from wholesalers and exporters, who control relationships with buyers and logistics. At the same time, exporters are not reinvesting profits by upgrading, lack the necessary skills as well as access to finance, and exert pressure on their suppliers to keep transaction costs low and revenues high. These findings suggest that process upgrading in product intensification and stakeholder organization as well as product upgrading through quality improvements, certifications, and empowering producers are the two most critical and immediate economic upgrading trajectories. Table 5.8 outlines the main short- to medium-term upgrading components and policy options.

NOTES

1. For individual country-level GVC analysis and relevant findings for Mali, Niger, and Chad, see Ahmed and Fandohan (2017, 2018a, 2018b). Further details are also provided in the individual chapters addressing GVCs in the country reports.
2. Subsidiary of Tata Group.

REFERENCES

Ahmed, G. 2018. "Upgrading Agricultural Value Chains in Mali, Niger, and Chad." Unpublished background paper, World Bank, Washington, DC.

Ahmed, G., and B. Fandohan. 2017. "GVC in Niger: Bovine and Onions." Unpublished background paper, *Niger: Leveraging Export Diversification to Foster Growth*, World Bank, Washington, DC.

———. 2018b. "Chad's Value Chains in Sesame Seeds and Gum Arabic." Unpublished background paper, *Chad: Leveraging Export Diversification to Foster Growth*, World Bank, Washington, DC.

———. 2018c. "GVC in Mali: Sesame Seeds and Cashew." Unpublished background paper, *Mali: Leveraging Export Diversification to Foster Growth*, World Bank, Washington, DC.

Ahmed, G., S. Nahapetyan, D. Hamrick, and J. Morgan. 2017. *Russian Wheat Value Chain and Global Food Security*. Durham: Duke Center on Globalization, Governance & Competitiveness at the Social Science Research Institute. https://gvcc.duke.edu/wp-content/uploads/2017/05/cggc -russia-wheat-value-chain.pdf.

Antràs, P., and D. Chor. 2018. "On the Measurement of Upstreamness and Downstreamness in Global Value Chains." NBER Working Paper 24185, National Bureau of Economic Research, Cambridge, MA. https://www.nber.org/papers/w24185.pdf.

Barrientos, S., G. Gereffi, and A. Rossi. 2012. "Economic and Social Upgrading in Global Production Networks: A New Paradigm for a Changing World." *International Labour Review* 150 (3–4): 319–40.

De Marchi, V., E. Di Maria, and S. Micelli. 2013. "Environmental Strategies, Upgrading, and Competitive Advantage in Global Value Chains." *Business Strategy and the Environment* 22 (1): 62–72.

FAO (Food and Agriculture Organization). 2018. Food and Agriculture Data. Retrieved from: http://www.fao.org/faostat/en/#data.

Gereffi, G. 2014. "Global Value Chains in a Post-Washington Consensus World." *Review of International Political Economy* 21 (1): 9–37.

Humphrey, J., and H. Schmitz. 2002. "How Does Insertion in Global Value Chains Affect Upgrading in Industrial Clusters?" *Regional Studies* 36 (9): 1017–27.

Neilson, J., B. Pritchard, and H. Wai-Chung Yeung. 2014. "Global Value Chains and Global Production Networks in the Changing International Political Economy: An Introduction." *Review of International Political Economy* 21: 1–8.

Pfeffer, J., and G. Salancik. 1978. *The External Control of Organizations: A Resource Dependency Perspective*. New York: Harper & Row.

Taglioni, D. 2018. "The Position of Mali, Niger, Chad, and Guinea in the Typology of GVCs." Unpublished background paper, World Bank, Washington, DC.

Taglioni, D., and D. Winkler. 2016. *Making Global Value Chains Work for Development*. Trade and Development Series. Washington, DC: World Bank.

World Bank. 2017. "Niger: Leveraging Export Diversification to Foster Growth." Report No. 120306-NE, World Bank, Washington, DC.

Wry, T., J. A. Cobb, and H. E. Aldrich. 2013. "More Than a Metaphor: Assessing the Historical Legacy of Resource Dependence and its Contemporary Promise as a Theory of Environmental Complexity." *Academy of Management Annals* 7 (1): 439–86.

6 Macro Foundations (1)
REVISITING TRADE POLICY AND LOGISTICS

ABSTRACT

- *Export diversification should address the trade policy framework defined by tariffs and other trade barriers that help determine the competitiveness of an economy. This is particularly important given the landlocked nature of these countries (except Guinea), geographic dispersion of the region's populations into local clusters across the vast landscape, and extensive informal trade.*

- *Three overlapping agreements (Economic Community of West African States [ECOWAS], West African Economic and Monetary Union [WAEMU], and Economic and Monetary Community for Central Africa [CEMAC]) govern their trade regimes based on a Common External Tariff (CET) featuring high tariff escalation and subject to excessive exemptions.*

- *Revisiting CETs with a view to eliminating exemptions and providing increased neutrality while bringing greater coherence to the three CET regimes would promote the reallocation of resources from resource-based nontradable to tradable goods and services, while encouraging trade along Sahel corridors connecting the four countries.*

- *Expected payoffs from tariff reforms are unlikely to fully materialize in the presence of multiple nontariff (parafiscal) barriers that have led to high informality in regional trade, high trade transaction costs, poor trade logistics, and poor market linkages.*

- *Addressing trade and transport related costs while also including complementary regional efforts in trade facilitation is required if these countries are to promote cross-border trade and deeper integration into more formal regional trade flows along the primary regional transit corridors and into global markets.*

BACKGROUND

Evaluating options for export diversification in the Mali, Chad, Niger, and Guinea (MCNG) economies first needs to acknowledge the high levels of informal trade that dominate intraregional trade in agricultural-based products (box 6.1). In developing global value chains (GVCs), the MCNG countries must make progress in promoting export diversification and intraregional and global trade through a policy framework that not only reduces their reliance on natural resources and fosters structural change but also facilitates the integration of informal trade into formal markets as opposed to a proper incentive framework defined by tariffs and other trade barriers that determine the allocation of resources. This chapter summarizes the key trade-related policy issues, challenges to export diversification, and policy recommendations that can best promote sustainable nonresource export growth in the region.

Exploring the right mix of trade policy prescriptions for formal export diversification in the MCNG economies should consider their regional integration. The four countries belong to three different and overlapping trade regimes defined by their respective Regional Economic Communities (RECs). Niger and Mali belong to the West African Economic and Monetary Union (WAEMU), together with Benin, Burkina Faso, Côte d'Ivoire, Guinea-Bissau, Senegal, and Togo. Meanwhile, most WAEMU countries, including Niger and Mali, are members of the Economic Community of West African States (ECOWAS), as is Guinea. Chad's trade is formally linked with the Economic and Monetary Community of Central Africa (CEMAC) along with Cameroon, the Central African Republic, the Democratic Republic of Congo, Equatorial Guinea, and Gabon, but not Nigeria, which is an ECOWAS member and perhaps the largest trading partner, at least for Niger and Chad. CEMAC countries, including Chad, also belong to the Economic

---

BOX 6.1

High informality in regional trade in West Africa

Intraregional trade (mainly of agricultural products) in West Africa consists largely of three sets of trade flows, much of which remains informal:

- *Cross-border trade*, carried out mostly by informal traders around natural market hubs based on excess local supply and demand conditions (such as local horticulture and other products) and enabled by porous borders;

- *Arbitrage trade*, much of it smuggling or trade deflection from third countries (for example, rice and poultry) designed to circumvent trade bans or highly restrictive tariff barriers and taking advantage of porous borders; and

- *Trade-based on complementarities*, largely in staple foods, where complementarities exist between production and demand (livestock, cereal grains and legumes, cassava) (Maur and Shepherd 2015).

A recent study estimates that about 84 percent of Chad's agriculture trade is informal (Diagnostic Trade Integration Study [DTIS] 2015). Niger is largely an agrarian economy, and much of its related trade, namely agricultural products and livestock, is informal and unrecorded (Raballand 2017). Furthermore, Hoffmann and Melly (2015) describe economic activity in border markets between Niger and Nigeria and estimate that the volumes of commodities traded informally between Nigeria, Niger, and the rest of Sahara-Sahelian region dwarf those of formal trade.

Community of Central African States, which has been established since 1983 but is virtually defunct as it is yet to be ratified. Each of the three regions is at various stages of integration, but all include their own Common External Tariffs (CETs).[1]

Yet, there remains much unrealized potential. Despite high market concentration (see chapter 1), a gravity model controlling for key economic factors shows unexploited trade potential. This is the case, for instance, of Chad and Niger in relation to their regional trading partners, the wider Sub-Saharan Africa region, and other major economies (figures 6.1 and 6.2). Using available data for these two economies, Niger appears to underexport to ECOWAS members such as Benin, Burkina Faso, and Nigeria as well as to larger markets such as France and China. In contrast, Niger's exports to Togo, Senegal, and Belgium are above what would be expected from geographic and other factors, a finding that is probably explained by proximity and trade complementarities as well as by its role as a re-export base for third countries. Similarly, despite the United States and India being major trading partners for Chad, it underexports to these economies as well as to other countries such as Japan and France. Chad also underexports to countries in East Asia such as Thailand and Singapore. As regards Niger and Chad, trade with neighbors is absent (or underreported vis-à-vis Nigeria) as these countries predominantly trade informally. On the other hand, the position of Rwanda and Ethiopia, which do not share borders with Chad, suggests unexplored market potential within the Sub-Saharan Africa region.

The recent announcement by African countries that they intend to proceed with a Continental Free Trade Area (CFTA), which aims to liberalize trade in goods and services and facilitate investment across the African continent, is likely to introduce an overarching policy and regulatory framework. The modalities for the CFTA tariff negotiations will need to effectively address specific trade and trade policy conditions prevalent in the African context. Different degrees of market integration across regional economic communities (RECs) as well as individual countries' intra-African trade patterns will affect the ease with which the parties will be able to engage in market opening under CFTA. It is important that credible liberalization objectives be set and an optimal way to reconcile

FIGURE 6.1

Chad's trading partners: Predicted vs. actual exports

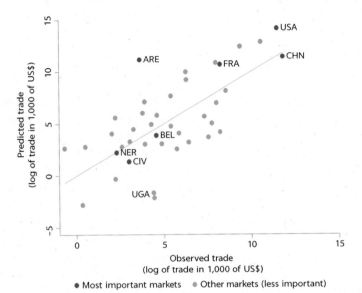

Source: World Development Indicators, World Bank, Washington, DC, https://databank.worldbank.org/source/world-development-indicators.
Note: ARE = the Arab Republic of Egypt; BEL = Belgium; CHN = China; CIV = Côte d'Ivoire; FRA = France; NER = Niger; UGA = Uganda; USA = the United States.

FIGURE 6.2

Niger's trading partners

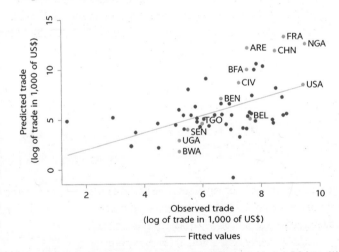

Source: World Development Indicators, World Bank, Washington, DC, https://databank.worldbank.org/source/world-development-indicators.
Note: ARE = the Arab Republic of Egypt; BEL = Belgium; BEN = Benin; BFA = Burkina Faso; BWA = Botswana; CHN = China; CIV = Côte d'Ivoire; FRA = France; NGA = Nigeria; SEN = Senegal; TGO = Togo; UGA = Uganda; USA = United States of America.

the parallel integration processes at REC, inter-REC and CFTA levels be found, including by ensuring continued monitoring, review, and follow-up.

PITFALLS IN THE TRADE POLICY FRAMEWORK OF MCNG COUNTRIES

Taxes on international trade continue to play an important role in overall taxation in MCNG countries. On the one hand, declining taxes on international trade still represent 12.8 percent, 28.2 percent and 14.9 percent of tax revenue in Mali, Niger, and Guinea, respectively. On the other hand, the importance of customs reform cannot be overstated as being plagued by exemptions. Customs revenue should in fact be higher: Extractive industries in these countries, especially Guinea and Niger, are heavily reliant on often exempted imported intermediate inputs and raw materials, which also explains two-digit current account deficits.

As part of regional customs reforms, the implementation of the CETs adopted by WAEMU, ECOWAS, and CEMAC is fraught with inconsistencies and exceptions. For instance, the CEMAC CET consists of five bands: (i) certain cultural products and products related to aviation (zero rated); (ii) essential items (5 percent); (iii) raw materials and capital goods (10 percent); (iv) intermediate goods and miscellaneous (20 percent); and (v) consumer goods (30 percent) (table 6.1). Meanwhile, the tariff applied by Chad in 2012 contains exceptions to the CEMAC CET on 45 tariff lines. However, these exceptions do not introduce new rates; rather, products are reclassified to another tariff category. For their part, ECOWAS member states have adopted a CET that came into effect in 2015, with four positive nominal rates (5, 10, 20, and 35 percent). Moreover, the most recent World Trade Organization (WTO) Trade Policy Review noted the presence of considerable exemptions to the CET at country level. For example, mining and other companies approved under Mali's Investment Code are exempt from customs duties. In Niger, imported raw materials and packaging are exempt if no domestic production exists. In 2015, its customs exemptions totaled around US$ 114 million (WTO 2017). Recent estimates indicate that fiscal (and tariff) revenues would increase significantly if Niger eliminated all tax exemptions and relied on customs tariffs (7.3 percent) and other taxes (2.4 percent) (World Bank 2017).

In 2015, ECOWAS members adopted the CET for 90 percent of tariff lines. The ECOWAS CET was based on the WAEMU CET, which has been implemented since 2004, but left the remaining 130 tariff lines subject to a 35 percent rate. The ECOWAS CET exceeds WTO rules in all member states except Guinea-Bissau and Togo. Furthermore, the additional 35 percent tariff band implemented under ECOWAS (for example, by Guinea) exceeds WTO rules; yet, estimates indicate that its elimination would have a negligible impact on revenues (IMF 2015). In addition, numerous other duties and levies imposed by member states are set at zero, creating a confusion. The latest available information for 2017 at the six-digit level shows Niger and Mali applying most favored nation tariff lines with multiple deviations from the CET, amounting to over 100 discrete tariff rates spread across the entire tariff

TABLE 6.1 Average tariff rates in Niger

TARIFF LINE	AVERAGE RATE
1. Simple average applied most favored nation rate	18.1
Agricultural products (WTO definition)	22.4
Nonagricultural products (WTO definition)	17.4
Agriculture, hunting, forestry and fishing (ISIC 1)	23.6
Extractive (ISIC 2)	11.2
Manufacturing (ISIC 3)	17.8
2. Effective applied tariffs	18.6
3. Tariff lines duty free (percent of all tariff lines)	0.6
4. Simple average rate (lines dutiable)	18.2
5. Non-ad valorem tariffs (percent of all tariff lines)	0.0
6. Tariff quotas (percent of all tariff lines)	0.0
7. National tariff peaks (percent of all tariff lines)	0.0
8. International tariff peaks (percent of all tariff lines)	48.1
9. Overall standard deviation of applied rates	9.6
10. Applied rates "nuisance" (percent of all tariff lines)	0.0

Sources: World Bank 2017.
Note: ISIC = International Standard Industrial Classification; WTO = World Trade Organization.

schedule, some with minor deviations from the five-band (0, 5, 10, 20, 35) structure, while other countries show more significant deviations.

Some simulations on adjusted CET rates in WAEMU find significant welfare and trade costs. The revision of the CET with the additional 35 percent band has potentially important consequences as it may increase the cost of living for households by 7 to 10 percent and therefore decrease their welfare by 2 to 5 percent (Gourdon and Maur 2014). In the case of Guinea, due to differing consumption patterns among households and the nature of the tariff structure, tariffs are regressive across the income distribution both for the four-band WAEMU tariff and the ECOWAS CET. For the former, average tariffs range from roughly 12 percent for the poorest to 9 percent for the richest, and for the CET from 13 to 10 percent. The impact on households is also regressive in the ECOWAS CET, with poor households disproportionately affected and the consumption-weighted average welfare cost amounting to 5 percent for the lowest 5th percentile compared to 3 percent for the 95th percentile.

In addition, the applied CEMAC, WAEMU, and ECOWAS CET rates display an escalating structure with (differences resulting from higher import duties on semiprocessed products compared to raw materials and higher still on finished products), thus distorting activity away from tradable toward nontradable and misaligning these economies with peer regions. CEMAC duties on intermediates and capital goods are above those seen in other regions and significantly above East Asian countries (EAC) and regions such as Association of Southeast Asian Nations (ASEAN), the latter being now among the most diversified and prolific exporters of industrial products and deeply integrated into GVCs (table 6.2). Providing increasing neutrality over incentives and aligning closely with world prices have been foundations of ASEAN's structural transformation. In contrast, the CET of the three MCNG-related regional blocs shows much higher tariffs on final products than on primary and intermediate inputs, a structure designed to promote outdated import substitution by providing tariff protection for the industrial production of final goods. High CET tariffs on consumer goods, with the aim of creating incentives for regional substitution, may encourage greater regional production, but at a high cost to consumers and at the expense of export diversification, both within the regional market and into GVCs. Moreover, while escalation is common across most African countries, variation is less pronounced in Sahel countries than in other Sub-Saharan Africa countries and regions as well as EAC (figure 6.3).

The presence of myriad and complex paratariffs in MCNG countries results in increasing unpredictability and reducing transparency while exacerbating the protective effect of tariffs. For example, Chad applies a range of other duties and levies such as a community integration tax, a community integration contribution, an Organization for the Harmonization of Business Law in Africa levy, and a statistical fee levied on all imports regardless of origin, all of which add between 5 percent and 8 percent ad valorem. In Niger, various border taxes apply: (a) a statistical import levy: 1 percent; (b) a value-added tax (VAT) set at 19 percent in WAEMU directives; (c) a WAEMU community solidarity levy: 1 percent; (d) an ECOWAS community solidarity levy: 1 percent;[2] (e) a special import tax on some

TABLE 6.2 Comparative simple and weighted tariffs in regional groupings, 2016

REGION	TYPE OF GOODS	SIMPLE AVERAGE	WEIGHTED AVERAGE
EAC	Primary	9.64	3.58
EAC	Intermediate	8.75	5.35
EAC	Consumer	17.07	7.72
EAC	Capital	4.97	4.48
ECOWAS	Primary	13.42	19.11
ECOWAS	Intermediate	9.96	9.37
ECOWAS	Consumer	18.36	13.78
ECOWAS	Capital	7.69	7.79
CEMAC	Primary	18.09	10.04
CEMAC	Intermediate	14.87	12.2
CEMAC	Consumer	24.84	19.99
CEMAC	Capital	12.68	12.82
SADC	Primary	4.37	0.65
SADC	Intermediate	4.49	2.26
SADC	Consumer	11.96	8.71
SADC	Capital	2.82	2.16
WAEMU	Primary	17.76	25.38
WAEMU	Intermediate	10.70	11.50
WAEMU	Consumer	17.51	14.47
WAEMU	Capital	7.94	7.76
ASEAN	Primary	5.33	2.72
ASEAN	Intermediate	4.49	4.08
ASEAN	Consumer	9.39	6.16
ASEAN	Capital	4.89	1.96
EU	Primary	5.64	n.a.
EU	Intermediate	0.03	n.a.
EU	Consumer	2.34	n.a.
EU	Capital	0.00	n.a.

Sources: Benjamin and Pitigala 2017; Pitigala 2018a, 2018b.
Note: n.a. = not available. ASEAN = Association of Southeast Asian Nations; CEMAC = Economic and Monetary Community for Central Africa; EAC = East Asian countries; ECOWAS = Economic Community of West African States; EU= European Union; SADC = Southern African Development Community; WAEMU = West African Economic and Monetary Union.

FIGURE 6.3

Average tariffs by stage of production, 2016

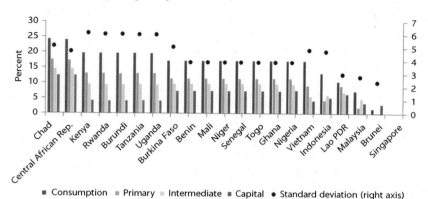

Consumption ■ Primary ■ Intermediate ■ Capital ● Standard deviation (right axis)

Sources: Benjamin and Pitigala 2017; World Bank 2018a, 2018b.
Note: PDR = People's Democratic Republic.

agricultural products: 10 percent of floor price; (f) an excise tax: between 15 and 45 percent depending on the product (for example, cigarettes and alcoholic drinks); (g) an import verification tax (TVI): 1 percent of the value of the goods to finance fees paid to COTECNA; (h) a preshipment inspection service; (i) an advance on the tax on industrial and commercial profits: 5 percent of the value of the goods for operators with no tax identification number (NIF); and (j) a 3 percent tax for operators with an NIF (DTIS 2015). Similarly, (k) a community solidarity levy of 1 percent, imposed on WAEMU member states on imports from countries outside ECOWAS, (l) the ECOWAS community levy of 0.5 percent, and (m) a statistical tax of 1 percent are also imposed by Niger. The absence of a domestic equivalent for these added duties and levies increases the protective effect of tariffs and exacerbates the escalated tariff structure, resulting in even higher rates of effective protection than suggested by the escalated tariff structure.

Thus, the currently applied tariff structures in MCNG economies worsen poverty and disincentivize agriculture exports. This is because high tariffs amplified by paratariffs imposed on basic agricultural goods add a substantial cost to consumers, especially poor households, which spend disproportionately on food. While this may protect these West African farmers against imports from outside the customs territory, it gives little protection in countries where imports are largely noncompetitive within respective regional arrangements. Thus, MCNG have considerable opportunities to increase and diversify their agro-exports products and, in some cases, to export high-quality processed products. A necessary condition for promoting higher-value-added processing is for inputs to production, including tools and equipment, to be allowed to enter at very low rates, which will also minimize intersectoral distortion. Moreover, if exports were directed at highly competitive markets, as could be the case for meat and hides and skins, zero or low tariffs on imports of inputs could generate sufficient competitiveness for these countries' exports.[3]

Similarly, high tariffs on manufactures and intermediate goods provide little by way of protecting Sahel producers because the contribution of domestic manufacturing of tradable goods is quite small, as is these countries' capacity for efficient import substitution. Those perceived as nascent industries, for example, fruit juice, textiles, or cement, which constitute the CEMAC regions' supply capacity, is not even sufficient to meet domestic demand in Chad, leading to extraregional imports, which in turn entail a substantial welfare loss resulting from high CET rates to consumers in Chad. Hence, the justification for maintaining such a high degree of escalation should be reviewed and linked to the performance of the industry in terms of competitiveness and ideally phased out over time.

In addition to standard and other ad hoc tariffs, other nontariff barriers (NTBs) impact trade, including barriers at borders through bans or quotas that are occasionally applied to sectors with domestic competing products. These largely apply to food products and can be imposed seasonally to protect local producers and industries. Some ECOWAS members have on occasion imposed short-term export restrictions, usually on grains, to help the country cope with temporary food security problems. Finally, efforts at regional harmonization, including for seed and other agriculture inputs, have not been fully implemented and continue to require duplicative certifications, while the lack of harmonized grades and standards on grains and legumes impedes the movement of staple foods from surplus to deficit regions and hurts the potential for agri-based GVCs.

Customs reform is a major priority. Perhaps the most significant NTBs are the complex, duplicative, and often unnecessary customs procedures (based on outdated manual systems). This complexity invites collusion and favors corruption among traders, officials, and intermediaries. It also provides incentives for extensive smuggling and informal trade. Customs officials also extract payments for goods in transit and impose lengthy procedures for clearance at border crossings, holding up shipments for days or even weeks. Even though ECOWAS made regional commitments to eliminate the need for certificates of origin for food products, some members continue to require them. In addition, despite ECOWAS countries signing technical agreements for mutual recognition of sanitary and phytosanitary certificates, border officials still require traders to obtain duplicate certificates. This may be in part due to a lack of information but also to interest in creating opportunities for collecting fees or bribes.

In parallel, opportunities exist for streamlining cross-border trade flows through border bazaars, similar to those implemented along parts of the India-Bangladesh or China-Kazakhstan borders (box 6.2). These bazaars, also known as *haat*, have as their main objective a simplified regime for trade transactions (with near absence

---

BOX 6.2

The role of border bazaars

Bazaars (or *haat*) play a vital role along the India-Bangladesh border. In 2011, the Governments of Bangladesh and India revived the border bazaar concept and opened a pilot *haat* near the Kurigram-Meghalaya border crossing. A *haat* is a makeshift bazaar held once a week, allowing border residents to trade eligible products free of customs duties as long as consignments do not exceed an agreed-upon threshold. Eligible products include local agricultural and horticultural products, spices, minor forest products (excluding timber), fresh and dry fish, dairy and poultry products, cottage industry items, wood furniture, and handloom and handicraft items. Such products are also exempt from local taxes. Since the pilot, a total of four border *haat* are now operational along the India-Bangladesh border in Meghalaya and Tripura. India has now proposed 27 new border *haat* across the 443 kilometer-long border.

The border bazaar model has been replicated in other regions. The Korgas bazaar on the Kazakhstan-China border is an exemplary case study. It is one of the region's largest cross-border bazaars, servicing some 1,300 traders each day. The bilateral regime allows visa-free entry for traders for the day and limited duty-free privileges (on up to US$ 1,000 of merchandise, with a flat rate applied thereafter). On the Kazakhstan side of the border, cross-border trading has become the most important source of employment in Zharkent, the largest border town in the district. Conservative estimates indicate that 10 percent of the local population works directly in cross-border trade activities. Estimates suggest that each trader generates employment for an additional one to two persons engaged in warehousing, local transportation, or sales within the bazaar. Moreover, the existence of the bazaar has generated spillover effects, creating new retail and other commercial opportunities (Kaminski and Mitra 2012).

Source: Kathuria and Malouche 2016.

of formal processes and duty- and tax-free transactions). Facilities also provide all required services, expand the reach of local markets, and create a direct stimulus for income generation and employment. Successful *haat* have allowed the transition from subsistence-level farming to small-scale commercial farming and related trade activities, including eventual integration into more formal supply chains for export, especially for cross-border communities along the long borders between Niger, Chad, and Nigeria, including in places such as Maradi, Zinder, Diffa, Birni-N'Konni, and Tahoua.

Geographically speaking, closer integration with Nigeria by Niger and Chad could contribute to MCNG trade growth in goods and services. The West Africa market is dominated by Nigeria, followed by Ghana, Côte d'Ivoire, and Senegal. Together, these countries account for 80 percent of regional gross domestic product (GDP) and 75 to 80 percent of agriculture imports and exports. Nigeria is the largest economy in Africa and is set to double in size by 2030. The size of the Nigerian economy, its diversity, demographics, and projected growth trajectory are likely to offer the greatest market potential in agriculture trade for MCNG countries. Anecdotal evidence points to substantial informal two-way exports, with staple foods and livestock exports dominating flows from Sahel countries to Nigeria and exports of millet and sorghum those from Nigeria to its neighbors. The scale of this informal trade provides clear evidence of strong complementarities with Nigeria and of substantial prospects for market synergies, positive externalities, and economies of scale that will improve efficiency and better allocate resources. While free trade theoretically takes place within ECOWAS, countries do not apply it, which means that ECOWAS exporters have to pay ad hoc duties and taxes when exporting within the region. Hence, rather than concentrating on tariffs, multilateral free trade arrangements (FTAs) should mainly correct burdensome and expensive NTBs and transit arrangements and thus unleash the true potential for multilateral trade between Nigeria and its neighbors, especially Chad and Niger. Moreover, such a development could spill over into services, including air connectivity, commercial collaboration, and financial services, with deeper integration facets likely to benefit all countries involved.[4]

Further potential for geographic trade diversification lies in North Africa. Despite the geography and politics of MCNG countries, which tend to orient them toward West rather than North Africa, the rapid expansion of technology, the digital economy, and a supply of professional services (banking, tourism) has created new opportunities for those countries to interact with North Africa, including partnerships with North African investors (especially from Morocco and Tunisia). Although lack of data prevented us from estimating the fiscal impact of such moves in all MCNG countries, box 6.3 presents those results for Niger.

TRADE LOGISTICS AND FACILITATION

Geography adds dramatically to the export diversification challenges faced by land-locked countries such those in the MCNG subregion (except Guinea) as the degree to which the trade and transit environment accentuates transaction costs may determine the countries' potential for both formal and informal trade. This is even more critical for exporters in fragile, conflict, and violent contexts, where any comparative advantage may be further eroded by conflict in certain production areas, resulting in additional distance between production and markets. These countries are entirely dependent on their neighbors' transit infrastructure and administrative procedures to transport their goods to seaports, the most expedient channel for international

BOX 6.3

Estimating the fiscal impact of trade reform: The case of Niger

This box examines the impact on imports and fiscal revenues of regional trade agreements in Niger. The country has committed to implementing the ECOWAS CET as well as the Economic Partnership Agreement (EPA) signed with the European Union (EU) in February 2014. Simulations show the limited impact of the trade preferential agreement, which is constrained by the country's extensive use of tax exemptions and the small share of imports originating from ECOWAS and European countries. Regarding the CET, as per customs data, in 2015, only 40 percent of imports entered Niger with the statutory most favored nation tariff rate, while 59 percent benefitted from partial exemptions (with uranium carrying only a 14 percent rate), and 1 percent were totally exempt. Moreover, EPAs were signed with only four ECOWAS countries (out of 14 ECOWAS countries exporting to Niger in 2013). In 2013, imports from ECOWAS and European countries represented 23 percent and 15 percent of total imports, respectively, both small ratios when compared to their shares in neighboring countries. Preferential access was used by 11 out of 14 ECOWAS countries (Nigeria being the most important, with a share of 6 percent of total imports).

There is wide diversity in tariff regimes and the taxes, which should be simplified. Myriad taxes are levied on imports: Among them, custom tariffs (5 bands: 0, 5, 10, 20, and 35 percent), two ECOWAS community taxes (1 percent each), a statistical tax (1 percent), excise taxes (alcohol: 45–50 percent; tobacco and cigars: 45 percent, other products: 8, 10, and 15 percent), TVI (1 percent), and VAT (0, 5, and 19 percent). As a result, in 2015, total tax revenue from Customs was dominated by VAT (49 percent), tariffs (30 percent), excise taxes (10 percent), and other taxes (11 percent). The mean duty on imports in Niger is 35.3 percent, while tariffs alone have an import-weighted mean of 15.4 percent (and a simple mean of 12 percent). The multiplicity of such taxes should also be considered when simulating the elimination of tax exemptions.

The EPA with the EU targets a market access of 75 percent liberalization over a 20-year transition period accompanied by an EPA development program of EUR 6.5 billion for the 2015–19 period (lower than the EUR 15 billion initially requested by the West African countries).

ECOWAS countries have also agreed to grant the EU any new favorable tariff treatment provided to other trade partners in the future provided the latter have a share of international trade higher than 1.5 percent and a sufficient degree of industrialization (above 10 percent in the year prior to the agreement's entry into force). These criteria would exempt any tariff preference granted to another African or African, Caribbean, and Pacific Group of States countries, while it could include any preference that would be granted to, for instance, China, India, or Brazil.

The World Bank's Tariff Reform Impact Simulation Tool was used to simulate the impact on Niger's import and fiscal revenues of removing tax exonerations and implementing the new CET and EPA. Two main results emerge:

- Not surprisingly, fiscal revenues increase significantly when eliminating all tax exemptions, either on customs tariffs only (7.3 percent growth rate) or on all taxes (20.4 percent growth rate), or CFA Franc (Communauté Financière Africaine; CFAF) raising from 153 billion to 164, or 184 billion, respectively. The downside from such a policy move, is that in the former case, the average level of tariff protection increases from 6.1 to 11.5 percent with the application of the most favored nation statutory tariff rates, which also reduces total imports by about 12.3 percent.

- For its part, the application of the CET seems at first sight almost irrelevant from the perspective of the expected lowering of the level of external protection and it is only slightly positive from the perspective of increasing imports from ECOWAS countries. In contrast, under the CET, the average level of tariff protection for Niger rather increases from 6.1 to 6.3 percent, with a negative impact on import growth rates (-0.5 percent) and positive fiscal revenue growth rates (+2.2 percent). These marginal small effects are a consequence of the small number of products affected as these products have been selected based on their strategic value to ECOWAS members. In addition, high tariffs target consumer goods consumed in proportionally greater quantities by the poorest segments of the population, thus potentially creating a nontrivial impact on the most fragile segments of the population.

Sources: Jammes 2017; World Bank 2017.

commerce. Niger primarily relies on Cotonou (Benin) as well as dry ports in Burkina Faso linked by rail to the seaports of Tema and Takoradi in Ghana. Chad mainly relies on Douala (Cameroon), while Mali ships its goods mainly through Dakar (Senegal) and Abidjan (Côte d'Ivoire). Countries also utilize other existing but far less functional trade corridors linking them to these major port cities. Overall, three types of parameters are relevant due to: (i) the quality of trade and transportation logistics; (ii) trade and transportation costs; and (iii) the availability of efficient transit corridors connecting them to other countries. It is also important to note that while natural resource exports are mainly transported via land to neighboring ports, other perishable goods may run into added obstacles. This is often the case of agri-based products traveling from dispersed and disconnected rural areas to larger urban markets.

The poor logistics competitiveness of Chad and to a lesser extent of Niger and Mali and their transit partners further reaffirms their weak trade environment. For example, Chad performs relatively poorly on key elements of the World Bank's Logistics Performance Index, including efficiency of customs and border management clearance, quality of trade and transportation infrastructure, competitiveness and quality of logistics services (trucking, forwarding, and customs brokerage), and ability to track consignments, with all three countries performing well below regional benchmark peers (Kenya, Uganda, and Tanzania). Further compounding Chad's problems, Cameroon does not perform much better in terms of Logistics Performance Index score (figure 6.4).

While Mali and Chad show a mixed performance in terms of trading costs, Chad also performs poorly in trading across borders compared with peers and faces exorbitant transactions costs with its transit partners (Cameroon, Nigeria) (table 6.3). The cost of being landlocked may be reflected in marked price differences between coastal and landlocked countries. Products sold in N'Djamena, Chad's capital, may be 30 percent higher than in neighboring Cameroonian cities. In fact, The World Bank's aggregate trade cost indicator also shows Chad as having the highest costs among landlocked countries, while Mali and Niger showed a decline in trade costs between 2004 and 2014.[5] However, the costs of exports (measured in US$ per container) are higher in Mali than the average for WAEMU and Sub-Saharan Africa countries, implying that the cost of domestic freight transportation in Mali is also higher due to the country's low performance in terms of documentary and border compliance costs. Compared to other landlocked and Sahelian countries in the West Africa region, Mali's cost performance is below that of Burkina Faso but superior to that of Niger.

Despite the multiplicity of (largely ineffective) bilateral and regional agreements,[6] severe issues prevent the availability of efficient transit corridors that might connect the countries involved.

- *Roads infrastructure is poor.* In Niger, the transportation infrastructure depends heavily on partially paved roads, which suffer from lack of maintenance. The entire network is approximately 19,000 kilometers long, of which less than 4,000 are paved. The Cotonou-Niamey corridor is almost entirely paved and is by far the

FIGURE 6.4

Mali, Niger, and Chad's logistics performance

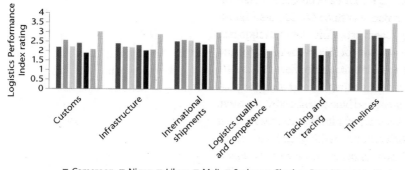

Source: Logistics Performance Index 2017, World Bank, Washington, DC, https://lpi.worldbank .org/.
Note: Highest scores means best performers. Ken = Kenya; Peer = peer countries; Tza = Tanzania; Uga = Uganda.

TABLE 6.3 **Trading across borders: Indicators**

	TIME TO EXPORT: BORDER COMPLIANCE (HOURS)	COST TO EXPORT: BORDER COMPLIANCE (US$)	TIME TO EXPORT: DOCUMENTARY COMPLIANCE (HOURS)	COST TO EXPORT: DOCUMENTARY COMPLIANCE (US$)	TIME TO IMPORT: BORDER COMPLIANCE (HOURS)	COST TO IMPORT: BORDER COMPLIANCE (US$)	TIME TO IMPORT: DOCUMENTARY COMPLIANCE (HOURS)	COST TO IMPORT: DOCUMENTARY COMPLIANCE (US$)
Cameroon	202	983	66	306	271	1,407	163	849
Chad	106	319	87	188	242	669	172	500
Central African Republic	141	280	48	60	98	209	120	500
Côte d'Ivoire	239	423	84	136	125	456	89	267
Guinea	36	310	48	105	72	405	32	37
Libya	72	575	72	50	79	637	96	60
Mali	48	242	48	33	98	545	77	90
Niger	48	543	41	39	78	462	156	457
Nigeria	135	786	131	250	284	1,077	173	564
Senegal	61	547	26	96	53	702	72	545
Sudan	162	950	190	428	144	1093	132	420
Peers (Botswana, Kenya, Uganda)	33	249	36	157	113	473	75	159

Source: Trading across Borders (time and cost) Index, Doing Business Indicators 2019, World Bank, Washington, DC, https://datacatalog.worldbank.org/dataset/doing-business.
Note: Peers = peer countries.

most utilized, accounting for more than 65 percent of goods traffic, but it is also very long, even if at 1,050 kilometers, it is shorter than Lomé-Niamey. The Chadian road network is 42,000 km long, of which 6,200 km are primary roads and only 996 km are asphalted roads, much of it in poor condition, especially in the north and east of the country. Unpaved roads are often inaccessible during the wet season, especially in the southern half of the country. The N'Djamena to Douala port route (1,800 km) is currently the main option for opening up Chad as nearly 90 percent of the total volume of international freight uses that corridor.

- *Road harassment at a multiplicity of checkpoints, where significant illegal payments are collected, is widespread.* The Improved Road Transport Governance initiative's report show that in the West African region, these hindrances—in terms of number of checkpoints, bribes, and delays during shipment of goods from gateway to place of delivery—are more significant in Chad and Mali, even though in the latter their magnitude has significantly decreased over recent years (table 6.4). Individual payments (bribes) at each checkpoint, though small, deter traders, mainly the poor and women, who prefer to deal in small volumes and informal trade.

- *Cross-border trade is expensive and inefficient.* This is due to the difficulty of obtaining import and export licenses as it takes an inordinate amount of time to file for licenses, and bribes or informal payments may be expected.

- *Domestic transportation markets are unorganized and fragmented.* The transportation sector in all three countries is dominated by a large number of

TABLE 6.4 **Road harassment in selected West African countries**

	NUMBER OF ROAD CHECKS PER 100 KM		BRIBES PER 100 KM		DELAYS PER 100 KM TRIP	
	2005	2013	2005	2013	2005	2013
Burkina Faso	5.5	1.6	4,410	2,140	22	17
Côte d'Ivoire	n.a.	1.9	n.a.	2,675	n.a.	8
Ghana	2	1.8	1,960	679	21	18
Mali	4.6	2.6	12,250	3,775	38	26
Senegal	n.a.	1.3	n.a.	1,614	n.a.	14
Togo	1.5	0.9	1,470	597	16	7

Sources: World Bank (2018b) calculations using Improved Road Transportation Governance (IRGT) Initiative data.
Note: Bribes are in amount of local currency. Delays are measured as average minutes lost due to road checks.
KM = kilometers; n.a. = not available.

individual or family-type transporters, using a fleet that is generally old and poorly maintained. Freight companies are estimated to account for less than 20 percent of transporters in Mali. The international freight-sharing quota schemes signed with the coastal transit countries coupled with the queuing system and various cartel practices constitute strong obstacles to increased market access and undermine transportation service quality. Codes of conduct and driving rules are at a nascent stage. This engenders a lack of reliability and predictability, two essential factors in the logistics supply chain. The result is a vicious circle of further informality.

The recently ratified WTO Trade Facilitation Agreement (TFA) provides its members, including MCNG as well as their neighbors with a robust, time-sensitive opportunity to address issues affecting regional and international trade. It does so by expediting the movement, release, and clearance of goods as well as transit issues across the region. All regional trading blocs (WAEMU, CEMAC, ECOWAS) are actively involved in the TFA. All three institutions received mandates from their respective member states to negotiate and play a key role in the preparatory stages and negotiation of the TFA. However, key trade partners such as Nigeria and Cameroon have yet to ratify the TFA.

POLICY OPTIONS

The key to exports diversification and facilitating a competitive tradable sector is to refine the incentive structure defined by trade, tariffs, and NTBs. Such policies would help MCNG countries better identify and exploit economic diversification opportunities while also creating sustainable employment opportunities and promoting an active role for the private sector in both domestic and international markets. Therefore, an active trade policy should be an integral part of the strategy. As the current trade regimes are excessively protective, appropriate sequencing of measures to be taken should be conducted in parallel with actions aiming to simplify the tariff structure, eliminate cumbersome NTBs, and improve customs procedures while introducing other reforms and regulations that deal with perceived constraints to the business environment. The following paragraphs summarize the key policy options shown in table 6.5.

- *Explore means of refining the CEMAC and WAEMU CETs to bring them closer to peers as means of reducing distortions and stimulating trade diversification. Restoring*

TABLE 6.5 **Matrix of policy interventions in trade policy for export diversification**

OBJECTIVES	RECOMMENDATIONS AND ACTIONS	LEAD INSTITUTIONS	RESULTS INDICATORS
Consistent CET structure across Sahel countries	Introduce CET 0, 5, 10, 20 across WAEMU and ECOWAS and include CEMAC as an interim step toward further rationalization and consistency	Ministries of Trade and Regional bodies	Improved trade environment and reduced smuggling
Improve governance and efficiency of incentives	Give authority to single interministerial committee to approve tariff exemptions Phase out inefficient tariff exemptions	Ministries of Finance, Customs, and Trade	Increased revenues and improved efficiency
Eliminate cross-border barriers and paratariffs	Eliminate illegal paratariffs and incorporate those remaining into the existing CET	Ministries of Finance and Trade	Reduced transactions costs and improved transparency
Stable commodity prices	Eliminate import and export restrictions on agriculture trade	Ministries of Agriculture and Trade	Increased investment in agriculture value chain
Develop ECOWAS-Nigeria trade and export development program	• Undertake a cost/benefit assessment of reducing tariffs bands to four as well as tariff exemptions, NTBs, and parafiscal levies under ETLS, especially with Nigeria • Present findings to negotiation committees at interministerial ECOWAS committees, Heads of Commerce meetings, and other forums	Ministries of Trade and Commerce and export promotion agencies	Expanded regional trade in agriculture, especially staple foods
Increase regional and extraregional markets in agricultural products	Define a strategy for a marketing program appropriate to each strategic sector for different regional and international markets	Ministries of Trade, Agriculture, and Foreign Affairs and export agencies	Increased export values, volumes, and share of agri-exports to countries
Promote diversification of exports to Asian markets	• Develop the capabilities of Chambers of Commerce, Industry, and Crafts to gather commercial information • Develop the capabilities of commercial counselors in respective overseas missions	Ministries of Trade and Commerce and export promotion agencies	Expanded exports to East Asian markets
Establish leadership in implement of WTO TFA	Establish the mandate of the NFTC and its lead role in steering TFA action plans, with mechanism for interagency coordination and public-private dialogue	Ministries of Finance and Commerce, PSP, CCIAN, SGG	New AFE standards promulgated and implemented
Take steps to operationalize the National Single Window	Expedite the harmonization of import and export documents among all relevant agencies and initiate business-oriented re-engineering of all trade-related processes and procedures	Prime Minister's Office, Ministries of Justice, Commerce, Economy, Finance, and Urban Development	Initial steps in establishment of single window
Simplify border control procedures	• Streamline data entry by eliminating repetitive records • Delete systematic scanning of records by adopting risk management principles	Customs	Reduced transit time at borders
Streamline customs regulations and revenues and introduce automation	• Introduce legislation necessary for the rationalization of documents and declarations and the development of teletransmissions • Allow electronic transmission of early transit declarations	Ministries of Commerce and Justice	Decrease in the number of paper-based transactions based
Include transit trade into computerization of customs revenues	• Develop infrastructure for computerization and strengthen centralized connectivity in all customs offices (import/export and transit) • Ensure migration to ASYCUDA World for UNCTAD	Ministries of Finance and Customs	Activation of centralized connections between customs offices for deployment of ASYCUDA World

continued

TABLE 6.5, *continued*

OBJECTIVES	RECOMMENDATIONS AND ACTIONS	LEAD INSTITUTIONS	RESULTS INDICATORS
Eliminate illegal fees and levies along trade corridors	• Launch an awareness campaign among traders of ECOWAS and WAEMU protocols with regard to transit traffic • Establish a reporting mechanism for traders encountering road harassment	Prime Minister's Office, Ministries of Trade, Justice, and Agriculture, and regional bodies	Enhanced trade, especially exports by SMEs and women traders
Promote a competitive and efficient transportation sector	• Implement harmonized regional rules of access and exercise of professions based on competence, training, and company solvency • Apply sufficient transitions time to gradually integrate the informal sector	Ministries of Transport	Improved transportation performance and reduced logistics costs

Note: AFE = Authorization for Expenditure; ASYCUDA = Automated System for Customs Data; CCIAN = Chambre de Commerce, d'Industrie, et d'Artisanat du Niger (Nigerien Chamber of Commerce, Industry, and Handicrafts); CEMAC = Communauté Économique et Financière d'Afrique Centrale (Economic and Monetary Community for Central Africa); CET = common external tariff; ECOWAS = Economic Community of West African States; ETLS = ECOWAS Trade Liberalization Scheme; NFTC = National Foreign Trade Council; NTB = nontariff barrier; PSP = Platform for Social Protection; SGG = Secrétariat Général du Gouvernement (Government Secretariat General); SME = small and medium enterprise; TFA = Trad Facilitation Agreement; UNCTAD = United Nations Conference on Trade and Development; WAEMU = West African Economic and Monetary Union; WTO = World Trade Organization.

the WAEMU CET to four bands (for example, 0, 5, 10, and a luxury goods rate of 20 percent) is recommended as a means of reducing welfare costs as well as reducing the anti-export bias as a step toward bringing these countries closer to the more competitive incentive structures seen in peer regions. A DTIS (2015) also recommended that the CEMAC CET adopt the four-band regime proposed above.

• *Phase-out exemptions.* Recent estimates in Niger suggest that customs services collect only one-third of revenues due to it as a result of both tax exemptions and smuggling. Phasing out exemptions while improving revenues significantly reduces incentives for rent-seeking and improves transparency.

• *Eliminate cross-border barriers and paratariffs.* The aim should be to eliminate all paratariffs with a phase-out period of 2–3 years and eventually integrate levies such as statistical fees into existing tariff bands in order to reduce costs and improve transparency. Anything less than 2 percent is considered a nuisance tariff as is implementation costs generally tend to exceed its benefits and should be eliminated in the short run.

• *Eliminate import and export restrictions.* Import restrictions affect crops such as maize, wheat flour, cassava, sugar, vegetable oil, rice, frozen and chilled fish, beef and poultry. Export restrictions are mostly applied to cereals, particularly maize, millet, and rice. Major reasons for governments to impose such restrictions are short-term food security concerns in periods of (expected) food shortages. Indeed, a large number of countries in the region banned exports during the 2007–08 food crisis. However, while this allows food to remain in the country in the short run, it can negatively affect the investment decisions of value chain actors and thus have an adverse effect in the long run. In certain cases, regional grain banks are an alternative option.

• *Promote implementation of regional standards.* Traders in agricultural products would profit from a clean implementation of WAEMU/ECOWAS rules on agricultural products, allowing tax-free transit for local products and regional recognition of product standards.

• *Promote a bilateral free trade agreement with Nigeria.* When countries such as Chad and Niger (with their small, landlocked, undiversified economies) share borders with Nigeria (a more diversified coastal country), incentive regimes tend to deviate, that is, higher consumer goods tariffs create sufficient rents for informal arbitrage both for bilateral and third-country trade, as seen from recent diagnostics, with large informal imports of consumer goods from Nigeria to Chad. Moreover, the presence of substantial informal trade with Nigeria due to both trade and other transactions costs suggests unexplored mutually beneficial trade. It is therefore in the interest of both Niger and Chad to consider mitigating or eliminating trade and transaction costs by negotiating a comprehensive FTA with a robust transit framework.

- *Create border bazaars to promote cross-border trade, especially for poor traders and women.* Given the geography of spatial markets linking Nigeria, Chad, and Niger, a regime aiming to ease the movement of goods and people engaged in subsistence-level trade needs to be encouraged using the border bazaar model. Border bazaars enable cross-border transactions with minimum formalities (limited by security protocols) and encourage retail trade between border communities and thus the development of postharvest infrastructure that can reduce harvest waste and increase returns to local communities. Participation in bazaars should be made easier, for example, through visa-free entry, exemptions from border taxes, reductions in documentation requirements, and adoption of good practices by agencies dealing with these procedures in order to ease flows through bazaars. Successfully implemented in India-Bangladesh border regions, such an initiative could be piloted at the Maradi, Zinder, Diffa, Birni-N'Konni, and Tahoua crossing points based on the density of communities along the border. A joint security arrangement in piloted border regions will likely protect cross-border trade and maintain access to productive territory around Lake Chad, which is likely to ease the burden of cross-border trade while reducing rent-seeking impacting border communities, particularly female traders, who are often more susceptible to security risks and harassment.

- *In terms of the second rung on the diversification ladder, all countries would benefit from making a concerted and comprehensive effort to deepen their regional and bilateral trade, especially with Nigeria.* As the largest market in the ECOWAS region, Nigeria alone could provide the engine MCNG countries need, especially for Mali, Niger, and Chad, in order to promote export growth. Whereas there is room for a comprehensive FTA, the focus should be on reducing transaction costs, increasing investments in regional transporting and energy infrastructure, and improving logistics services. To unlock such a strategy, a first necessary step would be to assess the mutual benefits flowing to both parties from mutually lowering tariffs and NTBs on key staples by removing barriers to trade in agricultural and livestock products. These measures should be discussed within both the ECOWAS forum and CEMAC channels. Greater joint efforts in security, bringing increased protection for people, land, and livestock along the long border with Nigeria, are also needed in order to expand access to productive territory. Finally, these efforts could include guaranteed access to the Lake Chad shores to promote the fishing sector.

- *Explore new emerging markets.* Develop institutions to facilitate commercial information about targeted Africa and Asian countries through overseas missions as well as the capabilities of respective export development agencies to explore value chain opportunities on the upstream side to export cotton to Bangladesh, India, the Republic of Korea, and Indonesia. In Europe, Germany, Switzerland, Austria, and Portugal are worth exploring in depth. This includes development of an Action Plan to promote agriculture products from Sahel countries to the targeted destinations highlighted above. There is also a need to explore the feasibility and available competencies for transitioning to the next tier of industrial ascendance for countries such as Niger and Chad in, for example, chemicals and plastics products derived from petroleum. Experience suggests that export promotion campaigns with a product-specific orientation tend to pay off. Promotion efforts should be supported by export promotion agencies and private sector organizations through identification of appropriate exhibitions and trade fairs as well as support for inward trade missions. In terms of resources, empirical evidence suggests that effort should be focused on large firms that are new or not yet exporters rather than on small firms and established exporters. For agricultural products, the success of the Global Shea Alliance and the African Cashew Alliance in integrating into international markets through export promotion, value addition, and improved standards provides examples of regional models that could be replicated.

- *Improve trade logistics so as facilitate entry into GVCs.* Improving trade and transportation logistics, the business environment (especially the rule of law), infrastructure, (telecommunication, roads, ports), and wage competitiveness are key determinants of entering GVCs. The service sector plays a crucial role in the competitiveness of manufacturing firms because it represents a key source of value added that could help to diversify Sahel economies and affects the chances of those countries to add value and climbing GVCs. Conditions for leveraging existing or nascent comparative advantages in manufacturing and services need to be supported by technology and knowledge transfers from other countries, most often in the form of foreign direct investment (FDI). Sectoral initiatives to promote integration with GVCs should include developing product quality and standards in order to connect with global players, establishing regional production networks, reducing NTBs, and increasing tariff liberalization.

- *Chad, Mali, and Niger needs a two-pronged strategy to address illegal payments and associated road harassment along transit routes.* First, in coordination through WAEMU, CEMAC and ECOWAS, these countries should negotiate a set of principles and guidelines governing transit traffic, specifying applicable service fees at each stage. Second, also in conjunction with WAEMU and ECOWAS, these two countries should develop and launch an awareness campaign designed to inform transporters and traders about such a set of guidelines along with a noncumbersome mechanism for reporting illegal fees. South Africa's nontariff barrier (NTB) reporting mechanism provides a robust best-practice guide to reporting NTBs, including transit-related harassment.

- *The recently ratified WTO TFA provides the region with a robust, time-sensitive opportunity to address issues related to regional and international trade.* It does so by expediting the flow, release, and clearance of goods, including transit issues, across the region. Both the WAEMU and ECOWAS trading blocs have been actively involved in setting up this TFA. In addition, the two institutions regularly organize national and regional seminars designed to build awareness of relevant provisions and to harmonize the application of common rules. Ratification and implementation of the TFA by Togo and Nigeria will likely boost prospects of both bilateral and transit trade for Niger. Once Benin and Burkina Faso become members, it will create a seamless transaction environment along existing trade corridors and open new, mutually beneficial market opportunities for all countries in the region.

• *Major interventions in customs modernization and simplification of procedures, personnel training, and increased automation are needed.* Together, these could significantly reduce rent-seeking as well as trading time and cost. Customs officials would benefit from increased trade flows arising from support from automation, communication, improved personnel management, and better data on actual trade transactions. Selected interventions that would support TFA implementation and facilitate regional trade include: (i) computerizing existing systems, including infrastructure to allow the transmission of data between customs agencies and facilitate transit trade; (ii) implementing a new Code of Ethics, such as that drafted by Chadian Customs; (iii) training customs officials; and (iv) providing IT infrastructure at key customs and other main transit points.

NOTES

1. WTO TPRs for WAEMU, CEMAC, and ECOWAS members (2013, 2015, and 2017).
2. The per capita income levy and special import tax could be lower under the ECOWAS CET as the per capita income levy was supposed to be replaced by a single ECOWAS levy.
3. This is more critical for agriculture-based products as recent estimates of real exchange rates based on agriculture prices in Sub-Saharan Africa countries found that the level of real appreciation is highest for Mali, Niger, and Chad (Zafar 2017).
4. The main impediment to formalizing trade with Nigeria, especially in staple foods, has been attributed to high tariffs, ranging from 5 to 35 percent, and to nontariff measures such as the overly restrictive standards maintained by Nigeria on agricultural imports from Niger and other ECOWAS countries. This takes place despite the ECOWAS Trade Liberalization Scheme as well as its structural domestic deficit in livestock, staple crops (including maize), and vegetable production. The ETLS (ECOWAS Trade Liberalization Scheme) eliminates tariffs, taxes, and nontariff barriers (customs duties, quotas, prohibitions, etc.) between ECOWAS members. Nigeria also applies ad hoc levies and duties of up to 45 percent on most imports, thus increasing the applied ad valorem tariff rates.
5. Aggregate trade costs are measured as the price equivalent of a reduction in international trade as compared to the potential implied by domestic production and consumption in origin and destination markets (Arvis et al. 2013). This measure encompasses several elements facing exporters and importers, which are then converted to ad valorem equivalents for ease of cross-country comparison.
6. Worth mentioning are the CEMAC framework for transit trade for Central Africa, the Interstate Transit in Central African Countries framework, and the UEMOA (Union Economique et Monetaire de l'Afrique de l'Ouest) and ECOWAS transit frameworks.

REFERENCES

Arvis, J.-F., B. Shepherd, Y. Duval, and C. Utoktham. 2013. "Trade Costs and Development: A New Data Set." *Economic Premise* 104, World Bank, Washington, DC.

Benjamin, N., and Pitigala, N. 2017. "Trade Diagnostic on Niger." Unpublished background paper, *Niger: Leveraging Export Diversification to Foster Growth*, World Bank, Washington, DC.

DTIS (Diagnostic Trade Integration Study). 2015. "Étude Diagnostique sur l'Intégration du Commerce au Niger." Niamey: Ministry of Commerce Private Sector Promotion. https://www.enhancedif.org/en/system/files/uploads/niger-edic-version_finale-post_atelier_dec2015.pdf?file=1&type=node&id=3903.

Gourdon, J., and J. Maur. 2014. "Estimating the Poverty Impact of the ECOWAS Common External Tariff." Unpublished paper, World Bank, Washington, DC.

Hoffmann, L. K., and P. Melly. 2015. *Nigeria's Booming Borders: The Drivers and Consequences of Unrecorded Trade*. London: Chatham House, The Royal Institute of International Affairs.

IMF (International Monetary Fund). 2015. "West African Economic and Monetary Union Common Policies of Member Countries." Country Report No. 15/100. IMF, Washington, DC.

Jammes, O. 2017. "TRIST-based Simulations of Tariff Changes in Niger." Background paper, *Niger: Leveraging Export Diversification to Foster Growth*, World Bank, Washington, DC.

Kaminski, B., and S. Mitra. 2012. *Borderless Bazaars and Regional Integration in Central Asia: Emerging Patterns of Trade and Cross-Border Cooperation*. Directions in Development—Trade. Washington, DC: World Bank.

Kathuria, S., and M. M. Malouche, eds. 2016. *Strengthening Competitiveness in Bangladesh— Thematic Assessment: A Diagnostic Trade Integration Study*. Directions in Development—Trade. Washington, DC: World Bank.

Maur, J.-C., and B. Shepherd. 2015. *Connecting Food Staples and Input Markets in West Africa: A Regional Trade Agenda for ECOWAS Countries*. Washington, DC: World Bank.

Pitigala, N. 2018a. "Trade Policy Options for Export Diversification of MCNG Economies." Background paper, World Bank, Washington, DC.

Pitigala, N. 2018b. "Trade Diagnostics and Policy Assessment of Chad." Unpublished background paper, *Chad: Leveraging Export Diversification to Foster Growth*, World Bank, Washington, DC.

Raballand, G. 2017. "Commerce informel et pertes douanières au Niger." Unpublished paper, World Bank, Washington, DC.

World Bank. 2017. "Niger: Leveraging Export Diversification to Foster Growth." Report No. 120306-NE, World Bank, Washington, DC.

——. 2018a. "Chad: Leveraging Export Diversification to Foster growth." World Bank, Washington, DC. https://openknowledge.worldbank.org/handle/10986/31839.

——. 2018b. "Mali: Leveraging Export Diversification to Foster Growth." World Bank, Washington, DC. https://openknowledge.worldbank.org/handle/10986/31829.

WTO (World Trade Organization). 2017. "Trade Policy Review for ECOWAS." WTO, Geneva.

Zafar, A. 2017. "Competitiveness Challenges in the CFA Zone in Sub-Saharan Africa." Unpublished paper, World Bank, Washington, DC.

7 Macro Foundations (2)
BUSINESS ENVIRONMENT AND FIRMS' PRODUCTIVITY

ABSTRACT

- *The Mali, Chad, Niger, and Guinea (MCNG) subregion is among the most difficult places in Sub-Saharan Africa for starting up and operating a business, not only because of prevailing structural conditions, including the region's fragility status and related security implications, but also because the region has a reform deficit in how countries design and implement policies geared toward improving the investment climate (IC).*

- *Most recent surveys reveal that their IC faces common issues related to political instability, corruption, informality, poor regulatory oversight, energy and other infrastructure gaps, and low access to finance. Given current trends, the subregion runs the risk of widening its competitiveness gap with regional and global comparators.*

- *Exporters perceive customs and trade regulations as well as access to finance as higher constraints than do nonexporters.*

- *Among the four MCNG countries, Niger recently recorded promising improvements on the Doing Business Index. Mali is a prime example of a country that has difficulties to sustain a systematic reform drive. Guinea and Chad are at preliminary stages in undertaking a holistic reform effort across IC issues.*

- *A productivity analysis finds that Mali, Niger, and Guinea's labor productivity is at about the level expected given their per capita income levels. Labor productivity among Guinea's firm shows about twice that of Mali and Niger. Exporters are also more productive in the three countries in this study. The median exporter in the three countries produces about twice as much per worker as the median nonexporter. However, this differential is due not to higher capital intensity of skills but rather to a higher presence of foreign firms. Niger firms are less likely to export than Guinean and Malian ones.*

- *Except for Niger, the single most important factor underlining these poor results is these countries' chronic lack of a sustained reform drive, with governments only engaging in ad hoc measures addressing isolated aspects of the IC and having no significant long-lasting impacts on firms' productivity.*

MAJOR OBSTACLES TO THE INVESTMENT CLIMATE OBSERVED IN THE MCNG COUNTRIES

Among the top constraints reported by firms in the region, those associated with low institutional capacity and poor governance figure among the top obstacles cited by managers. This should come as no surprise. In fact, the overall business environment, as captured by the ease of doing business score, and the quality of institutions are significantly better among nonfragile countries than among fragile countries such as Mali, Chad, Niger, and Guinea (MCNG) (World Bank 2019). Figure 7.1 shows the top five constraints in each country surveyed and points to common areas of investment climate (IC) that are problematic for firms operating in those countries. Political instability alone (followed by corruption) is ranked as the single most constraining factor in Mali, Chad, and Guinea and is among the top obstacles mentioned in Niger. In Mali, political instability is mentioned by 72.8 percent of businesses as a major to severe constraint in Mali and 68.1 percent in Guinea. This is followed by corruption, electricity, and unfair competition, with 70.6, 67.9, and 63.7 percent,

FIGURE 7.1

Top 5 major (or very severe) constraints in Chad, Guinea, Mali, and Niger

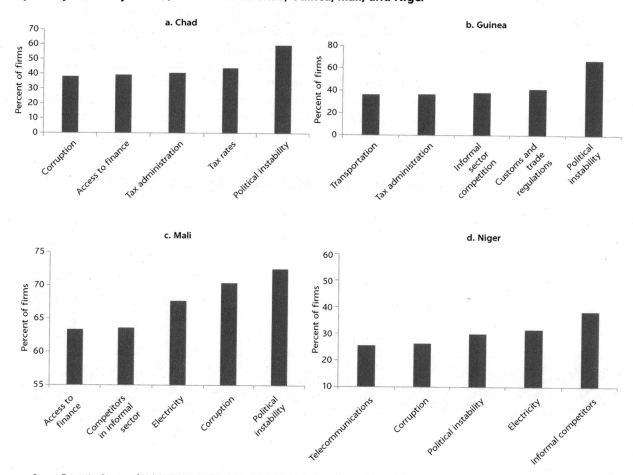

Source: Enterprise Surveys of Mali (2016), Niger (2017), Chad (2018), and Guinea (2016) prepared for this report, World Bank, Washington, DC, https://datacatalog.worldbank.org/dataset/enterprise-surveys.

respectively, of firms citing these as major or very severe. Likewise, informality figures among the top areas of concerns. Paradoxically and despite concerns with governance issues, the courts were not rated as among the top obstacles identified by enterprise surveys (ESs), which would indicate that disputes are settled out of courts. Similarly, the poor skills of the workforce were not mentioned as a major constraint across the subregion despite most surveyed firms reporting that they do not provide training for their employees, either because employees have the necessary skills or firms cannot afford to provide formal training.

There are various reasons that explain why political instability is ranked as the top concern in the subregion (figure 7.2). Nearly all countries surveyed experienced some form of internal or regional conflict within the past 10 years, followed by significant population displacements and a period of political transition. Mali is emerging from a violent and destabilizing period. Niger has had long-term issues with securing its borders. Guinea has been historically prone to regime change and, more recently exposed to the Ebola pandemic. Regional conflicts have also had a direct effect on population flows, exacerbating vulnerabilities in Chad and Niger. Chad has been a major recipient of inflows of refugees' and internally displaced populations (IDPs) over the years.

Given the fragile and uncertain environments in which firms operate, it is not surprising to find that corruption, and to some extent informality, are high in the ranking of IC constraints. Corruption is ranked as the second leading constrains in Mali, fourth in Niger, fifth in Chad, and ninth in Guinea. Regional comparators shown in figure 7.3 confirm that Malian firms are among the most concerned about issues of corruption. Quantitative indicators summarized in table 7.1 describe the challenging conditions for firms operating in those countries. Indicators measuring illicit practices indicate that nearly all countries surveyed engage in significant levels of corrupt practices compared to regional and global standards. However, specific illicit practices are more prevalent in some countries than others. In Niger and Mali, corruption seems to be biased toward the procurement of public contracts, with 46 and 63 percent, respectively, of firms expected to provide "gifts" to secure a government contract. This is far higher than in Guinea (25.3 percent), Chad (33 percent), or

FIGURE 7.2

Political instability: Rated as top-ranked obstacle to business operations

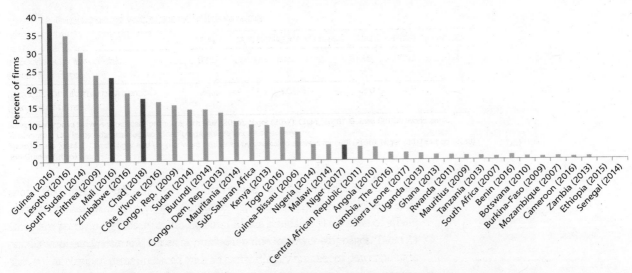

Source: Enterprise Surveys 2018, World Bank, Washington, DC, https://datacatalog.worldbank.org/dataset/enterprise-surveys.
Note: Results for Mali, Chad, Niger, and Guinea were produced by dedicated surveys for Mali (2016), Niger (2017), Chad (2018) and Guinea (2016).

the regional average (25 percent). While Guinean firms do not report high levels of corruption for obtaining permits or import licenses, the country tops the indicator measuring overall payments made by firms "to get things done," or almost twice as high as the regional Sub-Saharan Africa average. In contrast, Malian and Chadian firms stand out when it comes to corruption at the agency level, with 69.4 and 74 percent of firms, respectively, expected to provide payments to secure construction permits, well above the Sub-Saharan Africa average (22.5 percent).

Informality is closely associated with anticompetitive behavior and is considered the by-product of burdensome and costly administrative procedures. Informality is perceived as a major problem in most of the countries surveyed, with rankings of fourth in Mali, first in Niger, seventh in Chad, and third in Guinea (figure 7.4), or significantly higher than in other Sub-Saharan Africa nations. Moreover, all countries surveyed report that on average, over three quarters of firms compete against informal or unregistered firms (figure 7.5).

Additionally, responses regarding the regulatory burden find significant costs and delays imposed on firms in all four countries, thus providing them with strong incentives to evade their legal obligations. In Guinea, customs and trade regulations are ranked the second most burdensome constraint, with tax administration ranked third in Chad. Table 7.2 points to significant concerns affecting relations between the tax administrations and operators in Chad, particularly regarding the high proportion of firms subject to inspections as well as the high incidence of requests for informal payments.

The reliable and affordable provision of electricity is a distinctive problem for firms in the subregion. Except for Guinea, electricity is cited as a top-tier constraint in Chad, Mali, and Niger, thus underscoring the high degree of concern at firm level. Figure 7.6

FIGURE 7.3

Corruption: Rated as major or very severe constraint

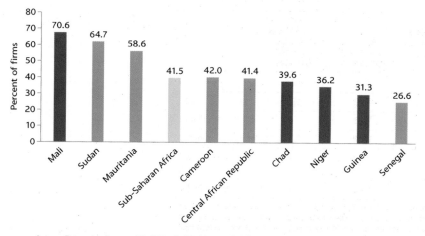

Source: Enterprise Surveys, World Bank, Washington, DC, https://datacatalog.worldbank.org/dataset/enterprise-surveys.
Note: Results for Mali, Chad, Niger and Guinea were produced by dedicated modules in the Enterprise Surveys for Mali (2016), Niger (2017), Chad (2018) and Guinea (2016).

TABLE 7.1 Selected corruption indicators: Comparators and Sub-Saharan Africa

	FIRMS EXPECTED TO GIVE GIFTS TO SECURE GOVERNMENT CONTRACT	GIFT EXPECTED TO SECURE A GOVERNMENT CONTRACT (% OF ITS VALUE)	FIRMS EXPECTED TO GIVE GIFTS "TO GET THINGS DONE"	FIRMS EXPECTED TO GIVE GIFTS TO SECURE OPERATING LICENSE	FIRMS EXPECTED TO GIVE GIFTS TO SECURE CONSTRUCTION PERMIT	FIRMS EXPECTED TO GIVE GIFTS TO SECURE POWER CONNECTION	FIRMS EXPECTED TO GIVE GIFTS TO SECURE IMPORT LICENSE
Chad	33	3.5	38	18.5	69.4	35.8	3.2
Niger	46	4.2	29.4	8.1	12.6	12.2	8.1
Mali	63	5.1	43.9	18.5	74	35.8	42.8
Guinea	25.3	0.4	48.7	n.a.	3.7	8.7	1.6
Sub-Saharan Africa	35.5	2.7	27.8	16.1	25.9	22.5	16.8
All ES countries	28.9	1.8	22	14.4	23.3	16.1	14.2

Source: Enterprise Surveys 2017–18, World Bank, Washington, DC, https://datacatalog.worldbank.org/dataset/enterprise-surveys.
Note: Results for Mali, Chad, Niger and Guinea were produced by dedicated surveys for Mali (2016), Niger (2017), Chad (2018) and Guinea (2016). ES = Enterprise Survey; n.a. = not available.

FIGURE 7.4
Informality: Rated as major or very severe constraint

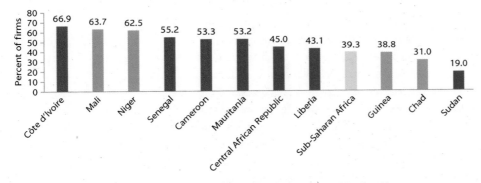

Source: Enterprise Surveys, World Bank, Washington, DC, https://datacatalog.worldbank.org/dataset
/enterprise-surveys.
Note: Results for Mali, Chad, Niger and Guinea were produced by dedicated modules in Enterprise Surveys for
Mali (2016), Niger (2017), Chad (2018) and Guinea (2016).

FIGURE 7.5
Firms competing against unregistered or informal firms

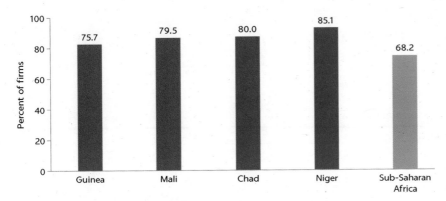

Source: Enterprise Surveys, World Bank, Washington, DC, https://datacatalog.worldbank.org
/dataset/enterprise-surveys.
Note: Results for Mali, Chad, Niger and Guinea were produced by dedicated modules in Enterprise
Surveys for Mali (2016), Niger (2017), Chad (2018) and Guinea (2016).

TABLE 7.2 **Interactions with tax administrations**

	CHAD	SUB-SAHARAN AFRICA	MALI	NIGER	GUINEA
Inspections by tax officials (percent of firms)	82.3	70.9	77.6	63.3	76.2
Requests for informal payments (percent of firms)	24.6	17.2	32.0	4.7	12.9

Source: Enterprise Surveys produced for this report: Mali (2016), Niger (2017), Chad (2018), Guinea (2016), World Bank,
Washington, DC, https://datacatalog.worldbank.org/dataset/enterprise-surveys.
Note: Results for Mali, Chad, Niger and Guinea were produced by dedicated surveys for Mali (2016), Niger (2017), Chad (2018)
and Guinea (2016).

shows that firms in Mali and Niger perform worse than the Sub-Saharan Africa average, an indication of the severity of the problem, while Guinea and to a lesser extent
Chad are performing closer to Sub-Saharan Africa standards. This state of affairs
entails associated costs and losses of production due to power stoppages. Table 7.3
shows that Nigerien firms are faced with an extraordinary number of power outages
(25.4 for a typical month vs. 8.5 for the Sub-Saharan Africa average), resulting in the
second highest costs (9.2 percent of sales lost due to power outages) and prompting
three in every four firms to meet over half their energy needs from generators (and

FIGURE 7.6

Electricity: Power outages rated as major or very severe constraint

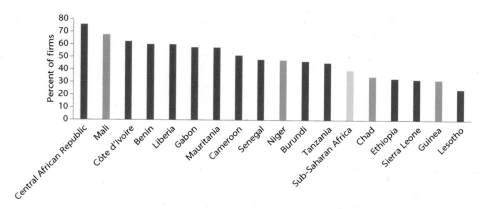

Source: Enterprise Surveys, World Bank, Washington, DC, https://datacatalog.worldbank.org /dataset/enterprise-surveys.
Note: Results for Mali, Chad, Niger and Guinea were produced by dedicated modules in Enterprise Surveys for Mali (2016), Niger (2017), Chad (2018) and Guinea (2016).

TABLE 7.3 **Electricity: Indicators**

	NUMBER OF ELECTRICAL OUTAGES (TYPICAL MONTH)	% OF FIRMS WITH GENERATOR	LOSSES DUE TO ELECTRICAL OUTAGES (% OF SALES)	ELECTRICITY FROM GENERATOR (% SELF-GENERATED)	% OF FIRMS EXPERIENCING ELECTRICAL OUTAGES
Niger	25.4	74.1	9.2	53.3	78
Mali	4.2	66.8	6.5	25.8	86.5
Chad	4.5	67.7	9.8	18.5	70.2
Guinea	4.5	56.8	4.7	26.6	84.2
Sub-Saharan Africa	8.5	51.3	8.5	28.2	78.7
All ES countries	6.4	33.4	4.7	20.4	59

Source: Enterprise Surveys, World Bank, Washington, DC, https://datacatalog.worldbank.org/dataset/enterprise-surveys.
Note: Results for Mali, Chad, Niger and Guinea were produced by dedicated modules in Enterprise Surveys for Mali (2016), Niger (2017), Chad (2018) and Guinea (2016). ES = Enterprise Survey.

featuring the highest proportion of generator ownership) compared to 28 percent for the regional Sub-Saharan Africa average. For their part, Chadian and Guinean firms report lower incidences of power outages, with 4.5 outages in a typical month compared to 8.5 for the Sub-Saharan Africa region (table 7.3).

Access to finance differ across countries both in terms of perception and in the way it affects firms. Access to finance is the fourth leading constraint in Chad, fifth in Mali, sixth in Niger, and tenth in Guinea. By regional standards, Malian and Chadian firms are in the first tier of countries reporting finance as a major constraint (figure 7.7). Table 7.4 indicates that the proportion of firms with a loan or line of credit stands at only 12 and 3.9 percent, respectively, in Chad and Guinea, compared to Mali and Niger, which report 27.6 and 26.3 percent, respectively, of firms having access to a loan, above the Sub-Saharan Africa average of 22.6 percent. In contrast, in terms of credit utilization (bank finance for investment or working capital), Mali and Niger perform slightly better than the Sub-Saharan Africa average. Yet collateral requirements in Chad (165 percent), Guinea (100 percent), and Niger (158 percent) are below average for the Sub-Saharan Africa region (206 percent).

- *Firms in Chad report access to finance as the fourth leading constraint.* The level of access to a loan is among the lowest (12 percent) compared to the world average.

FIGURE 7.7

Access to finance: Rated as major or very severe constraint

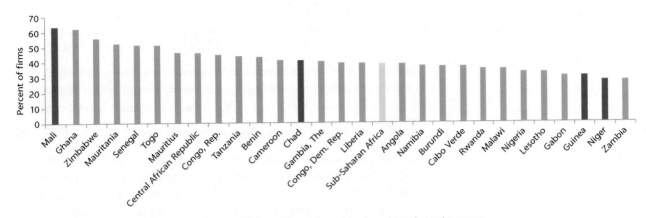

Source: Enterprise Surveys, World Bank, Washington, DC, https://datacatalog.worldbank.org/dataset/enterprise-surveys.
Note: Results for Mali, Chad, Niger and Guinea were produced by dedicated modules in Enterprise Surveys for Mali (2016), Niger (2017), Chad (2018) and Guinea (2016).

TABLE 7.4 **Selected access to finance indicators and regional benchmarking**

	CHAD	NIGER	GUINEA	MALI	SUB-SAHARAN AFRICA	ES
Firms with loan or credit line (%)	12	27.6	3.9	26.3	22.6	33.9
Value of collateral for loan (% of loan)	165	159.5	100	233.2	205.7	200
Firms not needing loan (%)	60.1	38.2	54.8	21.2	37.8	46.3
Firms with loan application rejected (%)	n.a.	7.3	14.8	10.5	15.8	11.2
Firms using banks to finance investment (%)	7.3	22.1	9.2	55.1	21	25.3
Firms using banks to finance working capital (%)	9.8	28.9	11.4	51.7	23.7	30.6
Working capital financed by banks (%)	2.4	12.6	3.9	15.0	9	11.7
Investment financed by banks (%)	1.6	14.1	2.8	19.0	10.3	14.3

Source: Enterprise Surveys, World Bank, Washington, DC, https://datacatalog.worldbank.org/dataset/enterprise-surveys.
Note: Results for Mali, Chad, Niger and Guinea were also produced by dedicated modules in Enterprise Surveys for Mali (2016), Niger (2017), Chad (2018) and Guinea (2016). ES = Enterprise Survey; n.a. = not available.

Chad is a typical case of self-exclusion in that a majority of firms (60 percent) reported that they did not need a loan and citing no need as a primary reason for not having one. This is supported with low credit utilization by firms.

- *Mali firms compare relatively well on most access to credit indicators.* Yet access to finance is mentioned as a major or very severe constraint by 63 percent of firms, one of the highest levels recorded in the Sub-Saharan Africa region (compared to a regional average of 40 percent). In a context of postconflict fragility, credit availability is limited, and the highest collateral requirements in the Sub-Saharan Africa region further restricts financial access for smaller firms.

- *Niger*. Firms have considerably higher access to loans or lines of credit compared to the region average as well as to other countries along with higher credit utilization rates to finance their operational and investment requirements. Similarly, Nigerien firms are less subject to rejection from banks.

- *Guinea* is a puzzling case in that although firms do not cite access to credit as among their main concerns, the level of firms accessing credit is among the lowest in the continent, with only 3.9 percent of firms having access to a loan or line of credit. At the same time, Guinea shows some of the highest rejection rates despite low collateral requirements (100 percent), suggesting voluntary exclusion from seeking bank financing.

- *Exporters in Niger and Mali* perceive access to finance (as well as customs and trade regulations) as higher constraints than do nonexporters.

MEASURING THE QUALITY OF BUSINESS REGULATIONS

In general, MCNG countries trail behind comparators due to the excessive compliance costs imposed on firms (especially regarding application processes for permits and licenses) and the complex and cumbersome procedures affecting the quality of the regulatory process by making it susceptible to unnecessary delays. Figure 7.8 shows the relative ranking and distance to frontier (DTF) for Mali, Niger, Chad, and Guinea relative to the Africa region and selected comparators on Doing Business 2018.[1] Chad stands out, with one of the poorest overall rankings (180th) in the DB Index as well as in terms of DTF (38). Mali and Niger perform slightly better than the Sub-Saharan Africa average, with rankings of 143rd and 144th, respectively, and DTF rates of 52.9 and 52.3, respectively. Guinea, with a ranking of 153rd and a DTF rate of 49.8, is slightly below the Sub-Saharan Africa standard. These results are in line with individual reform initiatives (or lack thereof) seen in recent years.

- *Niger has embarked on an ambitious reform program, which is showing promising results.* Niger's ranking has improved steadily from 160th in 2016 to 150th in 2017 and 144th in the 2018 DB report. The country has made clear strides on several indicators, including Creating a Business (+7.4 percent DTF), Dealing with Construction Permits (+7.3 percent DTF), and Registering Property (+4.1 percent DTF). Beyond these improvements in ranking, the impact of these measures at the firm level is not yet known.

- *Mali has taken concerted action at the national level through the Institutional Business Climate Improvement Mechanism and the National Council of Private Investors.* These initiatives accelerated the pace of regulatory reforms, starting in 2010. However, momentum has stalled over the last three years. Spotty, small-scale progress is noted on individual indicators such as Starting a Business, Reduction of Minimum Capital Requirements, Trading across Borders, and Obtaining Credit. However, the effectiveness of the creation of a credit bureau is yet to be demonstrated.

FIGURE 7.8

Comparative Doing Business rankings and distance to frontier

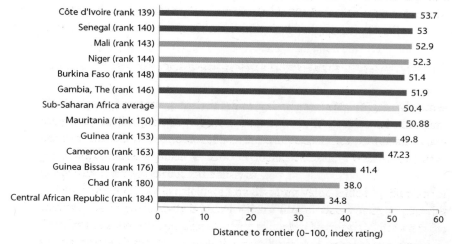

	Distance to frontier (0–100, index rating)
Côte d'Ivoire (rank 139)	53.7
Senegal (rank 140)	53
Mali (rank 143)	52.9
Niger (rank 144)	52.3
Burkina Faso (rank 148)	51.4
Gambia, The (rank 146)	51.9
Sub-Saharan Africa average	50.4
Mauritania (rank 150)	50.88
Guinea (rank 153)	49.8
Cameroon (rank 163)	47.23
Guinea Bissau (rank 176)	41.4
Chad (rank 180)	38.0
Central African Republic (rank 184)	34.8

Source: Doing Business Indicators, World Bank, Washington, DC, https://datacatalog.worldbank.org/dataset/doing-business.

- *Chad has yet to implement and sustain a more impactful DB reform program.* Chad's regulatory environment is among the most challenging in the world due to the high fees, social contributions, and taxes it imposes on firms. However, according to the DTF indicator, Chad has made some progress in the areas of Starting a Business and Registering Property.

- *Guinea ranks at the bottom by regional standards.* Guinea has yet to achieve a sustained reform drive. However, it has made modest progress in Obtaining Electricity and Starting a Business.

Individual indicators compare the relative ranking by regional and global standards.

- *Starting a Business:* Chadian firms are subject to the costliest and longest delays associated with the business creation process (table 7.5). In contrast, Niger is among the best performers in the Sub-Saharan Africa region as well as globally (DTF score: 93.6; rank: 24th). In between, Mali has made some progress by reducing minimum capital requirements, followed by Guinea.

- *Construction Permits:* Guinea is the best performer in this respect, with low costs and reduced delays and regulatory oversight superior to the regional standards (table 7.6). Along with Guinea, Chad has superior building quality institutions and procedures, though its costs remain high. Niger and to a lesser extent Mali trail behind and have yet to take serious steps toward reducing cost and delays.

- *Paying Taxes:* This indicator is problematic for all nations compared to standards (table 7.7). Chad stands out, with the worst ranking worldwide, and along with Guinea, the highest tax rates.

- *Obtaining Credit:* Mali, Niger, Chad, and Guinea have similar rankings in this respect (table 7.8). However, they are improving their credit information systems by introducing regulations that will govern the licensing and functioning of credit bureaus so as to comply with regional (West African Economic and Monetary Union [WAEMU], Economic and Monetary Community for Central Africa [CEMAC], and Economic Community of West African States [ECOWAS]) regulations.

TABLE 7.5 **Starting a business: Indicators**

	MALI	NIGER	CHAD	GUINEA	SUB-SAHARAN AFRICA	OECD
No procedures	5	3	9	6	7.6	4.9
Time (days)	8.5	7	69	8	24	8.5
Cost (% of per capita income)	58.4	8.3	171.3	67.5	49.9	3.1
Indicator ranking	104	24	125	125	n.a.	n.a.
Distance to frontier	82.3	93.6	50.2	81.7	76.8	n.a.

Source: Doing Business Indicators, World Bank, Washington, DC, https://datacatalog.worldbank.org/dataset/doing-business.
Note: n.a. = not available; OECD = Organisation for Economic Co-operation and Development.

TABLE 7.6 **Construction permits: Indicators**

	MALI	NIGER	CHAD	GUINEA	SUB-SAHARAN AFRICA	OECD
No procedures	13	15	13	15	14.8	12.5
Time (days)	124	91	226	161	147.5	154.6
Cost (% of warehouse value)	6.2	13.3	12	4.3	9.9	1.6
Building Quality Index (0–15)	5.5	6	11.5	12	8	11.4
Indicator ranking	134	163	153	75	n.a.	n.a.
Distance to frontier	61.3	53.7	56.7	69.9	56.9	n.a.

Source: Doing Business Indicators, World Bank, Washington, DC, https://datacatalog.worldbank.org/dataset/doing-business.
Note: n.a. = not available; OECD = Organisation for Economic Co-operation and Development.

TABLE 7.7 **Paying taxes: Indicators**

	MALI	NIGER	CHAD	GUINEA	SUB-SAHARAN AFRICA	OECD
Payments (number per year)	35	41	54	57.0	38.8	10.9
Time (hours per year)	270	270	766	440	304.2	163.4
Total tax rate (% of profits)	48.3	47.3	63.5	68.3	47.0	40.9
Post-Filing Index (0–100)	25.7	38	13	12.3	54.4	85.1
Indicator ranking	166	160	188	182	52.4	n.a.
Distance to frontier	51.5	48.4	17.9	38.9	n.a.	n.a.

Source: Doing Business Indicators, World Bank, Washington, DC, https://datacatalog.worldbank.org/dataset/doing-business.
Note: n.a. = not available; OECD = Organisation for Economic Co-operation and Development.

TABLE 7.8 **Obtaining credit: Indicators**

	MALI	NIGER	CHAD	GUINEA	SUB-SAHARAN AFRICA	OECD
Strength of Legal Index (0–12)	6	6	6	6	5.1	6
Depth of Credit Information Index (0–8)	0	0	0	0	3	6.6
Credit registry coverage (% of adults)	0.1	0.3	2.4	0	6.3	18.3
Credit bureau coverage (% of adult)	0.8	0.2	0	0	8.2	63.7
Indicator ranking	142	142	142	142	n.a.	n.a.
Distance to frontier	30	30	30	30	40.7	n.a.

Source: Doing Business Indicators, World Bank, Washington, DC, https://datacatalog.worldbank.org/dataset/doing-business.
Note: n.a. = not available; OECD = Organisation for Economic Co-operation and Development.

TABLE 7.9 **Access to electricity: Indicators**

	MALI	NIGER	CHAD	GUINEA	SUB-SAHARAN AFRICA	OECD
No procedures	4	4	6	4	5.3	4.7
Time (days)	120	97	67	69	115.3	79.1
Cost (% of per capita income)	2,794.6	5,632.6	9,821	5,639.8	3,737	63
Reliability of Supply and Transparency of Tariff Index (0–8)	0	0	0	0	0.9	7.4
Indicator ranking	154	162	177	158	n.a.	n.a.
Distance to Frontier	51.1	44.8	32.1	47.8	45.9	n.a.

Source: Doing Business Indicators, World Bank, Washington, DC, https://datacatalog.worldbank.org/dataset/doing-business.
Note: n.a. = not available; OECD = Organisation for Economic Co-operation and Development.

- *Access to Electricity:* Connection to the power grid poses significant problems in all countries, particularly with regards to its cost, with Chadian firms paying close to three times the regional average (table 7.9). Indexes also point to significant deficiencies in terms of the reliability and transparency of tariffs.

CROSS-COUNTRY COMPARISONS OF FIRMS' PRODUCTIVITY

The final section presents an analysis of firm performance in Mali, Niger, and Guinea compared with firm performance in other countries in West Africa and other comparators. This will give some idea of how these three countries' performance compares with countries at similar levels of development outside of West Africa. Due to lack of data, Chad was left out of the analysis.

Labor productivity is calculated by dividing value added by number of workers.[2] Labor productivity is higher when a firm produces more output with fewer workers and fewer purchased inputs. Labor productivity is higher when the firm uses more advanced technologies, is better managed, or has a better organizational structure. However, labor productivity, is also affected by a number of other

FIGURE 7.9

Labor productivity in Mali, Niger, Guinea, and comparator countries

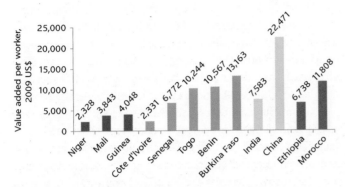

■ Countries of this report   ■ Representatives for West African neighboring countries
■ Global benchmarks   ■ Two good performers in Africa

Source: Clarke (2018) calculations based on data from Enterprise Surveys, World Bank, Washington, DC, https://datacatalog.worldbank.org/dataset/enterprise-surveys.
Note: Partial productivity measures are measured in and based on constant 2009 US$ (see Clarke 2018 for details). All data points are for the median firm on each measure of performance.

factors. First, it will be affected by the quality of the IC. Second, it will be lower when the firm's workers are poorly educated or unskilled. Third, it will be lower when firms are concentrated in unproductive sectors of the economy. Finally, it will be lower when firms do not use capital intensively. Firms that use capital intensively will often substitute capital for labor.

Labor productivity is higher in Guinea than in Mali or Niger. The median firm in Guinea produces about USD 4,000 of output per worker, nearly twice as much as in Niger (USD 2,300) and slightly higher than in Mali (USD 3,800).[3] But on a global perspective, labor productivity appears to be low in all three countries (figure 7.9). Their median firm produces less output per worker than in any of the other countries in West Africa except Côte d'Ivoire. Output per worker is also smaller than in comparator countries (India, China, Ethiopia, and Morocco). However, where workers are better educated and more highly skilled, firms are more capital-intensive, and the IC is more favorable, labor productivity tends to be higher in countries with higher per capita income. Taking this into account, Mali, Niger, and Guinea compare favorably with countries at similar levels of per capita income since their labor productivity appears to be at about the level expected given their per capita income (figure 7.10). Corroborating these findings, comparisons based on sales per worker are very similar to those for labor productivity,[4] with sales per worker lowest in Niger (about USD 3,800 per worker) and highest in Guinea (about USD 6,940), and Mali in between (about USD 4,611).

Differences in workers' skills can explain differences in labor productivity. However, because it is difficult in practice to measure worker skills directly, an indirect measure is labor costs. If labor markets were perfectly competitive, we would expect the marginal productivity of labor to be proportional to labor costs. Countries with high-quality workers would therefore receive higher wages. Although this measure is imperfect since wages also reflect local labor market conditions, it does provide useful information on worker quality.

Among the three countries, labor costs appear lowest in Guinea and Mali. The median firm in Guinea shows labor costs of USD 364 per worker, lower than in either Mali (USD 769) or Niger (USD 1,394) (figure 7.11). Labor costs in Guinea as well as Mali also appear low compared with comparator countries. Per-worker labor costs are lower in Guinea than in any of the comparator countries. Labor costs in Mali are also

FIGURE 7.10

Labor productivity in Mali, Niger, and Guinea compared to countries at similar levels of development

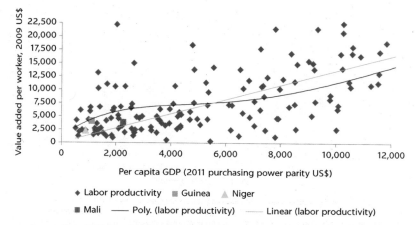

Source: Clarke 2018, based on data from Enterprise Surveys, World Bank, Washington, DC, https://datacatalog.worldbank.org/dataset/enterprise-surveys.
Note: 2009 US$ = based on constant 2009 US$. All data points are for the median firm on each measure of performance. The chart shows only countries with per capita GDP between US$0 and US$12,000. GDP = gross domestic product; Poly. = Political Economy index (proxy).

FIGURE 7.11

Manufacturing labor costs in Guinea, Mali, and Niger

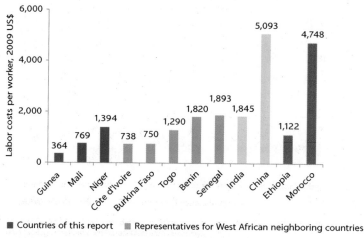

Source: Original analysis based on data from Enterprise Surveys, World Bank, Washington, DC, https://datacatalog.worldbank.org/dataset/enterprise-surveys.
Note: Partial productivity measures are in and based on constant 2009 US$ (see Clarke 2018 for details). All data points are for median firms on each measure of performance.

comparable to labor costs in Côte d'Ivoire and Burkina Faso but lower than in any of the comparator countries. Finally, labor costs in Niger are slightly higher than in Togo but below those of the median firm in Benin and Senegal as well as India and China.

Differences in firm size. As in most countries, larger firms in Guinea, Mali, and Niger are more productive on average than small firms. Median large firms produce about USD 40,989 per worker compared with USD 7,287 for median medium-sized firms and only USD 1,945 for median small firms (figure 7.12). Similar patterns can be seen in Mali and Niger. Unfortunately, there were too few firms in the Guinea sample to conduct a similar breakdown for Guinea. However, two additional patterns stand out. First, the gap between small and medium-sized firms is larger in Niger than in Mali, where the median medium-sized firm is about three times as productive as the median small firm. By comparison, the median medium-sized firm is about five times as productive in Niger. This leads to the second observation: whereas small firms in Niger appear relatively unproductive—about as productive as Mali's—medium-sized firms perform better, with the median medium-sized firm being more productive than similar-sized firms in Mali. These differences may be due in part to medium-sized firms being more capital-intensive than small firms in Niger, where the median medium-sized firm reports having about USD 10,000 of capital per worker compared with only USD 1,000 for median small firms. This is much larger than in Mali, where the median medium-sized firm has about USD 4,100 of capital per worker compared with about USD 800 per worker for the median small firm.

Differences in export status. Exporters are typically more productive than nonexporters in most developing countries, for two reasons. First, exporters may be more efficient than other enterprises because only the most productive enterprises are able to enter export markets (that is, the self-selectivity hypothesis). Second, the discipline of exporting directly might improve efficiency (that is, the learning-by-exporting hypothesis). Access to foreign markets forces firms to become more efficient or to benefit from technical advice from foreign buyers. Exporters are also more productive in these three countries. The median exporter in the three countries produces about twice as much per worker as the median nonexporter (USD 6,579 per worker compared with USD 3,330). Although there were too few firms to do similar breakdowns to those of Guinea and Niger, Mali shows a similar pattern, with the median exporter producing about USD 6,579 per worker compared with USD 3,843 for the median nonexporter (figure 7.13).

It is important to note that differences in productivity are not due to the fact that exporters use capital or skilled worker more intensively than nonexporters. For instance, median nonexporters in Mali have about USD 3,689 of capital per worker compared with about USD 1,188 for median exporters. Median exporters also pay their workers less than median nonexporters, or USD 620 per worker compared with USD 878 for nonexporters. This suggests that exporters operate mostly in areas that are neither skills- nor capital-intensive. This is surprising given that the three countries are unlikely to have a comparative advantages in skills or capital-intensive sectors. Furthermore, firms in Guinea and Mali are more likely to export than are firms in Niger: whereas about 27 percent of Guinean and Malian firms export, only 13 percent of Nigerien firms do so. Moreover, fewer manufacturing firms in Niger (13 percent) report that they export any part of their output than in any of comparator countries in West Africa or in China and India

FIGURE 7.12

Larger firms are the most productive in Mali, Niger, and Guinea

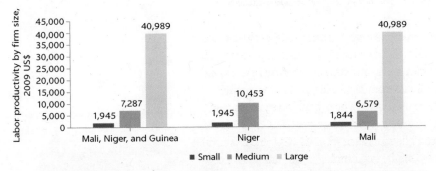

Source: Clarke 2018, based on data from Enterprise Surveys, World Bank, Washington, DC, https://datacatalog.worldbank.org/dataset/enterprise-surveys.
Note: Partial productivity measures are measured in and based on constant 2009 US$ (see Clarke 2018 for details). All data points are for median firms. The combined results for all three countries use data from all three countries. As fewer than five large firms provided information on Niger, this group is omitted.

FIGURE 7.13

Exporters are more productive than nonexporters in Mali, Niger, and Guinea

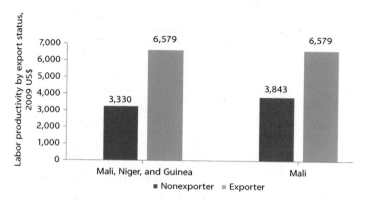

Source: Clarke 2018, based on data from Enterprise Surveys, World Bank, Washington, DC, https://datacatalog.worldbank.org/dataset/enterprise-surveys.
Note: Partial productivity measures are based on constant 2009 US$ (see Clarke 2018 for details). All data points are for median firms on each measure of performance.

FIGURE 7.14

Niger features a lower share of export-to-total firms than Mali and Guinea

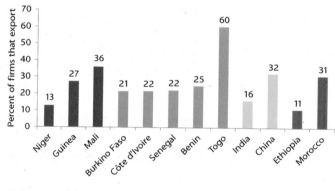

Source: Clarke 2018, based on data from Enterprise Surveys, World Bank, Washington, DC, https://datacatalog.worldbank.org/dataset/enterprise-surveys.

(figure 7.14). Similar comparisons hold for a broader sample of countries. Given that exporters are more productive than nonexporters in most developing countries, it is disappointing—though not surprising—to observe that Niger firms are less productive than in those in other MCNG countries while their unit labor costs are higher, suggesting that these firms are not very competitive.

Differences in foreign ownership. In many countries, foreign direct investment (FDI) is valued because foreign investors can give firms access to new technologies and markets. This is also the case for foreign and domestic firms in the three countries in this study (figure 7.15), where median foreign-owned firms produce nearly seven times as much output per worker as median domestic firms (USD 17,500 compared with USD 2,600). The pattern is similar in Mali. However, there are too few foreign-owned firms in Guinea or Niger to perform similar breakdowns for these two countries as only about 5 percent of firms in Niger and Guinea are foreign-owned compared to Burkina Faso or comparator

FIGURE 7.15

Foreign-owned firms are more productive in Mali, Niger, and Guinea than domestic firms

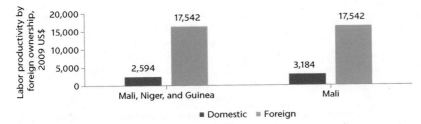

Source: Original analysis based on data from Enterprise Surveys, World Bank, Washington, DC, https://datacatalog.worldbank.org/dataset/enterprise-surveys.
Note: Partial productivity measures are measured in and based on constant 2009 US$ (see Clarke 2018 for details). All data points are for median firms on each measure of performance.

FIGURE 7.16

Few manufacturing firms in Niger and Guinea are foreign-owned

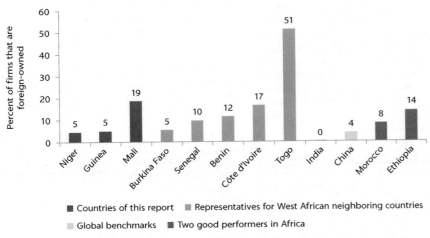

Source: Original analysis based on data from Enterprise Surveys, World Bank, Washington, DC, https://datacatalog.worldbank.org/dataset/enterprise-surveys.

countries in West Africa (figure 7.16). In contrast, foreign-owned firms are more common in Mali—about 19 percent of the manufacturing firms in the Mali sample were foreign-owned—higher than in most comparator countries inside or outside of West Africa. Broader comparisons with other countries at similar levels of development lead to similar conclusions. If foreign ownership is required to improve access to technologies and markets and hence improve firm performance, this conclusion is disappointing.

MAIN POLICY OPTIONS

A series of complementary business-oriented reforms should be undertaken, either simultaneously or sequentially. Before summarizing the key policies required by the DB report customized for each of the four MCNG countries (table 7.10), it is important to highlight a few key principles that need to be in place:

- *Up-front coordination* among the diverse institutions and actors within governments on the reform strategy as building a common vision will improve outcomes.

TABLE 7.10 **Main policy recommendations of Doing Business 2019**

REFORM SEQUENCE	SHORT TERM	MEDIUM TERM	COUNTRY-SPECIFIC MEASURES
Reform Track 1: Enable private sector dynamism and reduce informality **1.1 Simplify SME creation**	• Reduce notary fees • Lower the cost of registration to a flat fee • Pursue simplification of procedures (by simplifying steps and procedures)	• Eliminate all remaining professional and licensing taxes and other rent-derived forms of duties • Eliminate all minimum capital requirements	<u>Mali</u> *Short term* • Facilitate public access to the standard company statutes (available online or within the OSS website) *Medium term* • **Finalize computerization of the commercial registry office (RCCM) to accelerate firm registration** • Remove stamp duty of CFAF 9,750 collected by the tax administration for the registration of statutes <u>Chad</u> *Short term* • **Reduce minimum capital from CFAF 100,000 to CFAF 5,000** • Remove the requirement for a company seal • **Allow company creation notification in online registry** *Medium term* **Publish standard incorporation documents (OHADA) and improve the functioning of the RCCM** <u>Guinea</u> *Short Term* • Enable the online verification of the uniqueness of business name • **Operationalization of Synergui (business creation software for new functionalities and interconnection with agencies)** • Allow publication of legal announcements on the APIM website • Implement a toll-free number for business creators to follow up their files • **Complete the Interconnection between APIM's one-stop window and the national tax office** *Medium term* • Computerize the RCCM and the processing system in the National Social Security Fund (CNPS) • Complete interconnection between the RCCM and CNPS
1.2 Accelerate the delivery of construction permits	• Lower the cost of registration to a flat fee (5% of property value) • Make regulations and required documents for construction permits and all existing permits publicly accessible (website) • Reduce approvals procedures for simpler, low-risk projects	• Adopt and implement building codes based on best regional practices • Adopt risk-based approach (at municipal level) for inspections before start of construction and after construction (except large buildings)	<u>Mali</u> *Short term* • Reduce the number of days required to access geotechnical studies • Eliminate the cost of obtaining paper information for a connection to the water supply • **Reduce the number of days needed to obtain a certificate of compliance** *Medium term* Introduce a streamlined process for obtaining building permits for smaller buildings (single window) <u>Chad</u> *Short term* • **Set up a committee for construction permit issuance at municipal level** • **Reduce time needed for connection to public utilities networks (water) by setting specific services for business requests in STEE offices** • Ensure applications are complete at time of filing by establishing an information booth in the municipality *Medium term* **Reduce the cost of obtaining geotechnical studies currently carried out by a *laboratory* (LBTP or LABOGEC).**

continued

TABLE 7.10, *continued*

REFORM SEQUENCE	SHORT TERM	MEDIUM TERM	COUNTRY-SPECIFIC MEASURES
			<u>Guinea</u> *Short Term* • **Create a commission in charge of processing requests for construction permits** • Streamline the filing procedure by reducing the number of parties in the processing chain *Medium Term* **Establish a one-stop window for construction permits and streamline and computerize procedures**
1.3 Simplify tax collection	• **Simplify procedures and reduce delays associated with corporate tax and VAT compliance** • **Remove restrictions on VAT refund processes and make them operational**	• **Digitalize tax payment systems, starting with large and medium firms** • **Allow bank transfers for payment of taxes** • **Introduce self-filing and telepayment for large enterprises** • **Simplify tax codes and reduce tax holidays afforded to certain firms** • **Adopt a system of risk-weighted, randomized tax inspections** • **Transition to a flat fee with regards to stamp duty related to contracts**	<u>Mali</u> *Short term* • **Introduce a single form for social security payments to INPS** • **Reduce frequency of tax payments (4 vs. 12 returns)** <u>Niger</u> *Short term* Transition to a flat fee with regards to stamp duty related to contracts <u>Chad</u> *Short term* • Allow the option of quarterly filing of CIT, social security dues, and VAT (already implemented for mid-size firms) • **Introduce online application for tax identification number (NIF) with business registration** *Medium term* • **Implement a single tax payment window (CIT, social security, and VAT reimbursements procedures)** • **Unify NIF for all taxes and contributions (CNPS uses a different social security number)**
1.4 Improve access to credit	• **Collect information from institutional lenders (e.g., water and electricity companies) in addition to financial institutions** • **Lower the threshold for loans in the credit registry to 1% of annual income per person**	• **Improve SME capacity to provide adequate financial information** • **Enforce recovery legislation** • **Implement OHADA Uniform Act broadening a range of collateralized assets** • **Allow registered individuals to consult own credit information**	<u>All countries</u> Reforms to be undertaken within the framework of the BCEAO: *Short term* • **Approve the regulatory framework enabling the creation of a credit bureau** • Strengthen the capacity of the credit information team at the Central Bank *Medium term* • **Create a credit bureau** • **Create a collateral registry**
1.5 Facilitate trade	• **Fully implement online operation of SYDONIA WORLD** • **Full transition to risk-based management systems for customs inspection** • **Ease traffic backlog traffic by automatically sending goods requiring exemptions to the red channel**	• **Introduce single window (one-stop shop) systems for declarations and payments of duties** • **Approve legal framework to facilitate digital signatures** • **Allow export-oriented firms access to export guarantee schemes (export shipment finance guarantees) and remove restrictions related to letters of credits requiring amount equivalent to transaction to be mobilized**	<u>Mali</u> *Short term* • Reduce the time and procedures required to obtain a letter of credit • **Update the mapping of import and exports transactions procedures conducted in 2011 on the main Bamako-Dakar road corridor and undertake Bamako-Abidjan corridor** *Medium term* • **Set up a technical working group to propose a reform roadmap for export /import transactions** <u>Niger</u> *Medium term* • **Implement unilateral acceptance of internationally recognized quality certificates to reduce certification delays** • **Establish a reporting mechanism for operators facing road harassment at checkpoints or entry and exit points**

continued

TABLE 7.10, *continued*

REFORM SEQUENCE	SHORT TERM	MEDIUM TERM	COUNTRY-SPECIFIC MEASURES
			Chad *Short term* • Introduce electronic submission and processing of trade documents • Conduct mapping of import/export procedures and agencies *Medium term* • Eliminate official fees and charges levied on imports and exports, especially at the dry port of Ngueli • Pursue installation of customs scanners Guinea *Short term* **Reduce the number of documents needed for exports**
1.6 Improve reliability and access to electricity	• Prepare interim management contracts (2–3 years) recognizing the risks the management contractor or strategic partner can absorb • Simplify applications procedures for connection permits	• Strengthen powers of regulator and make it operational (where applicable) • Reduce the cost of supplies • Improve reliability (among others) through procurement of fuel for power generation	Mali *Short term* • Reduce from 120 to 20 days time needed for warehouse connections to the grid for 160 kVa subscribed power • Post connection costs and tariffs on billboards and online on EDM website *Medium term* • Measure the reliability of supply and the duration and frequency of power outages and time needed to restore supply Niger *Medium term* • Operationalize the unit dedicated to SME services Chad *Medium term* • Create a single window for SME payments and trackability Guinea *Short term* • Create a single window for local businesses *Medium term* • Simplify processes and reduce time and cost to connect businesses
Reform Track 2: Improve governance and limit rents 2.1 Fight corruption	• Approve salary increases for key public service positions	• Enforce sanctions provided by law in cases of proven corruption • Make internal audits of public agencies systematic	
2.2 Improve access to land	• Reduce property registration costs by pricing property transaction registration fees at the lowest level needed to ensure the land authority recovers operational and investment costs	• Streamline title registration processes • Modernize land registry or cadaster • Set criteria for public projects and long-term land use • Create stakeholders' committees to harmonize legislation on land allocation and tenure • Set threshold for plots to be sold per zone or administrative level	Mali *Medium term* • Introduce standardized contracts to allow operators to bypass notary services and fees • Establish transparent and predictable tax base assessment mechanism • Decrease legal fees associated with transferring property (notary's cost could be set per page and capped) Guinea *Short Term* • Establish a grievance resolution mechanism at the land registry and scan all property titles *Medium term* • Establish a one-stop shop for property registration • Establish a grievance resolution mechanism at the land registry

continued

TABLE 7.10, *continued*

REFORM SEQUENCE	SHORT TERM	MEDIUM TERM	COUNTRY-SPECIFIC MEASURES
2.3 Improve court effectiveness and proceedings		• **Enhance reliance on arbitration and mediation (Mali and Chad have a law regulating all aspects of mediation)** • **Increase the number of trained magistrates with curriculum in line with OHADA** • **Automatize and modernize processes within the court system** • **Create a website for commercial courts and publish decisions on commercial disputes cases**	<u>Mali</u> *Short term* • Reduce delays associated with trial proceedings and apply severe sanctions for the use of delaying tactics • Undertake mapping of court proceedings to identify bottlenecks • Establish electronic business management system to automatically update the status of filings reviewable by courts • Allow rapid detection of inactive cases based on a predetermined period and assist judges in performance evaluations *Medium term* • Develop tools to allow magistrates to refer small disputes (where stakes do not justify the costs of litigation) to mediation • Improve magistrate performance through specialization (commercial cases) and training for judges and court personnel <u>Niger</u> *Short term* • **Reduce the number of appeals to 2 and develop advocacy to inform services offered at CNAM** • Update the list of new mediators and conciliators and strengthen the capacity of staff at mediation center (CNAM) <u>Guinea</u> *Short term* • **Launch commercial court (including small claim court) and train commercial magistrates** *Medium term* • **Introduce electronic case management of court proceedings**
2.4 Strengthen corporate governance	• **Amend Commercial Code on disclosure of related party transactions** • **Set procurement rules (i.e., quotas for public contracts) to let SMEs submit individual or joint proposals**	• **Improve rules governing civil procedures (Shareholders Cases Index)**	<u>Mali</u> *Short term* • Eliminate technical procedures that allow recalcitrant debtors to delay enforcement of judgments to limit abuse of procedures for challenging or recovering confiscated goods *Medium term* • Allow minority shareholders the option of using legal channels when facing prejudicial regulated agreement <u>Niger</u> *Medium term* • **Strengthen duties of management in SOEs (due diligence, informed decisions, avoiding conflicts of interest)**
2.5 Increase digital financial inclusion		• **Develop low-cost transaction accounts that can enable digital payments and support credit reporting and cross-border payments** • **Develop backbone infrastructure, including financial ICT infrastructure and data collection capabilities** • **Facilitate user identification for digital financial services, including digital identify mechanisms for customers and support programs that enhance digital and financial literacy**	
Reform Track 3: Foster markets and the private sector 3.1 Competition	• **Increase regional cooperation (WAEMU, CEMAC) on cartel detection** • **Amend law on anticartels**	• **Improve operational capacity of competition agency tools (markets search and seizure capacity) and increase and enforce penalties and fines**	<u>Mali</u> *Medium term* • Strengthen effectiveness of national competition law and competition authority <u>Chad</u> *Medium term* • Modernize existing regulations on pricing and competition into a single national competition law • Establish competition regulatory and enforcement authority

continued

TABLE 7.10, *continued*

REFORM SEQUENCE	SHORT TERM	MEDIUM TERM	COUNTRY-SPECIFIC MEASURES
3.2 Strengthen PPP framework	• **Monitor financial sustainability of PPP projects** • **Strengthen capacity and expertise among PPP units** • **Ensure fiduciary and regulatory independence of PPP units** • **Set national public procurement regulation within legal PPP framework** • **Identify low-risk PPP projects as signal to investors, e.g. agribusiness**		<u>Chad</u> • Approve national PPP law and PPP unit in line with regional and international best practices • identify low-risk small-scale projects to be rolled out as pilots <u>Guinea</u> *Short Term* • Establish PPP unit

Note: Bold = most important; italics = those directly benefitting export diversification. APIM = Malian Investment Promotion Agency (Agence pour la Promotion des Investissements au Mali); BCEAO = Central Bank of West African States (Banque Centrale des États de l'Afrique de l'Ouest); CEMAC = Central African and Monetary Community (Communauté Économique et Financière d'Afrique Centrale); CFAF = CFA franc (Communauté Financière Africaine); CIT = corporate income tax; CNAM = National Arts and Crafts Center (Centre National des Arts et Métiers); CNPS = National Social Security Fund (Caisse Nationale de Prévention Sociale); EDM = Malian Electricity Company (Électricité du Mali); ICT = information and communications technology; INPS = National Social Security Agency (Institut National de Prévoyance Sociale); LABOGEC = Civil Engineering Laboratory (Laboratoire du Génie Civil); LBTP = Construction and Public Works Laboratory (Laboratoire du Bâtiment et des Travaux Publics); NIF = tax identification number (Numéro d'Identification Fiscale); OHADA = Organization for the Harmonization of Business Law in Africa; OSS = Sahara and Sahel Observatory (Observatoire du Sahara et du Sahel); PPP = public-private partnership; RCCM = Commercial and Real Estate Loans Registry (Registre du Commerce et du Crédit Mobilier); SME = small and medium enterprise; SOE = state-owned enterprise; STEE = Chadian Water and Electricity Company (Société Tchadienne d'Eau et d'Électricité); VAT = value-added tax; WAEMU = West African Economic and Monetary Union.

- *Prior consultation* with affected parties, especially the business community, to increase awareness, agreement, and ownership of the strategy and elicit suggestions.

- *Clear communication* of the strategy and its components as transparency is critical to avoiding misunderstandings and distortions, with citizens, businesses, and other stakeholders understanding both the "what" and the "why" of the overall program and its major components.

NOTES

1. Note that DB is not the only international ranking available to assess business regulations. More recently, a new global "Enabling the Business of Agriculture" index has ranked mainly the quality of a set of legal indicators and to a lesser extent a number of efficiency indicators. Of 62 countries, Mali and Niger, the only two MCNG countries ranked on this indicator, were in 52th and 49th position overall in 2017, lagging significantly in machinery, and seed and in information and communications technology (ICT) quality and in machinery, fertilizer, and seed quality, respectively. See: http://pubdocs.worldbank.org/en/929581534213514304/EBA17-Full-Report17.pdf.
2. Value added is sales less the cost of raw materials and intermediate inputs purchased by the firm to make its final product. Number of workers is the number of full-time workers at the firm.
3. Despite apparent differences, a caveat is that samples are very small for Guinea and Niger, which makes labor productivity estimates imprecise in these two countries, thus not statistically rejecting the null hypothesis that labor productivity is about the same in all three countries.
4. Sales per worker do not take purchased inputs into account.

REFERENCES

Clarke, G. 2018. "Firms' Performance in Guinea, Mali, and Niger." Unpublished background paper, World Bank, Washington, DC.

World Bank. 2019. "Africa's Pulse, No. 19: An Analysis of Issues Shaping Africa's Economic Future." (April), World Bank, Washington, DC.

8 Revamping Export Diversification Policies in MCNG Countries

A GVC 2.0 CLUSTER-BASED APPROACH

ABSTRACT

- Many global value chain (GVC) development projects undertaken by the World Bank Group in Mali, Chad, Niger, and Guinea (MCNG) countries have faced limitations resulting from their almost unidimensional approach, which focuses on a few poorly connected activities and a lack of dedicated efforts to upgrade producers' organizations, adopt international health and technical product standards, attract foreign firms, and foster participation from the private sector.

- MCNG countries can reinvigorate their agribusiness exports by initially specializing in lower-value-added areas in which they have comparative advantages along a given GVC while applying horizontal and vertical policies that would help them gradually develop comparative advantages in higher-value-added products.

- The standard practice of revisiting and making operational investment codes is needed but should be accompanied by institutional reviews and customized along with temporary, well-monitored packages of fiscal and nonfiscal market incentives.

- The four pillars of a GVC 2.0 cluster-based export diversification policy agenda are: (i) process, product, and market upgrading of strategic (and well-selected) GVCs; (ii) targeted investments (spatial dimension) in trade infrastructure and logistic corridors; (iii) revamped trade and logistic policies; and (iv) an e-business-friendly investment climate.

- This agenda can only succeed if strongly based on private (foreign and domestic) and public investment, which implies some sort of joint implementation plans designed to maximize financing for development where the roles of International Finance Corporation (IFC) in attracting foreign direct investment (FDI) and the World Bank Group in dealing with market failures will be key.

NEED FOR A NEW GVC 2.0 DEVELOPMENT APPROACH TO PROJECTS IN MCNG COUNTRIES

During the last decade, the World Bank has multiplied the number of projects supporting the development of selected agricultural value chains (VCs). In the Mali, Chad, Niger, and Guinea (MCNG) countries, these projects typically featured the following characteristics:

- In Niger, the ongoing 2012 *Competitiveness and Growth Support Project* aims to improve selected aspects of Niger's business environment, reinforce the capacity of supported enterprises, and support the development of the meat and butchery VC. The government wants to reduce the flow of live cattle vis-à-vis meat and meat by-products so as to increase the value added of livestock exports. The competitive advantages and opportunities in Niger's meat and butchery sector include: (i) high quality of Niger meat, which is highly sought by consumers in regional markets; (ii) existence of possibilities for fattening livestock along the Niger River and in urban centers; (iii) high and growing demand from Nigeria; and (iv) existence of centuries-old know-how in butchery that is well recognized in regional markets as well as high concentration of small, informal private entities. Niger has four refrigerated slaughterhouses, characterized by a lack of basic hygiene and poor organization. Moreover, the lack of maintenance of infrastructure and equipment has caused their progressive deterioration, resulting in previously automated work now being replaced by manual labor. The project initially supported three activities: (i) strengthening the Nigerian Export Promotion Agency (ANIPEX); (ii) concession of matching grants to small and medium enterprises (SMEs) developing VCs (operational assistance, credit, training); and (iii) rehabilitation of two slaughterhouses (Niamey and Maradi).

- In Chad, the ongoing 2014 *Value Chain Support Project* (restructured in 2017) aims to improve: (i) targeted aspects of the business environment; and (ii) the performance of agropastoral (meat and dairy) VCs. Chad has similar competitive advantages and challenges surrounding the meat industry as Niger. The project initially supported four activities: (i) strengthening the National Investment and Export Agency; (ii) concession of matching grants to SMEs developing VCs (operational assistance, credit, training); (iii) rehabilitation of meat infrastructure, including transportation and three slaughterhouses (Walia, Dighel, and Farcha) and three milk collection centers (Walia, Guilmey, and Linia; and (iv) support the Food Products Quality Control Center by providing equipment and agents for its new laboratories.

- In Mali, the 2005 *Agricultural Competitiveness and Diversification Project* (PCDA), which closed in 2015 (originally scheduled to last 5 years and benefitting of 2 years of additional financing in 2013–15) had a wider scope. It aimed at increasing rural incomes and economic opportunities through improvements to the investment climate and agricultural VCs. The project benefitted five regions (Bamako, Koulikoro, Mopti, Ségou, and Sikasso). The activities supported by the project were: (i) adoption of new irrigation techniques; (ii) introduction of new agricultural technologies; (iii) support to SMEs (commerce, exporters, artisans); (iv) training to key actors in the chain (mainly service providers); (v) matching grants and access to finance (risk management, guarantee fund); and (vi) support for participation in foreign commercial events. The project initially focused on eight value chains (five priority chains: onion, potato, mango, papaya, and meat; and three to be consolidated: banana, anacarde, and milk).

Past experience in MCNG countries allows for the identification of a few common features and gaps in past agricultural VC projects.

- The objective, which was to upgrade agricultural-based exports, was not made explicit. The only exception was a subordinated outcome expected in the case of the Niger (that is, replacing informal trade in live animals by formal meat exports). VC development was also essentially centered on the domestic market, perhaps under the assumption that as production increases and emerging higher-value-added products consolidate, firms would also develop the capacity to export.

- All projects have taken much longer than expected, often undergoing significant restructuring efforts. For instance, the Chad project cut the number of slaughter-houses as well as activities involved in their rehabilitation, while the Mali project had to concentrate on fewer products when it was realized that implementation of activities would take much longer than initially estimated.

- Performance on activities has been mixed. Implementation of matching grants had mixed results, while the rehabilitation of slaughterhouses was more difficult to achieve than expected.

- Articulation between components addressing either the investment climate or the development of VCs has been not straightforward. In some cases, efforts have concentrated on the broad Doing Business agenda, whose direct impact on agricultural VCs development has been minimal. In practice, both agendas have been implemented in parallel, with often disconnected efforts and carried out by different government counterparts.

- The focus on developing VCs has been almost unidimensional. Niger and Chad projects concentrated on a single or very few specific micro-issues in agricultural VCs, for example, slaughterhouses, transportation, rehabilitation, or equipment. The only (limited) exception was the multidimensional focus in Mali-PCDA addressing irrigation, finance, technology, small and medium enterprise (SME) strengthening, and foreign commercialization of a few VCs.

- Finally, dedicated efforts at upgrading producers' organizations, adopting international health and technical product standards, and attracting foreign firms and fostering private sector participation received little or no support from International Finance Corporation (IFC).

NEW GVC 2.0 DEVELOPMENT APPROACH: INTRODUCING CLUSTER-BASED POLICIES

As seen above, MCNG countries may reinvigorate their agribusiness-based exports by initially specializing in lower-value-added areas in which they have comparative advantages along a given global value chain (GVC) while actively investing in activities that would culminate in developing comparative advantages in higher-value-added areas at later stages. This is the underlying dynamics of the export diversification ladder (see chapter 3). Clearly, moving through steps 1 (intensive margin) and 2 (extensive margin) on the ladder mostly relies on the efforts made by private producers on a handful of emerging products where countries already have shown a degree of comparative advantage. However, a greater challenge relies in reaching steps 3 and 4, that is, gradually moving toward higher-value-added products as this process is not exempt from difficulties and requires a different approach based on past experience of developing VCs.

In considering how to reinvigorate VCs by turning them into higher-value-added activities, Baldwin (2011) acknowledges that nearly all manufacturing and agribusiness activities are taking place within GVCs. The fact is that many firms in various locations across the globe are involved in tasks ranging from research and development to final delivery of a specific product (or product set) to end users in the global market. Such tasks delink the process of innovation and product development from the production, employment, and commercialization processes themselves. The breaking down of the manufacturing process across GVCs straddling international borders should in principle make it easier for developing countries to industrialize than used to be the case. This is essentially the model China adopted and has pursued for the past three decades by combining an export-oriented growth strategy with a system of incentives for attracting inward foreign direct investment (FDI). The model is believed to have enabled Chinese firms to initially specialize in low-value-added segments of GVCs where they bundled low-skill labor services with globally recognized brands and advanced technology to sell them to global consumers. This placed Chinese firms at the center of a triangular trade within which they imported parts and components from Japan, Taiwan, China, the Republic of Korea, Singapore, and other East Asian economies, assembled them into finished products, and exported them to U.S. and European markets.

The apparent success of the model not only in China but also in Thailand, Vietnam, Cambodia, and other countries in East and South Asia makes it an attractive option as an initial step for MCNG countries. This seems timely especially when China and Thailand have transitioned to higher-value-added segments of GVCs and despite MCNG countries being among the most marginal relative to GVCs. The potential challenge faced by governments in the region in promoting participation of domestic firms in GVCs is thus one of designing a package of short- and medium-term policy initiatives that would facilitate the entry of foreign firms with strong GVC-related links into activities that maximize the countries' expected gains in terms of growth in per capita income and jobs. What is needed in the short run is a package of interventions that will both facilitate entry into GVCs in areas in which domestic firms have a comparative advantage, and attract selected FDI that will help provide the capital and technological input needed for their entry. Such a package would also include public and private investment in basic physical infrastructure along with reforms to trade policy and regulatory policy more generally as well as public and private investment in skills development programs, R&D institutions, and information and communications technology (ICT) infrastructure. Overall, there is a need for a set of interventions aimed at shifting the comparative advantage of domestic firms to activities with higher shares of value added in GVCs. This is the conceptual underpinning of the cluster approach.

A cluster approach initially explores the status of the four key determinants of GVC competitiveness: (i) factor conditions; (ii) demand conditions; (iii) the context of the GVC firm and its strategy; and (iv) the strength and quality of the linkages. Clusters involve multidirectional linkages involving suppliers, distributors, and companies (Porter 1998). Thus, the methodology identifies strengths, weaknesses, opportunities, and threats (SWOT) to competitiveness on those determinants. The methodology was applied to each of two selected GVC products for Mali (cashew and sesame), Niger (meat and onion), and Chad (sesame and gum arabic) in the Country Studies. By way of example, results for gum arabic and sesame (using the SWOT format) are shown in table 8.1.

Given limited financing resources in these countries, the policy framework should carefully ponder the scope of application, the type of instruments to utilize, and their period of application. In terms of scope, policies can be vertical (applicable to selected products or sector) or horizontal (applicable to all sectors). At the same time, the policy instrument may take the form of public input useful to private production or a market intervention that affects the behavior of firms. In addition, the case for targeted policy intervention should be temporary and carefully weighed against options and available resources. The 2x2 matrix below presents a classification of the mix of possible (horizontal and vertical) export diversification policies for MCNG countries (table 8.2). Although the list is not exhaustive and was customized for each Country Study, it offers a summary of the main policy areas to consider.

TABLE 8.1 SWOT study of Chad's sesame seed and gum arabic value chains

STRENGTHS	OPPORTUNITIES
• Chad's climate is potentially favorable to sesame • Chad is the second largest producer of gum arabic • Few players are exporting to key markets • Producers and processors are interested in developing both chains	• Global and regional demand increasing in high value markets • Stakeholders are keen to improve the sector • International assistance and government support are available for developing the agricultural sector • Growing sesame exports to Turkey and Olam's interest • Growing exports of gum arabic to India • Physical, linguistic, and cultural proximity to Sudan and the Middle East
WEAKNESSES	**THREATS**
• Low aggregate output constraints • Low human capital capacities • Lack of data on sesame and gum arabic • Poor organization and low investment across all segments and actors in the value chain • Insufficient orientation toward quality, certification, and traceability • Lack of branding • Nonexistent value addition • Producers are not getting optimal prices • Misaligned objectives of stakeholders • Misaligned objectives of policy, market realities, state actors, and value chain actors • Imbalanced market with fragmented producers and concentrated exporters • Poor research and lack of extension • Deficits in logistics, roads, and water infrastructure • Inadequate sequencing and continuity of aid programs	• Potential for market displacement • Growing competition from gum arabic belt countries with better enabling environment • Low aggregate amounts constrain exports and upgrading • Informal trading and cross-border exports do not reveal Chad's contribution to global trade • High insecurity • Government debt • Weak financial and marketing sector • Low capacities of government institutions

Source: Ahmed 2018.
Note: SWOT = strengths, weakness, opportunities, threats.

TABLE 8.2 Cluster-based typology of export diversification policies

	HORIZONTAL POLICIES	VERTICAL POLICIES
Public inputs	• Business climate enhancing reforms • Investment in infrastructure (spatially located in export production regions and along key logistics corridors)	• Quality, phytosanitary, and packing standards and controls • Matching grants to export-led SMEs • Specialized training programs for production
Market interventions	• Trade policy, customs and logistics reforms • Access to digital finance and competition policies • Research and development fund • Job skills programs	• Farm management upgrade support to SMEs with export growth potential • Temporary tax exemptions for investment in export-oriented GVCs • Incentives in Investment Codes • Land access concessions

Note: GVC = global value chain; SME = small and medium enterprises.

While this report does not take a stand between the two types of policies, it acknowledges that the selection of horizontal policies directly relies on the nature of the market failures identified, while vertical policies are more controversial because, though needed, they are not insensitive to vested interests. Policies of this type are frequently subject to a sector lobbying through entrepreneurs involved. These policies are often riskier because they concentrate benefits in certain beneficiaries (producers, intermediaries, or distribution firms) and may create rent-seeking opportunities. Hence, to prevent capture, a minimum institutional capacity is required to discipline private organizations by conducting a transparent selection process with clear criteria and monitoring performance (inputs received and outputs produced) so as to detect and remedy problems in a timely manner and prevent free-riding.

WHAT WORKS AND WHAT DOES NOT WITH MARKET INCENTIVES

The design of a customized package of policies per country is no simple task and is often wrongly limited to fiscal and nonfiscal vertical market incentives. In fact, all MCNG countries are in the process of revising their investment codes.[1] Until recently, all investment codes were outdated and, worst of all, implemented with wide discretion and distortions, resulting in major fiscal losses by MCNG governments. The slow ongoing updating of the codes and their implementing decrees does not prevent ambiguities, lack of knowledge, or uncertainties about the precise incentives firms (both foreign and domestic) obtain when intervening in key sectors. A generalized lack of transparency regarding the exact terms of foreign firms' contracts with the State is also the rule rather than the exception. Hence, performing an institutional review of recently approved or under review investment codes and their implementing decrees would not be premature despite the risk of this goal remaining unachieved in certain countries.

As an example, table 8.3 shows what is good and bad practice in the case of Niger. The table summarizes international good practices for investment incentives, which includes nine key principles (left-hand column). This is not an exhaustive list, and many other considerations and elements of good incentive policies could be taken into account regarding both their design and their management. These practices are then compared to the situation of Niger against each of these nine principles to see where there is a gap or areas for improvement in the incentive regime. No doubt other MCNG countries will uncover similar shortcomings in their own investment codes.

Lessons from countries that have achieved a degree of success with cluster-based approaches to export diversification are highly relevant. In this regard, Morocco's case is worth exploring as along with Turkey and Tunisia, the country features one of the most comprehensive and active set of horizontal and vertical policies to support export-oriented GVCs.

The most recent 2015 business survey conducted on the attractiveness of the Moroccan system (CMC 2016) reveals interesting findings. The survey shows that vertical market incentives to support investment are considered less important (coming in 13th place) than other policies addressing the investment climate and raising the efficiency of business procedures, the quality of justice, the burden of fiscal and social security costs, and the stability of macro fundamentals and of the Moroccan dirham (MAD).

TABLE 8.3 Comparing international good practices in investment incentives: Application to Niger

INTERNATIONAL GOOD PRACTICES FOR INVESTMENT INCENTIVES *(SELECTED AND SUMMARIZED)*	NIGER'S INCENTIVE REGIME *(SITUATION ANALYSIS AND DIRECTION FOR IMPROVEMENT)*
1. The incentive regime should be as clear and simple as possible.	The incentives regime is complicated and comprises multiple incentive regimes organized in multiple laws with general and sector-specific application along with their corresponding rules and procedures. *Direction for improvement: Simplification and consolidation of the multiple incentive regimes.*
2. Incentives should not be organized and provided in the Investment Code but in the relevant legislation (for instance, tax incentives should be placed in the tax legislation)	In Niger, the Investment Code is one of the laws organizing the incentive regime (which should not be the case). In addition, as mentioned above, many other laws (the tax and customs codes, several sectoral laws, law on PPP contracts, etc.) organize additional incentive regimes but different from that in the Investment Code. *Direction for improvement: Consolidate the various investment regimes and centralize them in one law, ideally the Tax Code (CGI).*
3. Administration of incentives: The process of application by investors and of granting incentives by the government should be simple and user-friendly and minimize discretion. Ideally, the process should be automatic or as automatic as possible (with ex-post verification rather than ex ante screening). There should be no negotiation on a case-by-case basis.	These processes are complicated, vary from one law from the other, and include significant room for discretion. There is not automaticity as incentive require an ex ante review process and decision. There are also no clear, objective criteria for decision-making. Some incentives can be negotiated (e.g., the contractual regime in the Investment Code. *Direction for improvement: Along with the consolidation of the various investment regimes into one law, ideally the Tax Code (CGI), and under one entity managing them, an effort should be made to simplify the award process, use more objective criteria, avoid case-by-case negotiation with investors, and move toward instruments that allow for a more automatic process and do not necessarily require ex ante reviews, instead using ex-post audits or controls.*
4. The fiscal cost of incentives should be systematically tracked and published.	The estimation of tax expenditures related to incentives has been mandatory since the 2011 Finance Law. This is also called for by WAEMU rules. Tax expenditure assessments have been conducted on an irregular basis by the Ministry of Finance, and to our knowledge, they have not been published. An ongoing assessment (2019) is being conducted by the Ministry of Finance with assistance from the IDA PCDS program, with a strong capacity-building component. *Direction for improvement: The ongoing study by the Ministry of Finance with World Bank Group assistance (PCDS project) should be completed. Ministry of Finance efforts should continue and be expanded. The scope of these estimations needs to include all incentive regimes and instruments within these regimes in order to give the government a complete picture of the fiscal costs of incentives. Another analytical expansion to consider is to include the benefits of incentives, including both elements of the cost-benefit ratio, and to see what incentives achieve best results in the most cost-effective manner. These assessments (of current tax expenditures or of future cost-benefit assessments, if adopted) should be published in a spirit of transparency. They should be used by policy makers to redesign the incentive regime in order to make it more cost-effective (among other objectives).*
5. Incentives should be designed in such a way as to minimize distortions to competition and align with international norms and best practices.	It does not appear that distortion minimization and alignment with international norms and best practices was a key objective when the current incentive regime were designed. *Direction for improvement: The multiple investment regimes should be revisited by the government, with assistance from its development partners (including the IMF and the World Bank Group) so as to align them with international norms, benefit from lessons of experiences and best practices, and thus improve them.*
6. Incentives should be linked to clearly defined policy objectives.	A clear strategy and specific policy objectives underpinning the incentive regimes seem to be lacking. *Direction for improvement: Before reforms to the incentive regimes can be implemented, there should be a comprehensive process to articulate a clear strategy with specific policy objectives set for these incentives regimes.*
7. To optimize benefits, incentives should be precisely targeted, focusing on the type of investors the country wants to attract, the type of behaviors it wants to foster, and the economic sectors and activities it wants to prioritize.	There is no obvious targeting at the moment in the sense that the objectives or results pursued are unclear (see Point 6 above) and incentive instruments are largely the same for all investors. Under the Investment Code, for instance, the difference between the three preferential regimes is not the type of incentives offered, which are identical under all three; rather, the difference is in the eligibility criteria and duration of the incentives.

continued

TABLE 8.3, *continued*

INTERNATIONAL GOOD PRACTICES FOR INVESTMENT INCENTIVES *(SELECTED AND SUMMARIZED)*	NIGER'S INCENTIVE REGIME *(SITUATION ANALYSIS AND DIRECTION FOR IMPROVEMENT)*
	Direction for improvement: As a process of revisiting or reforming the incentive regimes is launched, thought should be given to the sectors the government wants to promote through investment, the types of investments and investors it wants to attract, and the type of investor behaviors it wants to foster (see Point 6 above). It should then identify the needs and constraints of investors in these targeted or priority sectors and determine whether incentives can be part of the response and which type of incentives can be used to make a difference. In some cases, investors may not need tax incentives to invest in Niger; rather, they may need procedures to be streamlined or land with connection to utilities to be made available. These measures could constitute highly effective incentives to invest and be more helpful to investors than tax breaks.
8. Monitoring and evaluation mechanisms should be put in place to verify whether the policy objectives of incentives are attained and to evaluate the cost-effectiveness of the incentive regime.	There is no evidence of such an monitoring and evaluation mechanism being in place. *Direction for improvement: An element of the reform to the investment regimes that should be put in place is a robust monitoring and evaluation mechanism to ensure that the incentive regimes (revised or existing) are cost-effective and achieve the policy objectives that are (or will be) assigned to them.*
9. Information on the Incentive regime should be provided in a user-friendly and accessible format (single document, database, or inventory)	There is not a single location *or* document where investors (and other stakeholders) can find all of the information about all incentives currently available, procedures to access them, eligibility criteria, or reporting requirements. *Direction for improvement: Establish a central repository system and provide information to investors and stakeholders in simple, clear, user-friendly form. Use technology to allow online access. Update information on a regular basis as changes are introduced.*

Note: CGI = General Tax Code (Code Général des Impôts); IDA = International Development Association; IMF = International Monetary Fund; PCDS = Public Sector and Service Delivery Capacity and Performance Project (Projet de Capacités et de Performance du Secteur Public pour la Prestation de Services); PPP = public-private partnership; WAEMU = West African Economic and Monetary Union.

In taxation terms, Moroccan incentives seem not to feature major differences with those from Turkey and Tunisia. They can be summarized in four areas, also found with minor variations in the investment codes of MCNG countries:

- Firms (domestic and foreign) benefit from total 100 percent exemption (zero rate) in corporate income tax (CIT) for 5 years (approved in 2017).

- Firms also benefit from value-added tax (VAT) and customs duties exemptions for 36 months (permanently in Turkey) provided the minimum value of the investment is MAD 100 million (about USD 10 million).

- Firms established in Free Trade Zones (similar to the African area's *Agropoles*) benefit from CIT corporate and individual income tax exemptions during the first 5 years, followed by the application of a reduced tax rate over the following 20 years.

In contrast, in terms of nontax market interventions, Moroccan incentives lag behind those from Turkey and Tunisia. Table 8.4 provides a detailed account of these differences, which reflect a competitive edge among the three countries for attracting foreign firms.

IMPLEMENTING THE GVC 2.0 DEVELOPMENT APPROACH TO SUCCESS AND THE PRIORITY AGENDA

As seen above, there is no magic formula for export diversification. However, a cluster approach emphasizes that what matters to success with regard to GVC and

TABLE 8.4 Main nontax market incentives to global value chains in the manufacturing sector in Morocco, Turkey, and Tunisia

AREA	MOROCCO	TURKEY	TUNISIA
Land and equipment	• Support to land acquisition cost up to 20% of total land cost (FDI; large projects) and land leasing facilities at discounted prices. • Support to expenditure on external infrastructure up to 5% of total investment cost (FDI; large projects).	Land concessions according to incentive regime and regional development zone where project is located.	Bonus support to infrastructure expenses up to 85% of total cost, capped at TND 1 million according to the incentive regime of the regional development zone.
Investment contribution	• Bonus support to physical and nonphysical investment up to 30% of overall cost (FDI; ecosystems). • Annual bonus for import substitution up to 2% of total imported inputs (FDI; ecosystems). • State contribution of about 15% of total investment amount, capped at MAD 30 million (Fund Hassan II).	State contribution between 15% and 55% of total investment cost according to the incentive regime and the regional zone and its industrial development zone.	Bonus support to investment up to 30% of total investment costs capped at TND 3 million according to the incentives in force in the regional development zone.
Interest rate bonification		Interest rate support (discount) of between 1 and 7 points according to the incentive regime, the regional zone, and the type of loan.	
Employment and training	• State grant toward the firm's share of payments to the Social Security Agency and the professional training tax for a period of 24 months up to 10 employees per firm (Tahfiz Program). • Exemptions of payment by firms and workers to the Social Security Agency and of the professional training tax as compensation between MAD 1,600 and 6,000 (Idmaj Program).	State grant toward the firm's share of payments to the Social Security Agency either with no cap or capped at 10% to 35% for a period of 2 to 12 years according to the incentive regime of the regional development zone and its organized industrial zone.	State assumption of firm's contribution to Social Security regime during first 5 to 10 years of activity according to regional promotion zones. Permanent exemption from professional training tax and workers' contribution to the Housing Promotion Fund in regional development zone.

Source: Daki 2018.
Note: FDI = foreign direct investment; MAD = Moroccan dirham; TND = Tunisian dinar.

regional value chain (RVC) development is the need to deal with the integrality of the VC and not with isolated pieces of it. Hence, it is possible to summarize a carefully selected set of key complementary policies (already depicted in more detail in their corresponding previous chapters) under a theory of change framework (table 8.5). The table provides the fundamentals for a private-sector-driven export diversification in MCNG countries. These are grouped into four components (pillars) of complementary between micro and macro diversification-prone policies that compose the logical chain of the desired reform. The theory of change assumes that GVC or RVC development is a national priority, that is, a shared national vision with clear goalposts toward an export strategy both in terms of the few agribusinesses selected and of macro diversification ratios (openness ratios, export growth rates, jobs created, etc.).

TABLE 8.5 Theory of change of revamped main export diversification policies in Mali, Chad, Niger, and Guinea ("game changers")

MAIN CHALLENGES	KEY POLICIES AND MARKET INTERVENTIONS	MAIN OUTPUTS AND OUTCOMES	
Component 1: Upgrading Strategic Gvcs			
• Low process and product upgrading (participation in low value chain segments—live animals and raw products, producers' organizations at nascent stage, poor quality and lack of certification and control standards, deforestation)	• Introduce productivity and animal health enhancements (vaccine, fertilizer, certified seed, storage, sanitation, environment standards) [step 1] • Strengthen producers' organizations and management [step 1] • Training on quality certification and control and testing labs [step 1] • Financial support to higher value products: e.g., frozen meat, sesame oil, soap [step 1] • Digitization of agricultural financial transactions [steps 1–3] • Create risk-sharing facility for start-up exporters [steps 1–3]	• Process and product upgrades (with productivity enhancements) to selected GVCs • Improved farming techniques and producers' skills • Increased the number of export products complying with quality standards • Eligible exporters access to prefinancing	• Increased output and exports of selected products • Gradual diversification of export supply toward higher value-added goods (and services)
• Low market upgrading and global links (lack of market information, unskilled produced and workers)	• Develop information systems on foreign markets [step 2] • Consider smaller and better packaging and branding [step 2] • Financial support to explore new (niche) markets [step 2]	• Markets information upgraded • New brands developed for higher-value-added products	• Increased exports to new markets abroad
Component 2: Targeting investment in trade infrastructure and along main corridors			
• Infrastructure gaps in power, water irrigation, and roads • Unorganized domestic transportation • Logistics corridors in poor condition and trucking subject to road harassment • Cumbersome and corruption-prone customs and logistics procedures	• Financial support to off-grid solar power solutions and new irrigation techniques (pumps, drips) [steps 3, 4] • Rehabilitate and maintain 5 key corridors: Bamako-Dakar; Bamako-Abidjan; N'Djamena-Douala; Niamey-Cotonou; Niamey-Lomé [steps 3, 4] • Reduce road checkpoints [step 1] • Introduce single window for customs, supported by risk-based postaudit and e-payments [steps 3, 4]	• Increased access rates to power and water by rural populations • Lower transportation costs • Lower transit time and customs costs • Lower the number of corruption-prone transactions	• More conducive environment for GVC export development
Component 3: Revamped trade and access to financing policies			
• High anti-export bias with tariff exemptions and tariff escalation (despite move to CET) • Distortionary and corruption-prone use of NTBs	• Reduce CET to four bands (0, 5, 10, and 20) [step 1] • Redefine or phase out inefficient tariff exemptions [steps 1, 2] • Eliminate cross-border barriers and illegal paratariffs [steps 1, 2]	• Lower cost of imports and elimination of illicit custom fees	• Increased trade openness • Increased access to foreign markets • Greater financial inclusion • Reduced informality • Increased access to land • Lower cost and time for modern, more efficient trading
• Farmers' low access to formal bank accounts • Lack of awareness on digital finance • Lack of access to foreign markets by farmers	• Digitalize farmers' land registry and payments of some public inputs (seed, fertilizer) through mobile devices [steps 1, 2] • Digitize farmers organization's payments [step 3]	• Increased use of mobile money, digital money, and e-commerce • Better access to finance for farmers	

continued

TABLE 8.5, *continued*

MAIN CHALLENGES	KEY POLICIES AND MARKET INTERVENTIONS	MAIN OUTPUTS AND OUTCOMES
Component 4: Revamped trade and access to financing policies		
• Cumbersome procedures for SMEs creation	• Lower the cost of registration to a flat fee and reduce/eliminate capital requirements [step 1] • Finalize computerization of registry of firms [step 3]	• Reduced cost and time of registration
• Slow and corruption-prone concession of land permits	• Lower the cost of concession to a flat fee [step 1] • Reduce procedures and time for obtaining concessions [step 3] • Create a website for concessions granted [step 3]	• Reduced cost and time for obtaining land concessions
• Outdated trade IT systems	• Full implementation of SYDONIA WORLD in customs [step 2] • Update mapping of import/export procedures followed by electronic submission [step 3]	• Reduced cost and time for import/export transactions

Note: Shown in brackets, each policy action has a suitable sequence of intervention on the steps of the export diversification ladder. Steps 1–2: short term; steps 3–4: medium term. CET = common external tariff; GVC = global value chain; IT = information technology; NTB = nontariff barrier; SME = small and medium enterprise.

i. Effective, well-coordinated government interventions aiming at upgrading selected strategic bets in terms of product (and services) for RVCs and GVCs development. Key interventions should concentrate on: (a) improving production, yields, and quality in the strategic bets; (b) developing the capacities and organization of the chains actors; (c) complying with international certifications and traceability standards; and (d) attracting FDI investment in greenfield projects by lead regional and international firms.

ii. Spatially targeted investments in trade infrastructure (access to power and water) and rehabilitation and maintenance of key road corridors. Given the highly limited fiscal and external borrowing space in MCNG countries, investments should focus on increasing agricultural productivity and reducing transportation costs. Only about 4–6 key regional economic corridors should be prioritized. In Guinea, these investments should be accompanied by a thorough review of customs and port transit procedures.

iii. Revamped trade and logistic policies designed to reduce costs and allow the economy become globally competitive. Trade policy should remove any bias against exporting, ensure effective competition in product markets and in key services such as transportation, energy, and communications. Free trade agreements (FTAs) should foster exchanges with key commercial partners in the strategic bets. Digital technologies can lead to steep declines in transportation and communications costs and create significant opportunities to export services such as back-office processing. E-trade can also widen the range of mechanisms through which small producers in developing countries can grow through exporting, create jobs, and enhance productivity.

iv. Clear, transparent and predictable business-friendly investment climate that will facilitate adequate incentives to domestic and foreign private investors. Having a modern investment code or public-private partnership (PPP) laws are not enough to attract foreign or domestic private investment. Key policies and market interventions should aim to reduce the cost of registering business start-ups, simplify tax payments, accelerate the delivery of land and construction permits, especially those located in key producing areas, encourage access to credit and digital financial inclusion, improve court management and corporate governance, and develop the framework for an effective competition policy and PPPs.

MAXIMIZING FINANCE FOR DEVELOPMENT AND THE KEY ROLE IFC CAN PLAY IN ATTRACTING FOREIGN DIRECT INVESTMENT TO GVC 2.0 DEVELOPMENT

The importance of IFC in attracting FDI to the development of the GVC 2.0 cluster-based approach cannot be overstated. First, the vast number of SMEs currently producing either for consumption in the domestic market or selling their raw products in foreign markets have few linkages with the modern, mostly foreign-owned companies trading in the international markets and involved in vertically integrated trading. These SMEs have little or no access to modern technology or knowledge. In addition, the market incentives offered to both foreign-owned and domestic firms as well as to state-owned enterprises should be reviewed so as to foster a level playing field as experience indicates that these incentives are neither the best strategy for attracting FDI nor the only policies that matter to them (World Bank 2014). Second, successful case studies in Africa strongly advocate the key role played by international firms. For instance, after a decade of failed attempts to develop PPPs, Olam, the global leader in edible nuts, finally played a game-changer role in Côte d'Ivoire's cashew processing in 2008. The company was the first leading multinational to start processing cashew in the central city of Bouaké. Today, Olam's plant employs over 2,000 people, with another 1,000 working at a second facility. The processing of cashew nuts is labor-intensive, thus creating more jobs as the country expands cashew processing. Olam is now collaborating with the government and the private sector to support the African Cashew Alliance. Although Olam's example is far from unique, as we saw above (chapter 1), attracting FDI is an uphill challenge as in the last decade, none of the MCNG countries has received any efficiency-seeking export-oriented FDI favoring agribusiness or livestock development.

i. The World Bank Group recently developed the Maximizing Finance for Development (MFD) framework to leverage private investments and optimize the use of public funding. The MFD framework is supported by the cascade approach, which functions as its operating system (table 8.6). The World Bank Group initially prioritizes private sector solutions and inclusive business models through cost-effective commercial financing, supported whenever possible by IFC (step 1).

ii. Where markets show limited space for private investment, the World Bank Group focuses on policy reforms that address market failures and constraints to private sector solutions at the country and sector levels (step 2) and reduce the distortionary effects of public spending while improving incentives and reducing transaction costs (step 3).

iii. Where risks remain high, the cascade approach requires public investment to help crowd in private investment. This priority leads to focusing small investments in public infrastructure based on clear private sector needs such as public

TABLE 8.6 The cascade decision-making approach for agricultural value chains

Decision question		Spectrum of potential actions
Is the private sector doing it?	Yes →	**Spectrum of potential actions to promote responsible food and agriculture investments** • Strengthen country capacity to assess and mitigate/regulate environmental and social risks • Promote private sector alignment with the principles of responsible investment • Support inclusive business models to improve linkages among smallholders and firms for all sizes
↓ No		
Is this because of limited space for private sector activity?	Yes →	**Spectrum of potential actions to increase space for private sector investments** • Support competition and associated policy reform, including of state-owned enterprises • Strengthen investment policy and dialogue to open space for global investment • Reduce government intervention in agricultural financial markets to open space for private financial service providers
↓ No		

Is this because of policy and regulatory gaps or weaknesses?	Yes →	**Spectrum of potential actions to improve the policy and regulatory environment for private sector investments and to reduce the distortionary effects of public spending**
		• Reduce distortionary effects of public spending policies
		
		Improve incentives and reduce transaction costs
		  • Lower trade costs
		  • Improve policies and regulatory regimes of input markets
		  • Improve policy and regulatory environment for agri-finance
		  • Strengthen food safety systems
		
		Reduce private sector investment risk
		  • Ensure macroeconomic and political stability
		  • Improve the stability and predictability of policies
		  • Improve land tenure security and access to land
		  • Shift public policies from farm production support towards improving access for farms and agribusiness to risk management instruments that can increase lending

↓ No		

Can public investment help crowd-in private investment?	Yes →	**Spectrum of potential public investments to reduce private sector transaction costs and risk**
		
		Improve incentives and reduce transaction costs
		  • Invest in public infrastructure based on clear private sector needs
		  • Invest in public inspections and quality assurance
		  • Improve co-ordination to reduce transaction costs
		  • Consider public-private partnerships
		
		Reduce private sector investment risk
		  • Support political risk insurance for financial institutions and private investors
		  • Consider use of market pull incentive mechanisms
		  • Provide direct financing to value chain actors

↓ No		
Pursue purely public financing	→	**Use public resources to invest in public or quasi-public goods and services** Where there is no viable private sector return: • Invest agricultural public spending in public goods and services (such as rural roads, energy) to enable the • Support complementary public investment in other sectors (such as human capital, agricultural research) to enable the commercialization and competitiveness of national agricultural production, processing, and marketing

Sources: World Bank 2018a, 2018b.

inspections, quality assurance, or single-window agencies while de-risking tools such as guarantees and risk-sharing instruments (step 4). The project could also seek to establish a PPP framework with private operators.

iv. Where market solutions are not possible through sector reform and risk mitigation, public resources should be used to favor pure public or quasi-public goods (step 5). However, this step may be more relevant in the context of rural areas as these areas are less profitable for private operators and often require strong public interventions to finance the required infrastructures (roads, power, water, communication antennas, etc.).

Criteria for IFC intervention in agribusiness for Africa are well defined. IFC typically invests in projects whose total costs exceeds USD 10 million, except for projects financed by IFC's Private Sector Window.[2] In the agribusiness industry, IFC typically finances expansion of projects by an existing company rather than greenfield (start-up) projects, except where the sponsor (for example, a multinational firm) has significantly relevant experience. The project must be commercially and economically viable, thus offering IFC the potential for a commercial return while also providing development impact. In the case of exporters, the project's production should also be globally competitive. The project and its supply chain must be environmentally and socially sustainable. The project's sponsor is expected to inject equity representing 40–50 percent of total project costs. Adequate security and mortgage support for land as well as integrity and ethical standards on the part of sponsor and company are expected. Finally, the project must be consistent with the World Bank Group's country strategy (IFC 2018).

In practice, the new GVC 2.0 cluster-based approach has already being piloted in MCNG countries, especially in Mali, through a lighter instrument, namely Joint Implementation Plans (JIPs). JIPs are an illustrative example of the complementary role every institution in the World Bank Group should play in fostering the MFD approach. JIPs were introduced in 2014. Their aim can be summarized as follows: In countries where two or more World Bank Group institutions are engaged and pursue complementary goals in the same sector, teams may prepare a JIP. This management tool will help coordinate activities to ensure that they are directed, sequenced, and resourced so as to have the maximum sustainable impact. JIP implementation has been slow: of a total of 41 pilot JIPs that have been considered over the past four years, only 18 are reported to have reached the implementation stage, with Africa accounting for over half of those.[3] JIPs have been undertaken mainly in two sectors: energy and agribusiness. A preliminary assessment found that while there was significant support among senior World Bank Group management for initiating JIPs early on, few were actually initiated. However, as World Bank Group management shifts its focus toward the MFD agenda, JIPs may be used to encourage this agenda (World Bank 2018c).

Among JIPs pilots worldwide, the Mali plan is among the most advanced. Since 2017, a mango export project has been supported under the World Bank Group's JIP (figure 8.1). The project addresses four actors: producers, transporters, processors, and traders. While the Bank tackles infrastructure, logistical, and institutional bottlenecks, IFC handles SMEs agrifinance, the financing of the Africa Leasing Facility, and investment in the private African fruit processing company Centre d'Étude et de Développement Industriel et Agricole du Mali (Malian Center for Research and Industrial and Agricultural Development; CEDIAM),[4] while Multilateral Investment Guarantee Agency (MIGA) provides a political-risk guarantee. All JIP actors intervene in solving dedicated problems

FIGURE 8.1

Mali: Supporting large-scale pilot projects in the mango sector: How the Joint Implementation Plan is supporting the mango value chain

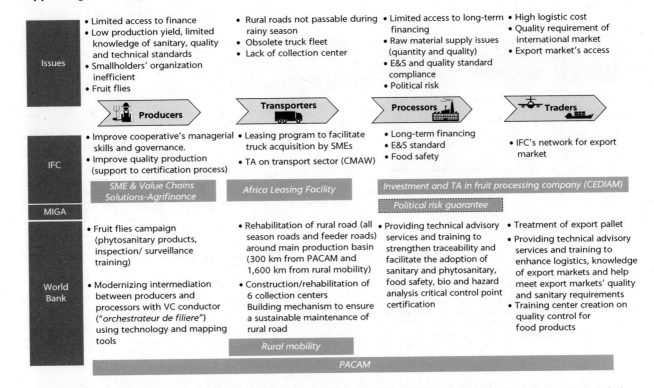

Note: CEDIAM = Malian Center for Research and Industrial and Agricultural Development (Centre d'Étude et de Développement Industriel et Agricole du Mali); CMAW = Creating Markets Advisory Window; E&S = environmental and social; IFC = International Finance Corporation; MIGA = Multilateral Investment Guarantee Agency; PACAM = Support Project for Agro-Industrial Competitivity in Mali (Projet d'Appui à la Compétitivité Agro-Industrielle au Mali); SME = small and medium enterprise; TA = technical assistance; VC = value chain.

under a learning-by-doing approach. Initially, Mali's Government requested public financing to experiment with new horticultural crops for which there is important market demand. These crops, in this case mango, are an opportunity for smallholders to produce and sell to CEDIAM. However, neither CEDIAM's resource nor IFC funding could prefinance new crop's testing as well as a smallholders' demonstration center, all of which was estimated at EUR 400,000. Hence, options discussed explored whether to use Bank funding from the West Africa Agricultural Productivity project, which deals with agri-innovations, the Support Project for Agro-Industrial Competitivity in Mali (PACAM), which supports horticulture development, or the innovative Tubaniso agri-investment platform under development to support new agri-projects.

A more pragmatic approach complementing the JIP under a country-customized multisectoral MFD reform agenda was recently agreed for Guinea. Following the visit by senior IFC management, joint preparatory work by IFC and World Bank staff led to the design of a reform-oriented MFD agenda focused on seven sectors (see table 8.7 for details).

A simpler, more innovative instrument for managing risk in fragile countries based in IFC and World Bank collaboration is the setting up of a risk-sharing facility (RSF) for exporters in Chad and SMEs in Mali. The RSF is a bilateral loss-sharing agreement between IFC (or World Bank-financed projects) and an originator of assets (normally a local bank or corporation). The RSF allows the originator and IFC (or World Bank project) to form a partnership, introduce a new business, or

TABLE 8.7 **Guinea: Customized MFD Reform Agenda for IFC and World Bank, 2019**

Agribusiness	• Introduction of e-vouchers in input markets • Setting up of an export quality system of technical norms • Support to specific global value chains	• IFC catalyzes foreign direct investment, • World Bank support policy changes and finance • creation of a quality certification agency • Joint advisory services
Energy	• Strengthen EDM financial health and management (tariff adjustments included) • Unfolding of Scaling Solar Program	• IFC catalyzes foreign direct investment • World Bank support policy changes
Low-Cost Housing	• Development of PPP strategy for low-income housing • Legal changes allowing joint-property.	• World Bank supports design of national strategy • IFC attracts financing for developers and banks
Transport	• Railroad development from Conakry port (urban decongestion) • Dry port rehabilitation • Rehabilitation of Conakry airport	• IFC catalyzes foreign direct investment
Access to Finance	• Strengthening SME financing infrastructure • Creation of a Credit Bureau	• IFC finances a guarantee fund • World Bank loan provides financing to MSMEs
Business Climate	• Operationalization of the Investment Code • Operationalization of PPP Law • Single Window for Real Estate	• World Bank provides TA
Taxes	• Introduction of digital tax declaration and payments • Creation of a fiscal mediator	• World Bank provides TA

Note: EDM = Malian Electricity Company (Électricité du Mali); IFC = International Finance Corporation; MFD = Maximizing Finance for Development; PPP = public and private partnerships; SME = small and medium enterprises; TA = technical assistance.

expand a target market (in addition to exporters, frequent targets are SMEs, energy efficiency-related projects, mortgages, etc.). Its objective is to support start-ups (for example, exporters with little historical experience of losses) on the basis of eligible criteria and to provide originators with credit risk protection but not funding (though it may eventually also allow prefinancing). The RSF typically reimburses the originator for a fixed percentage of incurred losses exceeding a predefined threshold (or first loss). Thus, its main features are: (i) the bilateral agreement; (ii) the portion IFC (or the World Bank-financed project) will reimburse on a pari passu basis to the originator for a portion of principal losses incurred in a pool of eligible assets (for example, merchandise exports), thus lowering the needs for collateral; (iii) exporters' eligibility to the RSF based on preagreed criteria; and (iv) assets covered and servicing procedures agreed for performing, delinquent, or defaulted assets. In practice, several options exist for structuring RSF transactions depending on the needs of the originator, its absorption capacity, and possible third-party participants (IFC 2018). Beside credit risk and eventual prefinancing, the RSF brings two added benefits: transfer of skills to local banks for adopting a prudent approach in their portfolio risk diversification, and setting standards for corporate governance and local business and exporter conduct. Details of IFC proposal for an RSF made available to Chadian exporters are shown in figure 8.2.

Other innovative instruments for risk management in fragile countries address larger FDI-financed firms as these tend to have better access to policy makers. These firms can raise the stakes in cases of failure if governments interfere in their operations and can be better placed to mobilize external support against political interference, including firms that support good corporate citizenship. For example, money transfers in Somalia, which align with religious principles and local values, provide useful services. Other examples include Chinese investors in Liberian construction looking for local capacity and creating jobs, and cocoa investors in Sierra Leone taking over the government's role in creating infrastructure (World Bank 2019).

FIGURE 8.2

Chad: Illustrative structure of a risk-sharing facility based on a collateral management agency

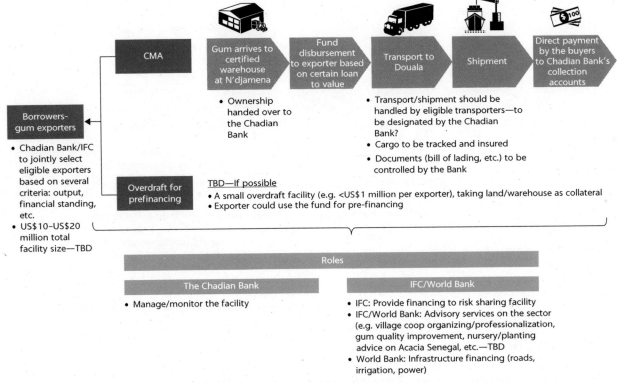

Source: Original analysis based on presentation by IFC to Chadian exporters in N'Djamena, February 18, 2019 (unpublished document).
Note: CMA = collateral management agency; IFC = International Finance Corporation; TBD = to be determined.

Other examples of cluster-based approaches applied to VCs development on a lower scale (and mostly oriented toward the domestic markets) encouraging private sector participation are already ongoing in Africa. Also called "agribusiness clusters" based on farmers' VC committees, these organizations are used to facilitate better coordination between VC actors, identify common interests, share knowledge, develop new business opportunities, and act as a lobby group for the common interest of its members. Figure 8.3 describes an example of the interactions between one nongovernmental organization (NGO) and farmers' organizations in developing a VC in horticulture in Bangladesh.

In a recent development, IFC contributed to developing a proven Scope Insight model for professionalizing agricultural organizations worldwide (SCOPE 2019). In the last decade, a global network of 60 global private partners, using nearly 600 assessors trained in 14 academic institutions, covering 39 countries (including Mali and Guinea), and reaching more than 7.2 farmers worldwide has come to define a global standard for farmers' organizations' professionalism in 2018 and set a standard metrics for measuring its key components. The main features of the Scope Insight model are as follows:

- Four types of assessment tools: (i) *Scope Pro* (for measuring access to markets and finance capabilities); (ii) *Scope Basic* (for measuring the level of professionalism in farmers' organizations; (iii) *Scope Agent* (for assessing the growth potential of farmers and field agents; and (iv) *Scope Input* (for gaining insights into the needs and opportunities of input retailers who supply inputs to farmers).

FIGURE 8.3

Example of integrated value chain developer: Sustainable Agriculture, Food Security, and Linkages (Solidaridad) in the aquaculture, dairy, and horticulture sector of Bangladesh

Approach:

- Finance non-governmental organization who acts as representative of farmers
- Start with establishing commercial demand for high value products, identify buyer requirements, and enter into agreements
- Target support at major binding constraints for the value chain to meet these requirements

Activities:

(1) Farmer training to comply with buyer requirements

(2) Facilitate farmer organization

(3) Finding buyers and input providers,negotiation, coordination of exchange, and enforcement

(4) Support to farm service providers [transport, (cold) storage, input distribution]

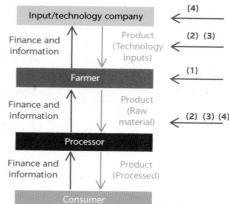

Preliminary results from double-difference impact evaluation show large effects on farm revenue and food security.

Source: Original analysis based on Swinnen 2018.

- A single weighted-average metrics for measuring farmers' organizations' professionalism, evaluating eight dimensions globally: (i) internal management; (ii) operations; (iii) sustainability; (iv) financial management; (v) production base; (vi) market; (vii) external risks; and (viii) enabling environment.

- Based on the strengths and weaknesses identified, design of customized technical assistance packages potentially addressing governance, financing, extension services, environment, and training needs.

While the metrics and potential for support unfolds worldwide, though still at the pilot stage, the type and number of these low-scale cluster-based public initiatives is growing,[5] which explains why there have been few rigorous studies of their benefits, with promising, though so far mixed results.

- A systematic review of farmer field schools found positive effects (yields +13 percent, farm incomes +19 percent) but only if these include both input and output market interventions (Waddington et al. 2014).

- Evidence of the effects of farmers' organizations on technology access, productivity, output market access, and incomes tend to be positive (for example, Verhofstadt and Maertens 2014).

- A systematic review of 26 contract farming arrangements in 13 developing countries by Ton et al. (2018) confirms positive income effects, with an overall pooled income effect between 23 and 55 percent.

- The systematic review of the benefits of certification per se by Oya et al. (2017) found that despite its positive effects on prices (14 percent increase) and farm revenue (11 percent increase), there is no evidence that, on average, certification schemes improve the total household income of participating farmers.

- Finally, Ashraf, Giné, and Karlan (2009) found that as a result of an integrated value chain developer (VCD) project targeted at farmers, farm income increased by 31.9 percent but that this effect later disappeared due to an exogenous factor when demand from the export market dried up.

An interesting local case of mixed VCD interventions among foreign firms and an NGO is that by Danone, Kinome, and SOS Sahel in gum arabic in Chad.[6] Conceived in 2009, the objective of the project was to introduce gum arabic extracted from *Acacia seyal* into Danone's yoghurts, thus replacing one of its chemical components. The project would have three main benefits: *economic,* as it would contribute to reducing poverty among Chadian collectors; *environmental,* as it would contribute to valorizing the Acacia tree and its conservation; and *social,* as it would empower women through better access to water, which is critical for production. The project is ongoing in four regions: Hadjer Lamis, Bata, Chari Baguirmi, and Guera. Despite the lack of formal evaluation of the pilot so far, the most significant difficulties it ran into have been facilitating access to basic services (water, electricity), increasing low returns for collectors when the collection area is far from water provision and the marketing center, and ensuring steady flows of a labor force due the nomadic character of the female population participating in the collection areas.

Finally, the spatial dimension is no less important in completing the cluster approach in fragile contexts, not because of having to avoid unsafe territories threatening the transportation of export products but because of its role facilitating a multi-set of policy interventions. For instance, a multiproduct agribusiness cluster is developing around Sikasso, Mali, exactly where the JIP is being implemented. This area also expects to take advantage of its connectivity to markets, vibrant urban center nearby, and its good arable land. Similarly, with tens of thousands of gravity-irrigated hectares, the Office project in Niger could become a critical agribusiness pole for products such as rice. The spatial dimension can thus help simultaneously tackle many of the constraints identified in this report (for example, connectivity infrastructure to facilitate access to input/output markets, access to well-serviced or irrigated land, etc.). To complement these provisions, auctioning land in selected areas could be a way to attract targeted leading FDI either on the basis of developing identified products or of letting investors decide which products they want to develop on a least amount of support or subsidy requested basis.

NOTES

1. Chad's Investment Code dates from 2008, but it took no less than six years to issue its implementing decrees. Mali's Code dates from 2012, Guinea's from 2015, and Niger's from 2017, but all still lack their implementing decrees, which leads to major problems of governance, delays, and investor uncertainty.
2. Private Sector Window-eligible projects may require a minimum of USD 2–4 million. All MCNG countries are Private Sector Window-eligible.
3. Burundi, Cameroon, Côte d'Ivoire, Mali, Mozambique, Nigeria, Senegal, Sierra Leone, other Sahel and Horn of Africa countries, Myanmar, the Philippines, Georgia, Turkey, the Arab Republic of Egypt, India, Nepal, and Pakistan.
4. Since 2012, CEDIAM has sourced mangoes for export, including processed mango concentrate and puree, to Europe. Its sponsors have invested EUR 18 million from own funds and had a EUR 13 million investment plan to secure sourcing of raw material supply and diversify the company's business to year-round operation. In 2015, CEDIAM sourced 11,000 tons of mangoes from over 2,000 producers and produced 5,000 tons of mango puree and concentrate, even though this represents only a 20 percent utilization of installed capacity. CEDIAM has developed a strong

client network in Europe for juice, concentrate, and puree thanks to its sponsor (an Italian investor) with over 20 years experience in the food sector.

5. Two cases worth exploring with MCNG countries in mind are the African Cashew Alliance and the Global Shea Alliance.

6. Danone is a leading global French firm operating in the agribusiness products and specializing in milk, bottled water, and medical nutrition products; Kinome is a French social enterprise firm working on deforestation prevention; SOS Sahel is an international NGO focused on food security in Africa.

REFERENCES

Ahmed, G. 2018. "Upgrading Agricultural Value Chains in Mali, Niger and Chad." Unpublished background paper, World Bank, Washington, DC.

Ashraf, N., X. Giné, and D. Karlan. 2009. "Finding Missing Markets (and a Disturbing Epilogue): Evidence from an Export Crop Adoption and Marketing Intervention in Kenya." *American Journal of Agricultural Economics* 91 (4): 973–90.

Baldwin, R. 2011. "Trade and Industrialization After Globalization's Second Unbundling: How Building and Joining a Supply Chain Are Different and Why It Matters." NBER Working Paper 17716, National Bureau of Economic Research, Cambridge, MA.

CMC (Moroccan Competition Council). 2016. "Système incitatif de l'industrialisation Marocaine: Vers des mesures ciblées et efficaces." Maroc Conjoncture Report 280, CMC, Rabat.

Daki, S. 2018. "Maroc: Système incitatif pour la promotion de l'industrie." Unpublished paper, Rabat.

IFC (International Finance Corporation). 2018. "Risk-sharing facility: Structured and securitized products." Unpublished paper, IFC, Washington, DC.

Oya, C., F. Schaefer, D. Skalidou, C. McCosker, and L. Langer. 2017. "Effects of Certification Schemes for Agricultural Production on Socio-Economic Outcomes in Low- and Middle-Income Countries: A Systematic Review." *3ie Systematic Review* 34.

Porter, M. E. (1998). "Clusters and the New Economics of Competition." *Harvard Business Review* 76 (6): 77–90.

SCOPE. 2019. "Insights into Impact: Transforming the Agricultural Sector in Emerging Markets." Presentation given to the World Bank (March), Strategic Community Agenda, Los Angeles.

Swinnen, J. 2018. "Inclusive Value Chains to Accelerate Poverty Reduction." Background paper, World Bank, Washington, DC.

Ton, G., W. Vellema, S. Desiere, S. Weituschat, and M. D'Haeseb. 2018. "Contract Farming for Improving Smallholder Incomes: What Can We Learn from Effectiveness Studies?" *World Development* 104: 46–64.

Verhofstadt, E., and M. Maertens. 2015. "Can Agricultural Cooperatives Reduce Poverty? Heterogeneous Impact of Cooperative Membership on Farmers' Welfare in Rwanda." *Applied Economic Perspectives and Policy* 37: 86–106.

Waddington, J., P. J. Morris, N. Kettridge, G. Granath, D. K. Thompson, and P. A. Moore. 2015. "Hydrological Feedbacks in Northern Peatlands." *Ecohydrologie* 8 (1): 113–27.

World Bank. 2014. "World Bank Group: A new Approach to Country Engagement." World Bank, Washington, DC.

——. 2018a. "Future of Food: Maximizing Finance for Development in Agricultural Value Chains." World Bank, Washington, DC.

——. 2018b. "Creating Markets for Sustainable Growth and Development." An Evaluation of World Bank Group Support to Client Countries FY 07-17, IEG, Unpublished approach paper (February), World Bank, Washington, DC.

——. 2018c. *The Human Capital Project*. Washington, DC: World Bank.

——. 2019. "Africa's Pulse, No. 19: An Analysis of Issues Shaping Africa's Economic Future." (April), World Bank, Washington, DC. doi:10.1596/978-1-4648-1421-1.

Bibliography

Ahmed, G., and B. Fandohan. 2017. "GVC in Niger: Bovine and Onions." Unpublished background paper, *Niger: Leveraging Export Diversification to Foster Growth*, World Bank, Washington, DC.

Benjamin, N., and N. Pitigala. 2017. "Trade Diagnostic on Niger." Unpublished background paper, *Niger: Leveraging Export Diversification to Foster Growth*, World Bank, Washington, DC.

Benyagoub, M., and L. Clark. 2017a. "Results from the Enterprise Survey and Module on Exporters in Niger." Unpublished background paper, *Niger: Leveraging Export Diversification to Foster Growth*, World Bank, Washington, DC.

——. 2017b. "Results from the Enterprise Survey in Mali and Module on Exporters." Unpublished background paper, *Mali: Leveraging Export Diversification to Foster Growth*, World Bank, Washington, DC.

——. 2018. "Results from the Enterprise Survey in Chad and Module on Exporters." Unpublished background paper, *Chad: Leveraging Export Diversification to Foster Growth*, World Bank, Washington, DC.

Forneris, X. 2019. "International Good Practices on Investment Incentives: An Application to Niger." Unpublished background note, *Leveraging Export Diversification in Fragile Countries: The Emerging Value Chains of Mali, Chad, Niger, and Guinea*, World Bank, Washington, DC.

Government of Niger. 2016a. "Renaissance." Unpublished paper, Government of Niger, Niamey.

——. 2016b. "Vision 2035: Economic Orientation." Unpublished paper, Government of Niger, Niamey.

——. 2017. "Plan de développement économique et social." Unpublished paper, Government of Niger, Niamey.

IFC (International Finance Corporation). 2018. "Introduction of IFC Agribusiness Activities in Africa." Presentation to the Seminar on Growth and Diversification, N'Djamena, November 17.

IMF (International Monetary Fund). 2017. "Central African Economic and Monetary Community (CEMAC): Staff Report on the Common Policies in Support of Member Countries Reform Programs." Country Report 17/176, IMF, Washington, DC. https://www.imf.org/~/media/Files/Publications/CR/2017/cr17176.ashx.

ITC (International Trade Centre). 2015. "Edible Nuts: Cashew." *Cashew Quarterly Bulletin*. http://www.intracen.org/uploadedFiles/intracenorg/Blogs/Cashew_Nuts_-_Main/Cashew%20quarterly%20bulletin%20Q3_Final.pdf.

——. 2017. International Trade Statistics. https://www.wto.org/english/res_e/statis_e/statis_e.htm.

Josserand, H. P. 2013. "Assessment of Volumes and Value of Regionally Traded Staple Commodities." Paper prepared for the Food Across Borders Conference, Accra, January 29–31. http://www.inter-reseaux.org/IMG/pdf/Josserand_-_Assessment_of_ATP_E-ATP_Trade_Data.pdf.

Lofgren, H. 2017. "Mining Export Prices and Public Investment: Alternative Scenarios for Mali." Unpublished background paper, *Mali: Leveraging Export Diversification to Foster Growth*, World Bank, Washington, DC.

López-Cálix, J. R., A. Garba, J.-C. Maur, and L. Razafimandimby. 2016. "Possible Impacts of Floating the Nigerian Naira on Niger's Economy." In *Demographic Explosion in the Sahel: Dividend or Burden?* AFCW3 Economic Update, Fall 2016, 33–39. Washington, DC: World Bank. https://openknowledge.worldbank.org/handle/10986/30952.

Manfred, L., K. Kanemoto, D. Moran, and A. Geschke. 2013. "Building EORA: A Global Multi-Regional Input-Output Database at High Country and Sector Resolution." *Economic Systems Research* 25 (1).

Prihardini, D. 2016. "Export Diversification Scenarios with a CGE Model." Unpublished paper, World Bank, Washington, DC.

Republic of Chad. 2017. "Vision 2030: Le Tchad que nous voulons." Ministère de l'Economie et de la Planification du Développement, N'Djamena.

Roster, K., and M. Cader. 2016. "Niger: Country Opportunity Spotlight." Country Analytics, IFC, Washington, DC.

Taglioni, D. 2017. "A Taxonomy of Global Value Chain Integration." Unpublished paper, World Bank, Washington, DC.

Torres C., and J. van Seters. 2016. "Overview of Trade and Barriers to Trade in West Africa: Insights in Political Economy Dynamics, with Particular Focus on Agricultural and Food Trade." Discussion Paper 195, European Center for Development Policy Management, Maastricht.

World Bank. 2019a. "On the IDA-18 Special Themes: Jobs and Structural Transformation." Unpublished paper, World Bank, Washington, DC.

———. 2019b "Mali JIP: Fourth Review." Unpublished paper, World Bank, Washington, DC.

———. 2020. *World Development Report 2020: Trading for Development in the Age of Global Value Chains*. Washington, DC: World Bank. https://openknowledge.worldbank.org/handle/10986/32437.

WTO (World Trade Organization). 2013. "Trade Policy Review: Countries of the Central African Economic and Monetary Community (CEMAC)." WTO, Geneva. https://www.wto.org/english/tratop_e/tpr_e/s285_e.pdf.

———. 2017. "Trade Policy Review: Niger." WTO, Geneva.

———. 2018. "Trade Policy Review 2017: WAEMU." WTO, Geneva.